English Silver at Williamsburg

THE

WILLIAMSBURG DECORATIVE ARTS SERIES

GRAHAM HOOD, *Editor*

The Williamsburg Collection of Antique Furnishings

New England Furniture at Williamsburg

English and Oriental Carpets at Williamsburg

English Silver at Williamsburg

ENGLISH SILVER
AT
WILLIAMSBURG

by
John D. Davis

Published by
THE COLONIAL WILLIAMSBURG FOUNDATION
Williamsburg, Virginia

Distributed by
THE UNIVERSITY PRESS OF VIRGINIA
Charlottesville, Virginia

LIBRARY OF CONGRESS CATALOGING IN PUBLICATION DATA

Colonial Williamsburg Foundation.
    English silver at Williamsburg.

    (The Williamsburg decorative arts series)
    Includes bibliographical references and indexes.
    1. Silverwork—Great Britain—Catalogs. 2. Sil-
verwork—Virginia—Williamsburg—Catalogs.
3. Williamsburg, Va.—History. I. Davis, John D.,
1938–   II. Title. III. Series.
NK7143.C64 1975   739.2′3′74207401554252 75-4814
ISBN 0-8139—0611-3 (Univ. Press of Virginia)
ISBN 0-87935-027-X (Colonial Williamsburg)
ISBN 0-87935-028-8 pbk.

CONTENTS

FOREWORD

UNLIKE MOST first-rate museum collections of English silver, the one herein cataloged can be seen to juxtapose the exceedingly rare with the thoroughly typical. This particular character was established in the earliest years of the collection's existence. Obviously, silver forms similar to those used in the colonial capital in private, public, and commercial capacities were necessary to furnish the series of restored buildings exhibited at Williamsburg. Such forms could be documented by archaeological discovery, written sources, and actual survival. Yet it was further obvious that these "representative" pieces could not be fully appreciated without reference to certain objects exemplifying the very highest attainments of the silversmith's art. Superb pieces such as the great chandelier made for William III, the Farren salver for George II, or the marquis of Rockingham's tureen (all worthy of any museum in the world) give this collection an undeniable importance.

That is not to imply that humbler objects are uninteresting. Among the simplest are a set of silver cockspurs complete with the names not only of the maker and original owner, but even of the birds they were attached to and where they fought—these are fascinating, surely. Nor is it to say that the objects for which we have only documentary evidence are all merely ordinary; the huge silver teakettle on stand that was listed in 1760 in the inventory of Henry Wetherburn, tavern-keeper, as weighing over 130 ounces must be extremely rare, and so also must the two silver "Branches with 4 Nozzles" owned by Lord Botetourt, penultimate royal governor, in 1770. We have yet to acquire either of these forms.

Perhaps in the future we shall acquire them—necessitating, it may be, a second edition of this book! Certainly, one of the virtues of the collection is that it is still expanding. Within recent months, for example, we have been fortunate enough to purchase two items associated with royal governors in Virginia. A pair of beakers that was made in London in 1735 for Lieutenant-Governor William Gooch, and engraved with his arms, would almost certainly have been sent to him in Williamsburg. A lovely silver-gilt jewel box and pin cushion, from a toilet service by John White, belonged to the sister of Lord Botetourt; as many of the latter's most private possessions were lost at sea, items such as this box may bring us, in material terms, as close to that gentle personage as we are likely to get. Also worthy of mention—although not included, as were the others at the very last minute, in the final section of this catalog—is a teaspoon by the Williamsburg silversmith, James Geddy, recently unearthed in the garden of the Peyton Randolph House.

Scholars will welcome, we believe, the accumulation of detail in this catalog. Perhaps the social historian, as much as the art historian, will find the evidence gathered here of the use of silver in colonial Virginia of special interest. It is this combination of the aesthetic and the social that is, we feel, one of the book's—indeed, one of Colonial Williamsburg's—chief qualities.

To the Ford Foundation we are extremely grateful for a grant to make the publication of this catalog possible. It is the second such publication on our collections that the Ford Foundation's excellent and thoughtful program has facilitated.

GRAHAM HOOD
Director of Collections

INTRODUCTION

Pure silver is too soft to be fully workable and to withstand in a domestic object the rigors of continual use. Since antiquity a base metal, almost invariably copper, has been used to harden pure silver to make it more malleable and more durable. In England beginning in 1300, repeated statutes have maintained the relative admixture of these two metals at 925 parts per 1,000 or 92.5 percent pure silver to 75 parts per 1,000 or 7.5 percent alloy. From then until now this mix has been known as sterling silver.

The necessary debasement of a precious metal has entailed the need of regulations to protect the client against illegal and excessive adulteration. The craft in England has developed under the strong control of the Goldsmiths' Company, one of the oldest of the English guilds. The company's charter of 1327 defined officially the powers it and its wardens had exercised for a number of years. Its primary responsibilities have been to assay new coin and to ensure that all wrought silver and gold are of the required fineness or standard.

The most visible evidence of the company's activity is the familiar grouping of hallmarks, accompanying the maker's mark, on English silver:

Leopard's head. The leopard's head, instituted in 1300, was the first hallmark ordered and used as a guarantee mark, and it became in time the distinctive mark of the London assay office.

Maker's mark. Silversmiths were first required in 1363 to have a mark of their own and to register that mark with the guild. Early maker's marks were often merely devices, but, increasingly during the seventeenth century, they incorporated the maker's initials. This mark, applied by the maker and not by the hall, is technically not a hallmark.

Date letter. The date letter was initiated in 1478. From then until now regular cycles of twenty letters, each cycle in a distinctive letter style, have been used to denote the year in which a piece was submitted for assay and marking. The marking periods since 1660 extend from May 29 of one year through May 28 of the following year, thus explaining the double-year references.

Lion passant. The third hallmark, the lion passant, was adopted in 1554 to specifically certify that a piece is of sterling fineness. Only in some provincial centers, such as Chester and Plymouth in the late seventeenth century and Cork and Limerick in the eighteenth century, does one encounter the word "sterling" stamped on a piece of English or Irish silver.

Sovereign's head. A fourth hallmark, the profile bust of the reigning sovereign, appears on English silver from 1784 until 1890, indicating that a duty of 6 pence per ounce had been paid by the silversmith at the time of assay.

These brief comments apply primarily to London silver; they do not account for the anomalies in the marking of provincial silver.

The only interruption in the use of the sterling standard since 1300 was the interlude of the Britannia standard from 1697 until 1720, when the required fineness jumped from 925 to 958 parts pure silver per 1,000. The government hoped thereby to restrain the wholesale translation of coin, as well as clippings from coin, into articles of wrought silver, which had taken place during the last decades of the century. On London silver of the Britannia standard, the lion's head erased replaced the leopard's head crowned, and the seated figure of Britannia replaced the lion passant. The law also stipulated that the maker's mark should incorporate the first two letters of his surname. After the reinstatement of the sterling standard in 1720 the Britannia standard remained optional, as it is to this day. Certain makers, notably Paul de Lamerie, the celebrated Huguenot silversmith, continued to work for a number of years in the richer metal; in fact, de Lamerie did not register a maker's mark for use on sterling silver until 1732.

* * *

From his plantation on the Potomac River in Stafford County, Virginia, William Fitzhugh wrote to his London agent in 1688: "I esteem it as well politic as reputable, to furnish my self with an handsom Cupboard of plate which gives my self the present use & Credit, is a sure friend at a dead lift, without much loss, or is a certain portion for a Child after my decease. . . ."[1] Fitzhugh was affirming the traditional virtues of silver as an accepted visible symbol of personal wealth and standing, a reasonably safe and pleasurable investment at a time before banking, and a means of passing on family fortune and identity. To Fitzhugh and doubtless to other affluent Virginians, silver was a significant constituent in the conscious emulation, though on a lesser scale, of the life style of the English gentry. Like books and paintings, politics and religion, silver—whether a teapot on a parlor table, a communion cup held in a cleric's hand, or a mace carried in a public procession—played a vital role in the transplanting of English ideals and institutions.

Customs records, inventories, business accounts, other manuscripts, advertisements in the *Virginia Gazette*, and the many surviving pieces of English silver with

---

1. Davis, R. B., p. 246. (See short-title list for full citations to this and other frequently cited works.)

long histories of ownership in local families and churches, all make clear that colonial Virginians acquired much of their silver from the mother country. Contemporary documentation and these surviving pieces also testify that in ordering silver from England they exercised little conscious concern regarding style and elaboration. Colonel Richard Lee, who traveled often to England and hoped to retire there, would appear an exception. On his return to Virginia in 1655, customs officials in England seized and temporarily held approximately two hundred ounces of silver articles that he had brought from Virginia a year and a half before to have made more fashionable.[2] Even Fitzhugh, who had systematically filled his cupboard with 122 pieces of silver before his death in 1701, told his agent in the same letter of 1688 that "what plate I design to have purchased, would be strong & plain, as being less subject to bruise, more Servicable & less out for the fashion. . . ."[3] He, like others, usually specified in his orders merely the objects he desired and only on occasion even their size or weight.

As might be expected, agents having only limited instructions supplied, in most instances, silver of standard appearance which they probably purchased from existing stock in the shops of the more obvious London makers and retailers. The unexceptional character of the bulk of the surviving silver of early Virginia ownership confirms this, and the makers of many of the mid-eighteenth-century pieces, in particular, are predictable: for example, cruet frames by Samuel Wood and Jabez Daniel; candlesticks by William Gould, Ebenezer Coker, and John Carter; and salvers by Robert Abercromby, William Peaston, John Swift, Ebenezer Coker, and John Carter.

* * *

The Virginia Museum of Fine Arts in Richmond gathered together many of these pieces for their 1940 silver exhibition, and Edward M. Davis III followed it with a useful article entitled "Historic Silver in Commonwealth of Virginia" in the April 1941 issue of the *Virginia Magazine of History and Biography*. The 1940 exhibition included only a small sampling of the rich body of seventeenth- and eighteenth-century silver in Virginia churches, which is much more impressive than its domestic counterpart. Numbering more than 120 pieces, almost entirely of English origin, the church silver features noble communion cups and flagons, particularly from Anglican parishes, and includes the work of such notable London makers as Pierre Harache, Sr., Benjamin Pyne, Francis Garthorne, Anthony

---

2. W. Noel Sainsbury, ed., *Calendar of State Papers, Colonial Series, 1574–1660* (Vaduz: Kraus Reprint Ltd., 1964), 1:430–31.

3. Davis, R. B., p. 246. It should be noted that Fitzhugh was writing when the thin-walled bodies of many pieces were high-chased in the Dutch manner and that he may not have had the means of repairing them. He makes specific reference to some candlesticks he acquired the previous year, which were probably of the wrought columnar type.

Nelme, Thomas Folkingham, George Wickes, Thomas Farren, Gabriel Sleath, and Thomas Heming.

E. Alfred Jones recorded many of these pieces in 1913 in his monumental volume, *The Old Silver of American Churches*, and more recently the Virginia Museum of Fine Arts assembled most of them for its 1970 exhibition of "Church Silver in Colonial Virginia," which was accompanied by an excellent illustrated catalog. The earliest pieces are a London communion cup and a pair of patens of 1618/19, presently at St. John's Church, Hampton, which have the longest history of use in this country of any church silver.[4]

Bruton Parish Church in Williamsburg acquired its silver in several ways. In 1694, when Williamsburg was called Middle Plantation, Governor Edmund Andros presented to the church a large salver of 1691/92 by Benjamin Pyne of London.[5] Upon the abandonment of the church at Jamestown in 1758, its London

communion cup with paten-cover of about 1660,[6] along with an alms dish of 1739/40 by Thomas Farren of London,[7] went to Bruton Parish Church. During the administration of Governor Francis Fauquier (1758–68), the church received as gifts a communion cup of 1764/65 and a flagon of 1766/67, both by Thomas Heming of London, as well as an alms dish of similar date (the marks were re-

---

4. Jones (d), pp. 204–5, pl. LXXI; Virginia Museum (b), pp. 20–21, ill.; Helen Scott Townsend Reed, "Church Silver in Colonial Virginia," *Antiques* 97 (February 1970):243–45, fig. 1.

5. Jones (d), p. 473, pl. CXLI; Virginia Museum (b), pp. 36–37, ill.

6. Jones (d), p. 231, pl. LXXIX, fig. 1; Virginia Museum (b), pp. 26–27, ill.

7. Jones (d), p. 232, pl. LXXIX, fig. 2; Virginia Museum (b), pp. 26–27, ill.

moved by an abbreviation of the rim about 1820), all engraved with the royal arms and the monogram of George III.[8] The most stunning piece of Virginia church silver and one of the few domestic forms (page 4) is the gilt two-handled covered cup of 1686/87 by Pierre Harache, Sr., of London. Lady Gooch, whose husband had served as lieutenant governor of Virginia between 1727 and 1749, willed it to the College of William and Mary, along with a gilt paten of 1751/52 by Richard Gurney and Thomas Cook of London, both engraved with the arms of her parents. These were transferred to Bruton Parish Church in 1905.[9]

* * *

The first piece of silver acquired by Colonial Williamsburg, appropriately, was a London slip-end spoon from the 1630s, that had been found near Jamestown (No. 174). Even more appropriately, it was the gift in 1930 of Dr. W. A. R. Goodwin, the rector of Bruton Parish Church, who had inspired John D. Rockefeller, Jr., to undertake the re-creation of an earlier Williamsburg. Eight years later Colonial Williamsburg made its most important purchase of period silver, selected pieces from the collection of William Randolph Hearst, including the magnificent chandelier and two sets of sconces, originally part of the English royal plate (Nos. 1–3), the majestic wine fountain by Joseph Ward (No. 31), three handsome seventeenth-century two-handled covered cups (Nos. 44–45, 47), and the splendid pair of gilt breadbaskets by Paul de Lamerie (No. 119). Since then the effort has been to form a broadly representative collection of English silver of the late seventeenth and eighteenth centuries of a character appropriate for the varied contexts of the exhibition buildings, whether it be the state dining room of the Governor's Palace, the Bull Head Room of Wetherburn's Tavern, or a workroom in one of the silversmiths' shops.

This catalog includes the entire collection except for duplicate forms, jewelry, watches, and various silver-mounted objects. Both for interpretive purposes and to permit easy comparison of related forms, the catalog is divided into large sections based on usage. Articles of fused silverplate ("Sheffield Plate") have been segregated. The name given under the object in the captions is that of the silversmith whose mark appears on the piece. It should be realized, however, that technically he may have only sponsored the piece for assay and hallmarking; in some cases an anonymous workman in his shop may have fashioned it or the master could have acquired the piece within the trade and have served as a go-between in its marking or as its retailer. All dimensions are maximum unless qualified. Weights are given in troy ounces, pennyweights, and grains. The entry "Pub-

8. Jones (d), pp. 496, 498, pl. CXL, fig. 1; Virginia Museum (b), pp. 92–93, ill.

9. Jones (d), pp. 496–98, pl. CXL, fig. 2; Virginia Museum (b), pp. 32–33, ill.; Reed, "Church Silver in Colonial Virginia," pp. 244–45, fig. 2. The finial is a replacement.

lished" in the captions is used only to indicate when and where the specific piece under discussion has been previously published. References to frequently cited works have been abbreviated, full bibliographical information being given in the short-title list. A separate index of silversmiths represented in the collection precedes the general index, which includes categorical entries for collectors and collections, dealers, donors, former owners, and silver with histories of Virginia ownership.

ACKNOWLEDGMENTS

MANY INDIVIDUALS have been helpful in the preparation of this catalog. I am particularly indebted to John Graham, Milo Naeve, and Graham Hood, successive curators under whom I have worked at Colonial Williamsburg, who have enlarged the silver collection and encouraged its study, as well as to Carlisle Humelsine, president of the Colonial Williamsburg Foundation, whose commitment to the publication of the collections ultimately made this volume possible. I am grateful to those who have examined the collection and graciously shared their knowledge: Kathryn Buhler, Michael Clayton, Edwin Firestone, Arthur Grimwade, John Hayward, Mrs. G. E. P. How, Thomas Lumley, Charles Oman, and Eric Shrubsole. I also want to thank Mr. and Mrs. Oliver Ramsey, who have stimulated our interest in "Sheffield Plate" and through generous gifts from their extensive collections have helped correct a deficiency in ours. William de Matteo and Philip Thorp, our silversmiths, must be admired for their patient indulgence of a novice's questions on technical matters. To Delmore Wenzel and Hans Lorenz, who took the photographs, Thomas K. Ford, who edited the manuscript, and Richard Stinely, who designed the catalog and oversaw its production, I extend my thanks. And, of course, an affectionate tribute to Ginny and the children for their interest and patience.

SHORT-TITLE LIST

BANISTER

Judith Banister. *English Silver* London: Ward Lock & Company Ltd., 1965.

BOTETOURT INVENTORY

"An Inventory of the Personal Estate of his Excellency Lord Botetourt began to be taken the 24th of Octo^r 1770." MS, Botetourt Papers, Virginia State Library, Richmond; photostat copy in Department of Research, Colonial Williamsburg Foundation.

BRADBURY

Frederick Bradbury. *History of Old Sheffield Plate.* London, 1912. Reprint. Sheffield: J. W. Northend Ltd., 1968.

BUHLER

Kathryn C. Buhler. *Mount Vernon Silver.* Mount Vernon, Va.: Mount Vernon Ladies' Association of the Union, 1957.

CHARLESTON

R. J. Charleston. "Petitions for Patents Concerning Porcelain, Glass and Enamels with Special Reference to Birmingham, 'The Great Toyshop of Europe'," Part 2B. *English Ceramic Circle Transactions* 6 (1966):107–19.

CHRISTIE'S

Christie, Manson & Woods, Ltd. Sale catalogs. London.

CLAYTON

Michael Clayton. *The Collector's Dictionary of the Silver and Gold of Great Britain and North America.* London: Country Life Ltd., 1971.

COMSTOCK

Helen Comstock. "Williamsburg Revisited." *Antiques* 68 (November 1955):I–VIII.

COOPER

Wendy A. Cooper. "The Purchase of Furniture and Furnishings by John Brown, Providence Merchant. Part II: 1788–1803." *Antiques* 103 (April 1973):734–43.

DAVIS, E. M.

Edward M. Davis III. "Historical Silver in Commonwealth of Virginia." *Virginia Magazine of History and Biography* 49 (April 1941):105–24.

DAVIS, J. D.

John D. Davis. "The Silver." *Antiques* 95 (January 1969):134–37.

DAVIS, R. B.

Richard Beale Davis, ed. *William Fitzhugh and His Chesapeake World, 1676–1701: The Fitzhugh Letters and Other Documents.* Chapel Hill, N. C.: University of North Carolina Press, 1963.

DELIEB

Eric Delieb. *Investing in Silver.* New York: Clarkson N. Potter, Inc., 1967.

GRIMWADE

Arthur G. Grimwade. "The Garrard Ledgers." *Proceedings of the Society of Silver Collectors* (1961):1–12.

HACKENBROCH

Yvonne Hackenbroch. *English and Other Silver in the Irwin Untermyer Collection.* Orig. edn. New York: Metropolitan Museum of Art, 1963. Rev. edn. New York, 1969.

HAYWARD

John F. Hayward. *Huguenot Silver in England, 1688–1727.* London: Faber and Faber, 1959.

HOW

George Evelyn Paget How and Jane Penrice How. *English and Scottish Silver Spoons, Medieval to Late Stuart, and Pre-Elizabethan Hall-marks on English Plate,* 3 vols. London: Privately printed, 1952–57.

HUGHES

G. Bernard Hughes. *Small Antique Silverware.* London: B. T. Batsford Ltd., 1957.

JACKSON

Charles James Jackson. *An Illustrated History of English*

Plate, 2 vols. London, 1911. Reprint. New York: Dover Publications, Inc., 1969.

JONES (a)

E. Alfred Jones. *Catalogue of the Collection of Old Plate of William Francis Farrer at No. 7 St. James's Square, London*. London: St. Catherine Press, 1924.

JONES (b)

———. "More Old English Silver in the William Randolph Hearst Collection." *Connoisseur* 88 (December 1931): 395–401.

JONES (c)

———. *The Old Plate of Cambridge Colleges*. Cambridge: University Press, 1910.

JONES (d)

———. *The Old Silver of American Churches*. Letchworth, Herts.: Arden Press, 1913.

MACQUOID AND EDWARDS

Percy Macquoid and Ralph Edwards. *The Dictionary of English Furniture from the Middle Ages to the Late Georgian Period*, 3 vols. Rev. edn. by Edwards. London: Country Life Ltd., 1954. Shorter edn. London, 1964.

MULLINER

H. H. Mulliner. *The Decorative Arts in England During the Late XVIIth and XVIIIth Centuries*. London: B. T. Batsford Ltd., 1923.

OMAN (a)

Charles C. Oman. *Caroline Silver, 1625–1688*. London: Faber and Faber, 1970.

OMAN (b)

———. *English Domestic Silver*. 5th edn. London: Adam & Charles Black, 1962.

OMAN (c)

———. *English Silversmiths' Work, Civil and Domestic; An Introduction*. London: Her Majesty's Stationery Office, 1965.

PARKE-BERNET

Sotheby Parke Bernet Galleries Inc. (formerly Parke-Bernet Galleries Inc.). Sale catalogs. New York.

PHILLIPS

Philip A. S. Phillips. *Paul de Lamerie, Citizen and Goldsmith of London: A Study of His Life and Work, A.D. 1688–1751*. London, 1935. Reprint. London: Holland Press, 1968.

ROWE

Robert Rowe. *Adam Silver, 1765–1795*. London: Faber and Faber, 1965.

ROYAL NORTHERN HOSPITAL

Royal Northern Hospital. *Catalogue of a Loan Exhibition of Old English Plate and Decorations and Orders*. London: Country Life Ltd., 1929.

ROYAL ONTARIO MUSEUM

Royal Ontario Museum. *English Silver: A Catalogue to an Exhibition of Seven Centuries of English Domestic Silver*. Toronto: Royal Ontario Museum, 1958.

SEAFORD HOUSE

Seaford House. *Queen Charlotte's Loan Exhibition of Old Silver*. London: St. Catherine Press, 1929.

SNEYD PLATE

"List of Plate At Keele Hall April 1854." MS, Sneyd Papers, Box 79, Manuscript Collection, Keele University, Staffordshire; copy in Department of Collections, Colonial Williamsburg Foundation.

SOTHEBY'S

Sotheby & Co. Sale catalogs. London.

VIRGINIA MUSEUM (a)

Virginia Museum of Fine Arts. *An Exhibition of Silver: French, British, American, Modern*. Richmond: Virginia Museum of Fine Arts, 1940.

VIRGINIA MUSEUM (b)

———. *Church Silver of Colonial Virginia*. Richmond: Virginia Museum of Fine Arts, 1970.

WENHAM

Edward Wenham. "The Anglo-French Silversmiths—Part 7. Paul Crespin and the Felines." *Antique Collector* 16 (November–December 1945):202–7.

WESTOVER PLATE

"List of the Plate at Westover August 10th, 1769." MS, Charles City County, Deeds & Wills, 1766–1774, p. 193, Virginia State Library, Richmond; microfilm copy in Department of Research, Colonial Williamsburg Foundation.

WILLIAMSBURG (a)

Colonial Williamsburg Foundation. *A Recent Gift*. Williamsburg: Colonial Williamsburg Foundation, 1973.

WILLIAMSBURG (b)

"Williamsburg Issue." *Antiques* 63 (March 1953).

THE CATALOG

Lighting Equipment and Accessories

1 CHANDELIER
Daniel Garnier
London. 1691–97

Maker's mark only on underside of inner ends of seven arms (inside shaft when assembled). Iron suspension rod with silvered upper end and ring. Iron nuts and bolts securing arms.

H: 27″ (68.6 cm); W: 33″ (83.8 cm). Wt: 721 oz. 9 dwt. 9½ gr.

PROVENANCE: English royal collections; Sneyd family, Keele Hall, Staffordshire (sold at Christie, Manson & Woods, London, 1924); William Randolph Hearst (sold by Parish-Watson & Co., New York, 1938)

PUBLISHED: "The Silver Plate of the Sneyds of Keele Hall," *Country Life* 55 (June 21, 1924):1023, fig. 2; Christie's (June 24, 1924), lot 82, ill.; E. Alfred Jones, "Old Silver in the Possession of the Duke of Buccleuch, K.T.—1," *Old Furniture, A Magazine of Domestic Ornament* 6 (April 1929):220; Williamsburg (b), p. 259, ill.; N. M. Penzer, "The Plate at Knole—II," *Connoisseur* 147 (May 1961): 183; Alice Winchester, Preface, *Antiques* 75 (June 1964): 265, frontispiece; Clayton, p. 59, and fig. 118, p. 61; Christie's (June 27, 1973), lot 48; Frank Davis, "A Feast of Gold Boxes," *Country Life* 154 (July 26, 1973): 219; John Herbert, ed., *Christie's Review of the Season 1973* (London: Hutchinson & Co. Ltd., 1973), p. 228

Daniel Garnier fashioned this magnificent chandelier for William III. It bears only the maker's mark; silver made for royal or ambassadorial use was freed from the obligation of being sent to the Goldsmiths' Hall for full marking.[1] Despite the absence of a date letter, the chandelier can be securely placed between 1691 and 1697. In the former year Garnier entered at the Goldsmith's Hall his first mark, which appears on this piece, its crowned fleur-de-lis and two pellets or *grains de remede* betraying his French background. In the latter year he entered his second and third marks, incorporating—as required by law during the period of the Britannia standard (1697–1720)—the first two letters of his surname rather than his initials. The chandelier exhibits the visual clarity found in the more refined Huguenot work. The strong baluster and vase forms of the shaft and the bold scrolls of the arms are tightly composed and firmly controlled. The decorative means are economical, gadrooned bands, placed at precise intervals to create a forthright contrast between plain and embellished surfaces.

The earliest mention of this chandelier appears in the 1721 inventory of royal plate, which lists it as "One 10 nozzelld Branch . . . 730.0.0.," and places it "At St. James's/In the Lodgings."[2] A notation on the document relating to the formal transfer of plate in 1727, shortly after the accession of George II to the throne, locates it in "the little drawing Room" of the palace.[3]

Precisely when or how this chandelier and the following two sets of sconces left the royal collections and entered those of the Sneyd family is not known. It probably took place in 1808, when the Prince of Wales set aside suitable apartments in Kensington Palace for his estranged wife. The estimate of the silver needed to furnish her quarters was so great that the Lord Chamberlain suggested melting down silver in the royal collections "neither available for service in its present form nor valuable from its antiquity or workmanship." With the consent of an ailing George III in September of that year, he released selected pieces at their bullion value to Rundell, Bridge and Rundell, the royal goldsmiths. Instead of melting them down, that firm sagaciously sold them to its leading clients, such as William Beckford, the 1st Earl Brownlow, the earl of Lonsdale, the duke of Buccleuch, and probably Walter Sneyd. Unfortunately, no list of the silver and its purchasers survives.[4]

It was at this time that Walter Sneyd (1752–1829) acquired a town house in London. He may have purchased the chandelier and sconces from Rundell, Bridge and Rundell as part of its furnishings, or to augment those of Keele Hall, the family seat in Staffordshire. He was then in command of the Staffordshire Regiment at Windsor and lieutenant colonel of the King's Bodyguard there. George III served as godfather to several of his daughters.[5]

The chandelier is first noted as "1 Silver Chandelier" in the Sneyd family papers in 1849, and five years later referred to as "1 Chandelier 10 Arms."[6] It remained in the family until William Randolph Hearst purchased it at the sale of the Sneyd heirlooms at Christie's in 1924.

Silver chandeliers appear to have had only limited use in England. The 1721 inventory of royal plate contains only five chandeliers. Aside from the Williamsburg example, only one other of these is known, that which George Garthorne of London made for William III in about 1690 and which still hangs at Hampton Court.[7] Other English examples include an unmarked one of about 1670 owned by the duke of Buccleuch,[8] an unmarked pair of about 1700 at Knole,[9] a pair of 1703/4 and 1704/5 by John Boddington of London,[10] two of 1734/35 by Paul de Lamerie of London in Russia,[11] and one of 1752/53 by William Gould of London at the Fishmongers' Company.[12] An English or Dutch chandelier of about 1694 still hangs at Chatsworth.[13] A pair of chandeliers, made by Behrens of Hanover in 1736/37 after a design by William Kent for George III's palace at Herrenhausen, are at Anglesey Abbey, Cambridgeshire.[14] The Williamsburg chandelier is the only early English example in an American collection. An Irish one of about 1742 is in the Henry Francis du Pont Winterthur Museum in Delaware.[15]

1938-42

1. The maker's mark was not discovered until the chandelier was disassembled and closely examined in 1964 by Charles C. Oman, then of the Victoria and Albert Museum, London, and Kathryn C. Buhler, then of the Museum of Fine Arts, Boston. It had been sold in 1924 as "A Queen Anne Chandelier" with no indication of the maker's mark or its early history. Mr. Oman was able to document its royal pedigree.

2. "An Account of all His Majesty's Plate in any of his Majestys Palaces or elsewhere together with the respective denominacions and weights of each piece or Parcell, as also of all Plate, now remain[g] in his Maties Jewell Office," dated September 1721 (MS, Public Records Office, London, L.C. 5/114; photostat copy, Department of Collections, Colonial Williamsburg Foundation).

3. MS, Public Records Office, London, L.C. 9/44 f. 288.

4. Charles C. Oman "Caddinets and a Forgotten Version of the Royal Arms," *Burlington Magazine* 100 (December 1958):435; Christie's (May 29, 1963), p. 5; John F. Hayward, "Rundell, Bridge and Rundell, *Aurifices Regis*: Part 1," *Antiques* 99 (June 1971):862; ———, "Royal Plate at Fonthill," *Burlington Magazine* 101 (April 1959):145. Hayward discusses two pieces known to have been bought from the group by Beckford.

5. Sylvia England, "Report on Sneyd Documents at Keele University" (unpublished report, prepared for Colonial Williamsburg Foundation, 1964); J. M. Kolbert, *The Sneyds & Keele Hall* (Keele, Staff.: Keele University, 1964).

6. "Inventory of Plate left at Messer Garrard Co. 31 Panton St. London," dated June 16, 1849 (MS, Sneyd Papers, Box 79, Manuscript Collection, Keele University; copy in Department of Collections, Colonial Williamsburg Foundation); Sneyd Plate.

7. Macquoid and Edwards, rev. edn., 1:328, fig. 6; shorter edn., p. 176, fig. 6; Hayward, pp. 64–65, pl. 77.

8. E. Alfred Jones, "Old Silver in the Possession of the Duke of Buccleuch, K.T.—1," *Old Furniture, A Magazine of Domestic Ornament* 6 (April 1929):219, fig. 1; Oman (a), p. 56, pl. 66.

9. Macquoid and Edwards, rev. edn., 1:328, fig. 5; shorter edn., p. 176, fig. 5; N. M. Penzer, "The Plate at Knole—II," *Connoisseur* 147 (May 1961):182–83, fig. 18.

10. Christie's (June 27, 1973), lot 48, ill.; Frank Davis, "A Feast of Gold Boxes," *Country Life* 154 (July 26, 1973):218–19, fig. 4; John Herbert, ed., *Christie's Review of the Season 1973* (London: Hutchinson & Co. Ltd., 1973), pp. 228–30, ill. One of the pair was exhibited at the Royal Ontario Museum in 1958 (Royal Ontario Museum, p. 38, no. F.3).

11. E. Alfred Jones, *The Old Plate of the Emperor of Russia* (Letchworth, Herts.: Arden Press, 1909), pp. xlviii, 54–57, plates XXVII and XXVIII; Jackson, 2:863–65, fig. 1127; Phillips, p. 96, plates XCIII and XCIV.

12. Macquoid and Edwards, rev. edn., 1:328, fig. 7; shorter edn., pp. 176–77, fig. 7; G. W. Whitman, *Halls and Treasures of the City Companies* (London: Ward Lock & Co. Ltd., 1970), p. 48; Clayton, p. 59, and fig. 119, p. 61.

13. James Lees-Milne, "Chatsworth, Derbyshire—III: A Seat of the Duke of Devonshire," *Country Life* 143 (April 25, 1968):1044, fig. 7.

14. W. W. Watts, "Silver Chandeliers Made for George II," *Connoisseur* 100 (November 1937):232–34, figs. I and II.

15. Joseph Downs, *American Furniture: Queen Anne and Chippendale Periods* (New York: Macmillan Company, 1952), color pl. II; John A. H. Sweeney, *The Treasure House of Early American Rooms* (New York: Viking Press, 1963), ill. p. 44.

2 EIGHT SCONCES
London. About 1670

2

Originally unmarked. Second arm on seven added by Robert Garrard of London in 1856/57 (second arm on eighth missing and replaced by Colonial Williamsburg) and marked with varying completeness on undersides of drip pans and on large central leaves at juncture of arms with backplates.

H: 18½″–19½″ (47 cm–49.5 cm); W: 11¾″–13″ (29.8 cm–33 cm); D: 8¾″–9¼″ (21.4 cm–23.5 cm). Total wt: 989 oz. 8 dwt.

PROVENANCE: English royal collections; Sneyd family, Keele Hall, Staffordshire (sold at Christie, Manson & Woods, London, 1924); William Randolph Hearst (sold by Parish-Watson & Co., New York, 1938)

EXHIBITED: "In Virginia," Virginia Museum of Fine Arts, Richmond, 1971

PUBLISHED: "The Silver Plate of the Sneyds of Keele Hall," *Country Life* 55 (June 21, 1924):1023–24, fig. 3; Christie's (June 24, 1924), lot 80, ill.; Jones (b), p. 397, pl. III; Williamsburg (b), p. 254, ill.; "In Virginia," *Arts in Virginia* 3 (Winter 1963):31, ill.; Macquoid and Edwards, rev. edn., 3:48, fig. 7; shorter edn., p. 427, fig. 5; Oman (a), p. 55; John F. Hayward, "Rundell, Bridge and Rundell, *Aurifices Regis*: Part 1," *Antiques* 99 (June 1971):860, fig. 1; Clayton, p. 248; Sotheby's (June 27–28, 1974), lot 1

These massive sconces consist almost entirely of cast elements, adding greatly to their weight and initial expense. Chandeliers, sconces, and other imposing forms, such as wine fountains (No. 31) and mon-

teiths (Nos. 32 and 33), evidence the extravagant use of silver for domestic purposes after the restoration of the Stuart monarchy in 1660. John Evelyn, the diarist, observed that Charles II "brought in a politer way of living, which soon passed to Luxurie & intollerable expense."[1] So much coinage was translated into plate—to replace pieces melted down or left unmade during the Civil War and the Commonwealth and to satisfy the great demand for new and ostentatious forms—that the crown enacted the higher Britannia standard in 1697 to retard the process and to maintain sufficient bullion for the mint. Such extravagance is seen in Evelyn's enumeration of 1683 of the silver in the dressing room of the duchess of Portsmouth: "huge *Vasas* of wrought plate, *Tables, Stands, Chimney furniture, Sconces, branches, Braseras* &c they were all of massive silver, & without number."[2]

These sconces, among the earliest surviving English examples,[3] are of the most common, late Stuart type with a large, shaped, oval backplate in the form of a baroque cartouche; a broad decorative border frames the central reflecting area. The swirling leaf border with cherubs was a popular baroque device, and it can be seen in a more conventional treatment in the chased sides of the pincushion of the same period (No. 214).

In comparison to silver chandeliers, silver sconces were produced in relatively large numbers from the reign of Charles II through that of Queen Anne. The 1721 inventory of royal plate contains no fewer than 196 sconces with an aggregate weight of 14,315 ounces.[4] Made for royal use during the reign of Charles II, the eight examples of the Williamsburg set, like a number of others of that period, have been altered. The cypher of William and Mary and possibly the royal crown were probably added during their joint reign between 1689 and 1694. Devices, most likely of armorial or emblematic character, have been removed from above and below the festoons of the backplates, revealing holes for their mounting, as well as stamped set numbers. Other holes in both of these areas have been plugged. Further, the cherubs hold in their outstretched arms remnants of swags of oak leaves and acorns, which originally extended the full length of the sides of the backplates. Finally, this set had but a single arm until Robert Garrard of London added second arms in

1856/57. The missing second arm on one of the sconces was replaced by Colonial Williamsburg in 1938. These changes preclude linking the sconces to entries in the 1721 inventory of royal plate.

The Sneyd family probably acquired these, the following two sconces, and the chandelier in 1808 when the royal plate was drastically and unfortunately thinned (see No. 1). The sconces are first mentioned in the Sneyd family papers in 1849 as "8 Silver Sconces,"[5] and they are referred to as "8 Sconces" in 1854.[6]

Stamped set numbers 1, 2, 3, 5, 6, 8, 11, and 12 appear on the backplates, on both the inner ends of the arms and the backplates where they attach, and on the undersides of the crowns, indicating that they were once part of a set of at least twelve. Four sconces at Buckingham Palace, virtually identical to these, retain side swags of oak leaves and acorns, as well as clusters of grapes on the vines entwining the arms.[7] Whether or not they are the other four from this set or four from an even larger set used in different royal residences and not numbered or fitted with the same devices is difficult to say. They do not bear the missing set numbers, though these could have been polished out. Subsequent gilding has made it impossible to determine whether holes for applied devices have been plugged.

Two other series of set numbers from 1 through 8 are engraved, one of simple roman numerals on the reverse of the backplates and the other of shaded arabic numbers both on the inner ends of the arms and the backplates where they attach and on the undersides of the large leaves used to mask the attachment of the arms to the backplates. This latter series dates from after the rearrangement of the arms in 1856/57.

A pair of similar sconces without royal crown and cypher were in the collections of H. H. Mulliner and William Randolph Hearst.[8]

1938-34, 1-8

1. E. S. de Beer, ed., *The Diary of John Evelyn* (Oxford: Clarendon Press, 1955), 4:409–10.

2. Ibid., p. 343.

3. The earliest are a group of ten in the collection of the duke of Buccleuch, four of which bear the date letter for 1668/69. They are discussed and illustrated in Oman (a), p. 54, pl. 63A.

4. "An Account of all His Majesty's Plate in any of his Majestys Palaces or elsewhere together with the respective Denominacions and weights of each piece or Parcell, as also of all Plate, now remaing in his Maties Jewell Office," dated September 1721 (MS, Public Record Office, London, L.C. 5/114; photostat copy in the Department of Collections, Colonial Williamsburg Foundation).

5. "Inventory of Plate left at Messer Garrard Co. 31 Panton St. London," dated June 16, 1849 (MS, Sneyd Papers, Box 79, Manuscript Collection, Keele University; copy in the Department of Collections, Colonial Williamsburg Foundation).

6. Sneyd Plate.

7. Oman (a), p. 55, pl. 54B.

8. Mulliner, fig. 79; Jones (b), p. 396, fig. II; Sotheby's (June 27–28, 1974), lot 1, frontispiece.

3 PAIR OF SCONCES
Philip Rollos
London. 1700/1701

3

Fully marked on sides of each console; lion's head erased on each socket and arm.

Cypher of William III, with royal crown above, engraved on outer face of each arm.

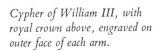

English makers, who felt threatened, a number of these *immigré* craftsmen soon established themselves in business, among them Daniel Garnier, the maker of the chandelier (No. 1) and Philip Rollos, the maker of these sconces; others worked in anonymity as journeymen in London shops. By 1700, they had established a distinct strain in English silver. The sconces exhibit superb craftsmanship and give some indication of the Huguenot makers' high technical competence. They share with other Huguenot silver a formal approach to baroque design and a preference for small scale ornament. The elegant enrichment of the undersides of the saucers is totally French in character and of a type repeated on a broad range of forms during ensuing decades.

H: 15¾″ (40 cm); W: 4½″ (11.4 cm); D: 8½″ (21.6 cm). Wt (no. 1): 59 oz. 10 dwt. 6 gr. ("59=17=N 1" engraved on underside of backplate); (no. 2): 56 oz. 10 dwt. ("57=3=N 1" engraved on underside of backplate).

PROVENANCE: English royal collections; Sneyd family, Keele Hall, Staffordshire (sold at Christie, Manson & Woods, London, 1924); William Randolph Hearst (sold by Parish-Watson & Co., New York, 1938)

PUBLISHED: "The Silver Plate of the Sneyds of Keele Hall," *Country Life* 55 (June 21, 1924):1023–24, fig. 3; Christie's (June 21, 1924), lot 79, ill.; Jones (b), p. 397, pl. LV; Macquoid and Edwards, rev. edn., 3:48, fig. 7; shorter edn., p. 427, fig. 5; Clayton, pp. 248–49, fig. 500

Sconces of this type with a narrow rectangular backplate, often, as in this instance, of embellished console form, appear to have been introduced in the closing years of the seventeenth century by the Huguenot silversmiths. Although encountering resistance from

The small hand and fleur-de-lis flanking the rim of the royal crown of the cresting further indicate French character. They often occur in this position in the emblazonments of the royal arms of France as the upper terminals of the two sceptres placed in saltire behind the shield. The tasseled banner below with bell flowers is purely decorative with no heraldic significance.[1] Two full sceptres, both with fleur-de-lis terminals, appear below the crown on a pair of very similar sconces made the previous year by

from 1768 to 1770, listed among "Plate, in the Pantry":

 2 [Silver] Branches with 4 Nozzles,
 2 ditto ditto with 2 ditto
 2 ditto ditto with 1 ditto[7]

These were probably either sconces or candelabra, or merely the arms to convert candlesticks into candelabra.

1938-35, 1–2

---

1. Information provided by Conrad Swan, York Herald of Arms, College of Arms, London, 1971.
2. Royal Northern Hospital, no. 782, pl. LI; Seaford House, p. 54, no. 463, pl. LXIX; Edward Wenham, "The Anglo-French Silversmiths—Part 4: David Willaume & His Pupils," *Antique Collector* 16 (May–June 1945):83–84, fig. 5.
3. "Inventory of Plate left at Messer Garrard Co. 31 Panton St. London," dated June 16, 1849 (MS, Sneyd Papers, Box 79, Manuscript Collection, Keele University; copy in Department of Collections, Colonial Williamsburg Foundation).
4. Sneyd Plate.
5. Arthur Oswald, "Trumpton Hall, Nottinghamshire—II," *Country Life* 125 (May 28, 1959):1197, fig. 9.
6. Jackson, 1:269–70, figs. 286–87.
7. Botetourt Inventory.

David Willaume, Sr., another Huguenot silversmith working in London; they were owned in 1929 by Lord Brownlow.[2]

Philip Rollos fashioned these sconces for William III, whose cypher with crown is engraved on the arms. They, like the preceding chandelier and sconces, probably left the royal collections and entered those of the Sneyd family in 1808 (see No. 1). Colonial Williamsburg acquired four of them in 1938 and disposed of two in 1972. They first appear in the Sneyd family papers in 1849 as "4 Bracket do [sconces]"[3] and again as "4 Bracket Sconces" in 1854.[4] They remained at Keele Hall until they were sold along with a considerable quantity of family plate in 1924.

A pair of identical sconces—presumed to be from a set of four—hang in Trumpton Hall, Nottinghamshire.[5] Apparently unmarked, they could also be the work of Philip Rollos. Other similar sconces include a single example by Rollos of about 1700, published when owned by the earl of Ilchester,[6] and the pair of 1699/1700 by David Willaume, Sr., mentioned previously.

The inventory of the furnishings of the Governor's Palace in Williamsburg taken after the death of Lord Botetourt, who served as governor of the colony

4 FOUR CANDELABRA
Thomas Pitts
London. 1759/60

H (no. 1): 14¼″ (36.2 cm); (no. 2): 14⅞″ (37.8 cm); (no. 3): 15½″ (39.4 cm); (no. 4): 15⅝″ (39.7 cm); W (no. 1): 14⅛″ (35.9 cm); (no. 2): 13⅞″ (37.8 cm); (no. 3): 14″ (38.1 cm); (no. 4): 13¼″ (33.7 cm). Wt (no. 1): 77 oz. 19 dwt.; (no. 2): 80 oz. 17 dwt. 6 gr.; (no. 3): 83 oz. 0 dwt. 6 gr.; (no. 4): 81 oz. 3 dwt. 18 gr.

PROVENANCE: George Nathaniel Curzon (1859–1925), 5th baron and 1st viscount Scarsdale and 1st marquess Curzon of Kedleston, Derbyshire; Richard Nathaniel Curzon (b. 1892), 2nd viscount Scarsdale, Kedleston, Derbyshire (sold at Christie, Manson & Woods, London, 1930; purchased by S. H. Harris Ltd., London); Garrard & Co. Ltd., London

PUBLISHED: Christie's (July 16, 1930), lot 66; Comstock, p. VI, ill.; Clayton, pp. 37–39, fig. 66

These remarkable rococo candelabra are, to my knowledge, unique, having no mid-eighteenth-century counterparts in English silver. Even though human figures had long been used in candlestick design, they had usually formed an integral part of the

4

Fully marked on side of each base; maker's mark and lion passant on neck of each socket.

stem and had visually supported the socket and candle, as in the set of four plated candlesticks (No. 246).[1] The use of a figure group on the base as a vignette without a supportive function became a characteristic treatment in nineteenth-century candelabra and centerpieces. The overall handling of these candelabra, in particular the modeling of the figures and bases, is reminiscent of porcelain figure groups, especially some French ones of the third quarter of the century on similar rockwork bases

from such factories as Sèvres, Vincennes, Mennecy, and Tournay, but no specific ceramic prototype or print source, either for the individual groups or the overall scheme, has been determined. William Ince and John Mayhew did include in their *Universal System of Household Furniture* a large candlestand in the form of a naturalistic tree with a figure group at its base.[2]

1954-633, 1–4

1. John F. Hayward, "Candlesticks with Figure Stems: Some Important English and Continental Examples," *Connoisseur* 152 (January 1963):16–21; Shirley Bury and Desmond Fitz-Gerald, "A Design for a Candlestick by George Michael Moser, R.A.," *Victoria and Albert Museum Yearbook* 1 (1969):27–29.

2. William Ince and John Mayhew, *The Universal System of Household Furniture* (London, 1759–62), pl. LXIX (facsimile reprint edn. by Ralph Edwards [London: Alec Tiranti, 1960]).

5 PAIR OF CANDLESTICKS
London. 1694/95

5

Fully marked on underside of each base; maker's mark overstruck.

H: 4⅞″ (12.4 cm); W (base): 3⁷⁄₁₆″ (16.4 cm). Total wt: 15 oz. 4 dwt. 20 gr.

PROVENANCE: Crichton Bros., London

Cast candlesticks with baluster stems appear to have been introduced into England from France. Judging from extant examples, their introduction coincides with the arrival of the early Huguenot silversmiths, for among the earliest-known English candlesticks of this type are a set of four at Althorp House and a smaller pair, formerly owned by Sir John Noble, all made by Pierre Harache, Sr., of London in 1683/84.[1] By the turn of the century, such candlesticks had supplanted the less substantial wrought ones of co-

lumnar form (No. 6). Cast candlesticks with baluster stems remained fashionable through the mid eighteenth century. Even though casting permits repetition, candlesticks of this period (Nos. 7–17, 19) show amazing variety and responsiveness to changes in taste.

These candlesticks of small size were probably intended for use on a dressing table.

1936-450, 1–2

---

1. Arthur G. Grimwade, "Silver at Althorp—II: The Candlesticks and Candelabra," *Connoisseur* 152 (March 1963):159, fig. 1. Grimwade states that the baluster stem appears in French candlesticks as early as 1636. Further, he notes a pair of Paris candlesticks of 1678/79 with sockets and stems almost identical to those of the Harache candlesticks at Althorp House.

6 PAIR OF CANDLESTICKS
William Denny and John Bache
London. 1698/99

6

Fully marked on underside of each base.

H: 8¾" (22.2 cm); W (base): 5⅛" (13 cm). Total wt: 25 oz. 12 dwt. 1½ gr. ("26=14" engraved on underside of each base).

PROVENANCE: Garrard & Co. Ltd., London (purchased from J. C. Lowe, London, 1962)

The predominant form of late seventeenth-century candlestick is architectural in character with a columnar stem, either fluted, as in this instance, or of clustered gothic type. Such candlesticks were fashioned from sheet with the fluting and gadrooning chased. Their lack of sturdiness may have prompted William Fitzhugh to write his London purchasing agents in 1688 from his plantation on the Potomac River in Stafford County, Virginia, "the plate that I would have bought pray let it be plain and strong . . . A pair of silver Candlesticks less than them sent last year by Mr. Hayward but more substantiall."[1]

A pair of similar candlesticks by Thomas Jenkins of London (1699/1700) is also in the Colonial Williamsburg collection (1936-444, 1–2).

1962-188, 1–2

---

1. Letter from William Fitzhugh to John Cooper and Nicholas Hayward, dated June 1, 1688. Davis, R.B., p. 244.

7 PAIR OF CANDLESTICKS
John Jackson
London. 1709/10

Fully marked on underside of each base; lion's head erased on each socket.

H: 6¹³⁄₁₆" (17.3 cm); W (base): 4 9⁄32" (10.9 cm). Total wt: 26 oz. 4 dwt. 7 gr. ("13=12" and "13=15" engraved on undersides of respective bases).

PROVENANCE: Garrard & Co. Ltd., London (purchased from C. J. Vander Ltd., London, 1953)

1954-519, 1–2

8 PAIR OF CANDLESTICKS
Thomas Merry
London. 1712/13

7

8

Fully marked on underside of each base; lion's head erased on each socket.

Unidentified crest engraved on face of each base.

9

Fully marked on underside of each base; lion's head erased on each socket.

H: 7⅜″ (18.7 cm); W (base): 4 1/16″ (10.3 cm). Total wt: 21 oz. 6 dwt. 13 gr.

PROVENANCE: Garrard & Co. Ltd., London (purchased from David Udy, Hinton House, Amersham, Buckinghamshire, 1957)

PUBLISHED: Advertisement, Hinton House, *Apollo* 65 (July 1957):iii, ill.; "Accessions of American and Canadian Museums, July–September, 1958," *Art Quarterly* 21 (Winter 1958):444, ill.

The maker's mark on these candlesticks was long thought to be that of Lewis Mettayer. Recent research by Arthur Grimwade and Stanley Percival has resulted in the reattribution of this mark to Thomas Merry, who entered it at the Goldsmiths' Hall on June 19, 1701.[1] A very similar pair of candlesticks with only minor variations by Edward Winslow (1669–1753) of Boston are also in the Colonial Williamsburg collection (1962-263, 1–2).[2]

1957-152, 1–2

---

1. Stanley T. B. Percival, "Thomas Merry, Citizen and Goldsmith of London," *Connoisseur* 74 (August 1970):270–74.
2. Joseph T. Butler, *Candleholders in America, 1650–1900* (New York: Crown Publishers, 1967), p. 33, fig. 15.

9 FOUR CANDLESTICKS
Thomas Folkingham
London. 1720/21

H: 6½″ (16.5 cm); W (base): 4⅛″ (10.5 cm). Total wt: 53 oz. 14 dwt. 2½ gr.

PROVENANCE: The Goldsmiths & Silversmiths Co. Ltd., London (now Garrard & Co. Ltd.) (1950); Sotheby & Co., London (1962)

PUBLISHED: *The Connoisseur Souvenir of the Tenth Antique Dealers' Fair and Exhibition* (June 1950), p. 55, ill.; advertisement, Goldsmiths & Silversmiths Co. Ltd., London, *Connoisseur* 126 (October 1950):xxxi, ill.; "Sotheby's March Sales," *Burlington Magazine* 104 (March 1962):xxvii, ill.; Sotheby's (March 15, 1962), lot 134, frontispiece; *Sotheby's Annual Review, 218th Season, October, 1961–August, 1962* (London: Sotheby & Co., 1962), p. 110, ill.; Hackenbroch, rev. edn., p. 67

Folkingham continued to work, as did several makers, in the higher Britannia standard after it had become optional with the reinstatement of the sterling standard in 1720. These handsome candlesticks with bold moldings and unusual ribbed decoration are an elegant variation, favored by Folkingham, of this basically plain, polygonal type of candlestick. Two pairs of candlesticks of identical design of 1718/19 by Folkingham, one pair of smaller size, and an earlier pair (1715/16) of similar form with ribbed stems and related radiate base decoration, are in the Untermyer collection.[1] A pair of candlesticks of 1714/15 by Folkingham, virtually identical to those of the following year in the Untermyer collection, were advertised for sale in 1947 and 1952.[2] Possibly the earliest candlesticks of this type by Folkingham are a pair of 1712/13 with ribbed stems and a molded panel on the upper face of and repeating the plan of their bases.[3]

1962-136, 1–2; 137, 1–2

---

1. Hackenbroch, p. 69, no. 144, pl. 150; rev. edn., p. 67, no. 128, ill. The pair of 1715/16 is not included in the first edition. The two pairs of 1718/19 are also illustrated in an advertisement of the Goldsmiths & Silversmiths Co. Ltd., London, *Antique Collector* 18 (July–August 1947): unp.

2. Advertisement, Biggs of Maidenhead, *Connoisseur* 120 (December 1947):xxxv, ill.; advertisement, Goldsmiths & Silversmiths Co. Ltd., London, *Antique Collector* 23 (June 1952):104, ill.

3. Christie's (July 19, 1967), lot 221, ill.

10 FOUR CANDLESTICKS
David Green
London. 1723/24

Fully marked on underside of each base.

H: 6¼″ (15.9 cm); W (base): 3¹³⁄₁₆″ (9.7 cm). Total wt: 39 oz. 11 dwt. 5 gr. Set numbers "I," "II," "III," and "IIII" engraved on undersides of respective bases.

PROVENANCE: Museum of Fine Arts, Boston

PUBLISHED: Edith Gaines, "The Buildings," *Antiques* 95 (January 1969):92–93, ill.

1954-326, 1–4

11 PAIR OF CANDLESTICKS
James Gould
London. 1727/28

10

11

Fully marked on underside of each base.

H: 6⅜″ (16.2 cm); W (base): 3⅞″ (9.8 cm). Total wt: 23 oz. 15 dwt.

PROVENANCE: Garrard & Co. Ltd., London (purchased from Lady Kroyer Kielburg, London, 1958)
1958-637, 3–4

12 PAIR OF CANDLESTICKS
Silver-gilt
Paul Crespin
London. 1727/28

12

Fully marked on underside of each base; removable nozzles of later date unmarked.

H: 9¾″ (24.8 cm); Diam (base): 5⅛″ (13 cm). Total wt: 52 oz. 6 dwt. 8½ gr. ("25=13" and "24=14" engraved on undersides of respective bases).

PROVENANCE: William Randolph Hearst (sold by Parish-Watson & Co., New York, 1938)

PUBLISHED: Williamsburg (b), p. 250, ill.

These candlesticks, totally in the French taste, illustrate the classical tendencies of the Huguenot style. Not only is the ornament of classical derivation (the acanthus bandings of socket and base, the Roman portrait busts of the stem, and the guilloche banding of the knop of the stem), but also the disposition of form and ornament is classical in attitude. The form is balanced and restrained, and the ornament is formally disposed.

Arms of Sir Edward Kerrison (1774–1853) quartered with those of Barnes and Thornes engraved on exterior of each base with crest on nozzles. Arms were engraved after his elevation to baronet in 1821 and before a grant of honourable augmentation to his arms in 1841.

Candlesticks of this type first appear in English silver in the early years of the eighteenth century. Twelve such candlesticks, engraved with the arms and cypher of Queen Anne, two of which bear the legible date letter for 1702/3, were part of the plate provided to Robert Harley as speaker of the House of Commons between 1701 and 1705.[1] Most candlesticks of this pattern, however, date from the 1720s. These later candlesticks, the Williamsburg pair included, were probably modeled after examples by Nicolas Besnier, the noted Parisian silversmith. Interestingly enough, there is a similar candlestick of 1723/24 by Besnier with a long history of English ownership. It is part of a large suite of French silver acquired by Viscount William Bateman and his wife, Lady Anne Spencer, in the years immediately following their marriage in 1720.[2]

Among similar candlesticks of the same year by Crespin are a set of fourteen with engraved royal arms. They were owned by Philip Dormer Stanhope, 4th earl of Chesterfield, and may have formed part of his plate as ambassador to The Hague from 1728 to 1731.[3]

1938-29, 1–2

1. E. Alfred Jones, *Catalogue of Plate Belonging to the Duke of Portland, K.G., G.C.V.O. at Welbeck Abbey* (London: St. Catherine Press, 1935), p. 60, pl. v. A pair of very similar candlesticks of 1705/6 are illustrated in an advertisement by S. J. Phillips, London, *Apollo* 91 (February 1970):liii.

2. Faith Dennis, *Three Centuries of French Domestic Silver, Its Makers and Its Marks* (New York: Metropolitan Museum of Art, 1960), 1:64, fig. 56; *French Master Goldsmiths and Silversmiths from the Seventeenth to the Nineteenth Century* (New York: French & European Publications, 1966), pp. 88–89, fig. 5.

3. These, at least in part, were acquired by William Randolph Hearst at auction (Christie's [May 11, 1927], lot 63, ill.). Four of them were sold by Hearst in 1939 (Parke-Bernet [January 7, 1939], lot 251, ill.). Four candlesticks from this large set, perhaps the four sold by Hearst, are illustrated in Wenham, p. 203, fig. 4. Other pairs of candlesticks of this type of the same year by Crespin are illustrated in Sotheby's (May 20, 1965), lot 142 and in an advertisement by de Havilland Ltd., London, *Apollo* 88 (November 1968): cvii. Paul de Lamerie fashioned similar candlesticks.

13

13 PAIR OF CANDLESTICKS
Matthew Cooper
London. 1729/30

Fully marked on underside of each base.

Crest of Jackson, Cumberland and Oxfordshire, engraved on exterior of each base.

H: 6½″ (16.5 cm); W (base): 4¹⁄₁₆″ (10.3 cm). Total wt: 23 oz. 1 dwt. 18 gr.

PROVENANCE: Garrard & Co. Ltd., London

These candlesticks were acquired with a practically identical pair of the same date by Thomas Mann of London (1967-166, 1–2).

1967-167, 1–2

14 PAIR OF CANDLESTICKS
William Gould
London. 1741/42

Fully marked on underside of each base.

14

15

H: 7⅟₁₆″ (17.9 cm); W (base): 4³⁄₁₆″ (10.6 cm). Total wt: 27 oz. 6 dwt. 7½ gr.

PROVENANCE: Garrard & Co. Ltd., London (purchased from C. J. Vander Ltd., London, 1954)

1954-551, 1-2

15 FOUR CANDLESTICKS
William Gould
London. 1741/42

Fully marked on underside of each base; lion passant on each socket; removable nozzles unmarked.

H: 6⅞″ (17.5 cm); Diam (base): 4⅜″ (11.1 cm). Total wt: 60 oz. 8 dwt. 18 gr. ("1 16," "2 15=8," "3 15=8," and "4 15=5" engraved on undersides of respective bases).

PROVENANCE: P. A. E. Archer of Trelaske, Launceston, Cornwall (apparent descent in family; sold at Christie, Manson & Woods, London, 1958; purchased by C. J.

Vander Ltd., London); Garrard & Co. Ltd., London

PUBLISHED: Christie's (June 4, 1958), lot 140, pl. VIII

Arms of Archer, Cornwall, engraved on exterior of each base.

A pair of candlesticks of the same year, probably by James Gould, of virtually identical design except for plain nozzles and the inclusion of shells in the recesses of their bases are engraved with the arms and crest of the Nelson family of Virginia and have descended with other family silver known to have been owned by Thomas Nelson (1677–1745) of Yorktown, who married Margaret Reade in 1710. These candlesticks are on loan to the National Park Service.

1958-475, 1-4

16 PAIR OF CANDLESTICKS
Probably William Gould
London. 1748/49

16

Fully marked on underside of each base; lion passant on each socket; nozzles unmarked.

Arms of the Lightfoot family of Virginia engraved on exterior of each base with crest on each nozzle.

H: 8½″ (21.6 cm); W (base): 4⅜″ (11.1 cm). Total wt: 36 oz. 16 dwt. 19½ gr.

PROVENANCE: Miss Elise H. Bolling, Richmond, Virginia

These candlesticks, as well as a snuffer tray of 1749/50 by Simon Jouet of London (No. 30), are both engraved with the arms of the Lightfoot family of Virginia. They are believed to have been originally owned by William Lightfoot (1722–before 1771) of Teddington, Charles City County, and Yorktown, and to have descended in the Lightfoot, Minge, and Bolling families. These were acquired with snuffers of about 1785 by William and George Richardson of Richmond, Virginia (1955-164).

1955-162, 1–2

17 PAIR OF CANDLESTICKS
John Cafe
London. 1750/51

17

Fully marked on underside of each base; removable nozzles unmarked.

H: 8½″ (21.6 cm); Diam (base): 5¼″ (13.3 cm). Total wt: 34 oz. 14 dwt. 16 gr.

Arms of Churchman impaling Harvey engraved on exterior of each base.

PROVENANCE: Garrard & Co. Ltd., London (purchased from Bracher and Sydenham, Reading, 1954)

John Cafe and to a lesser extent his brother and former apprentice, William, like the Goulds, were prolific makers of candlesticks during the middle decades of the eighteenth century. Four identical candlesticks by John Cafe (two 1752/53, one 1754/55, and one 1759/60) are also in the collection (1947-425, 1–4).

1954-574, 1–2

18 PAIR OF CANDLESTICKS
John Holland
London. 1755/56

Fully marked on underside of each base; removable nozzles unmarked.

Unidentified crest engraved on face of each nozzle and base.

H: 12⁷⁄₁₆″ (31.6 cm); W (base): 5¾″ (14.6 cm). Total wt: 28 oz. 16 dwt. 15½ gr. ("N° 3 14 ‖ 10" and "N° 4 14 ‖ 12" engraved on undersides of respective bases indicating an original set of at least four candlesticks).

PROVENANCE: Stair and Andrew Ltd., London

These unusual candlesticks are of hybrid form. Their bases correspond closely with those of late seven-

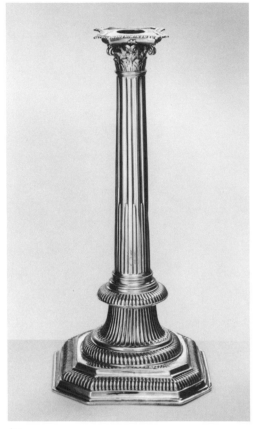

18

teenth-century columnar candlesticks, even including the pronounced knop at the bottoms of their stems, a vestige of the still earlier drip pan (see No. 6). Their stems of Corinthian columnar form with articulated capitals for sockets, on the other hand, anticipate fully architectural candlesticks, such as the set of four of 1761/62 by John Robinson of London (No. 20). A set of four very similar hybrid candlesticks of 1754/55 by John Wirgman of London are recorded.[1] Other related hybrid candlesticks, without knops at the bottoms of their stems and with plainer bases of shaped octagonal form with gadrooned edges, include a set of four of 1754/55, probably by William Justus of London,[2] a pair of 1754/55 by David Willaume, Jr., of London at Clare College, Cambridge,[3] and a pair of 1755/56 by Peter Werritzer of London at Merton College, Oxford.[4]

1936-443, 1–2

---

1. Advertisement, S. J. Shrubsole Ltd., New York and London, *Antiques* 98 (November 1970):723, ill. and *Connoisseur* 179 (March 1972):91, ill.

2. Christie's (November 29, 1972), lot 67, ill.

3. E. Alfred Jones, *Catalogue of the Plate of Clare College, Cambridge* (Cambridge: University Press, 1939), pp. 26–27, pl. XVII.

4. E. Alfred Jones, *Catalogue of the Plate of Merton College, Oxford* (Oxford: Oxford University Press, 1938), pl. 7. A set of four candlesticks of this pattern of the same year by Werritzer are illustrated in Sotheby's (February 24, 1966), lot 153.

Unidentified crests engraved on each base and nozzle.

A very similar candlestick of 1771/72 by Ebenezer Coker of London is among the Carter family silver at Shirley, Charles City County, Virginia.

1954-536, 1–4

19 FOUR CANDLESTICKS
William Cafe
London. 1760/61

19

Fully marked on underside of each base; maker's mark and lion passant on exterior of each socket and on bezel of each nozzle.

H: 9¾″ (24.8 cm); W (base): 4⅞″ (11.3 cm). Total wt: 91 oz. 6 dwt. 21½ gr.

PROVENANCE: Viscountess Bertie of Thame (sold at Christie, Manson & Woods, London, 1954; purchased by Garrard & Co. Ltd., London)

PUBLISHED: Christie's (June 30, 1954), lot 81, ill.

20 FOUR CANDLESTICKS
John Robinson
London. 1761/62

20

Fully marked on underside of each base; maker's mark and lion passant on bezel of each removable nozzle.

Unidentified crest engraved on each base and nozzle.

H: 12⅞″ (31.6 cm); W (base): 5³⁄₁₆″ (13.2 cm).
Total wt: 98 oz. 8 dwt. 2 gr.

PROVENANCE: Henry Philip Strause, Richmond, Virginia (sold by Thalhimer Brothers, Richmond, 1945)

This standard type of columnar candlestick, usually in the Corinthian order, was fully developed by the late 1750s. An early set of four such candlesticks of 1756/57 by Thomas Gilpin of London are at Althorp House.[1] Candlesticks of this type are often considered solely a function of the neoclassical movement, and, indeed, their sheer quantity after 1760 and their obvious formal derivation have made them emblematic of the movement. There are, however, earlier eighteenth-century columnar candlesticks with a pretention towards architectural correctness, which are expressions of the classical strain in Palladian taste, such as the pair of 1755/56 by John Holland (No. 18), as well as related examples noted in regard to them, and a set of four in the Ionic order with stepped square bases of 1745/46 by Paul de Lamerie.[2] Further, one encounters columnar candlesticks from the 1740s and 1750s with their stems twisted in a baroque manner and supported on rococo bases.[3] The presence of these earlier candlesticks as prototypical material, the standard renderings of the orders in many eighteenth-century design books, and the obvious and appropriate choice of such models, help explain the early incidence of fully developed columnar candlesticks in silver in the neoclassical style.

A pair of similar candlesticks in the Corinthian order from a set of at least four with a history of ownership in the Byrd family of Virginia have survived. Probably made by Ebenezer Coker of London in 1765/66 and engraved with the Byrd family crest, they were originally owned by William Byrd III (1728–1777) of Westover, Charles City County, and his wife, Mary Willing Byrd (1740–1814). They are privately owned by a descendant. William McCaa of

Norfolk advertised for sale in the *Virginia Gazette* for January 18, 1770, among other silver, "Two pair of neat silver candlesticks, with fluted Corinthian pillars and capitals, &c. (65 ounces and a half)" and "A pair of fluted silver tea candlesticks with pillars and capitals to match the large (about 11 ounces and a half)." These candlesticks testify to the use of silver of neoclassical design in Virginia before the Revolution.

This form of candlestick strongly appealed to the classical sensitivities of Thomas Jefferson. After his house in Paris was robbed in 1789, he wrote to John Trumbull in London:

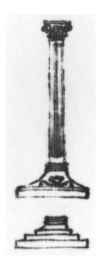

One article they took obliges me to trouble you. This was my candlesticks, all of which I lost. I have searched every shop in Paris and cannot find a tolerable pattern: therefore I will beg the favor of you to send me 4. pair plated from London. Mine were plated and came from there, and I am sure the pattern is common there. It was a fluted Corinthian column, with the capital of it's order, and the bottom of the candlestick was of the form in the margin. I recollect to have once seen the undermost form, which I thought very handsome. Mine were about 12. Inches high. I must trouble you therefore to find one of these patterns for me, and indeed I think no form is so handsome as that of the column. . . .[4]

Trumbull acquired these for Jefferson, who used them in Paris and brought them back with him to Monticello. Unfortunately, their present location is not known.[5]

1945-5, 1–4

1. Arthur G. Grimwade, "Silver at Althorp—II: The Candlesticks and Candelabra," *Connoisseur* 152 (March 1963):163, fig. 5.
2. Advertisement, Thomas Lumley Ltd., London, *Antique Collector* 22 (January–February 1951): back cover, ill.
3. Representative of these are sets of four of 1747/48 by Peter Archambo, Sr., of London (Christie's [January 29, 1969], pl. 16; Hartman Galleries Inc., *English Silver of Four Centuries, 1585–1835* [New York, 1969], no. 35), and of 1759/60 by Lewis Hearne and Francis Butty of London (Christie's [December 2,

1964], lot 10, ill.; advertisement, S. J. Phillips, Ltd., London, *Connoisseur* 176 [April 1971]:23, ill.).

4. Julian P. Boyd, ed., *The Papers of Thomas Jefferson*, 19 vols. to date (Princeton: Princeton University Press, 1950–), 15:335. Marginal drawing courtesy of Library of Congress, Washington, D.C.

5. James A. Bear, Jr., *Report of the Curator to the Board of Directors of the Thomas Jefferson Memorial Foundation* (Monticello, 1962), pp. 17–18.

21 PAIR OF CANDLESTICKS
John Winter & Co.
Sheffield. Retailed by John Carter of
    London
Overstruck London hallmarks of 1774/75

Maker's mark on bezel of each removable nozzle (partially obliterated by filing); retailer's mark and London hallmarks overstruck on Sheffield hallmarks on edge of each base; retailer's mark and London lion passant overstruck on that of Sheffield on bezel of each nozzle. Bases and stems weighted with resin.

Crest of the Custis family of Virginia engraved on each base and nozzle.

21

H: 11 11/16″ (29.7 cm); W (base): 5″ (12.7 cm).

PROVENANCE: John Parke Custis (1755–1781), and his wife, Eleanor Calvert (1758–1811); their son, George Washington Parke Custis (1781–1857), and his wife, Mary Lee Fitzhugh (1768–1853); their daughter, Mary Anne Randolph Custis (1808–1873), and her husband, General Robert E. Lee (1807–1870); their son, William Henry Fitzhugh Lee (1837–1891), and his wife, Mary Tabb Bolling (b. 1850); their son, Robert E. Lee III, and his wife, Mary Memminger; their nephew and his wife, Mr.

and Mrs. Beverly Middleton; and James C. Barrett (sold at Parke-Bernet Galleries, New York, 1969)

PUBLISHED: Parke-Bernet (October 28, 1969), lot 103, ill.; *Art at Auction: The Year at Sotheby's & Parke-Bernet, 1969–70, The Two Hundred and Thirty-sixth Season* (New York: Viking Press, 1970), p. 370, ill.

These neoclassical candlesticks are from an original set of six and are part of an impressive group of silver acquired by John Parke Custis and his wife, Eleanor Calvert, shortly after their marriage in 1774.[1] He was born at White House, New Kent County, not far from Williamsburg. When he came of age, he inherited this and other properties in and about Williamsburg. His widowed mother, Martha Custis, married George Washington in 1759, and he was raised as a boy at Mt. Vernon. Serving as an aide to Washington, he contracted camp fever at Yorktown and died in 1781. His silver, listed before his death, amounted to 762 oz. 18 dwt.[2] The other four candlesticks of the set are at Mount Vernon, on loan by descendants.

These were not made in the traditional manner with relief decoration chased with hammer-driven punches. Rather, they are assembled of parts stamped out by steel dies. The development of the die-stamping industry in Sheffield made it the principal center in England for the production of candlesticks in the neoclassical taste. Die-stamping greatly lowered the cost of candlesticks and other items with overall raised decoration. The parts could be stamped out of a relatively thin gauge of silver, and the whole, as in this instance, strengthened and weighted by loading the interior with resinous material.

John Winter & Co., the principal firm in the Sheffield candlestick trade, wholesaled much of its production to London retailers. Before the establishment of an assay office in Sheffield, silver had to be sent to London or another assay office for marking. That was a convenient arrangement for London silversmiths, such as John Carter—a specialist maker of candlesticks himself, who depended on supplementing his own wares with those from Sheffield. He and other London silversmiths testified before committee hearings in the House of Commons against granting an assay office to Sheffield. It was established in 1773, however, and given its own distinctive marks. Thereafter many Sheffield candlesticks, such as these, were overstruck by John Carter, the principal figure in this practice, and a cooperative London hall.[3]

Predicated on the free use of a variety of classical forms and detail, with little attention to classical precedent for their overall scheme, these candlesticks exemplify contemporary neoclassical treatment. The main section of the stem is actually not a classical tripod, since an additional leg has been added for the convenience of the design. This free use of classical elements was reinforced by the commercial nature of the production of such candlesticks. When one examines other candlesticks and trade catalogs of the period, one can readily see that these and other factory-made candlesticks, both sterling and plated, are often random combinations of interchangeable sockets, stems, and bases.

These candlesticks, as well as some of the other Custis plate, further document the use of neoclassical silver in Virginia before the Revolution (see No. 20).[4]

A pair of identical candlesticks of 1774/75 with the maker's mark of George Ashforth & Co. of Sheffield are in the Victoria and Albert Museum, London.[5] A pair of candlesticks of this pattern in fused silverplate are at Temple Newsam House, Leeds.[6]

1969-246, 1–2

1. Buhler, pp. 24–33.

2. "A List of Plate with the Weight of the Different Articles belonging to JP Custis Jany. 26 1781" (MS, privately owned; copies at Mount Vernon and in the Department of Collections, Colonial Williamsburg Foundation).

3. Bradbury, pp. 189–90, 219; S. W. Turner, "The Establishment and Development of the Silver and Plate Industry in Sheffield," *Apollo* 96 (December 1947):143–45, 149; Rowe, pp. 37, 67–68, 84–85. Bradbury illustrates several dies for stamping candlestick parts (pp. 102–3).

4. Other Custis silver in the neoclassical taste, all London, 1774/75, includes: a hot water urn, a two-handled covered cup, a hot water jug, and a cruet frame by John Carter; a sugar basket and two tea canisters by William Sumner; and a breadbasket by Burrage Davenport (Buhler, pp. 24–33).

5. Victoria and Albert Museum, *Adam Silver* (London, 1953), fig. 6; Oman (c), fig. 156.

6. *Leeds Art Calender*, no. 58 (1966):4, pl. 2.

22 PAIR OF CANDLESTICKS
John Wakelin and William Taylor
London. 1782/83

22

Fully marked on side of each base; removable nozzles unmarked.

Owner's cypher engraved on each nozzle and base.

H: 11¼" (28.6 cm); Diam (base): 5⁹⁄₁₆" (14.1 cm). Total wt: 23 oz. 5 dwt. ("№ 1 11–16" and "№ 2 11–13" engraved on rims of respective sockets).

PROVENANCE: Henry Philip Strause, Richmond, Virginia (sold by Thalhimer Brothers, Richmond, 1945)

1945-4, 1–2

23 HAND CANDLESTICK
London. 1683/84

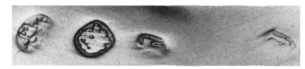

Fully marked in saucer; maker's mark on underside of handle.

Owner's initials engraved on underside of saucer.

L: 8⅜" (21.3 cm); Diam (saucer): 5¹⁵⁄₃₂" (13.9 cm). Wt: 6 oz. 6 dwt. 11 gr.

PROVENANCE: Sotheby & Co., London (1963)

PUBLISHED: Sotheby's (June 27, 1963), lot 9, ill.

Seventeenth-century hand or chamber candlesticks are quite rare; something less than twenty examples survive.[1] The piercing of the socket, often of decorative design, to facilitate the removal of candle stubs is customary on early examples. Such candlesticks

were produced in ever-increasing quantities. By the late eighteenth and early nineteenth centuries, examples, both sterling and plated, are quite common.

1963-137

---

1. Clayton, p. 44. The earliest hand candlestick cited by Clayton dates from 1652/53. It was sold in 1903, and its present location is unknown.

24 HAND CANDLESTICK
James Gould
London. 1734/35

24

Fully marked on underside of saucer; lion passant on socket.

Fully marked on underside of base.

Arms of Manlove impaling those of unidentified family engraved in saucer.

Unidentified crest engraved on exterior of base.

L: 6⁷⁄₃₂″ (15.8 cm); Diam (saucer): 5¼″ (13.3 cm). Wt: 8 oz. 6 dwt. 15½ gr.

PROVENANCE: Garrard & Co. Ltd., London (purchased from C. J. Vander Ltd., London, 1954)

1954-572

25 TAPERSTICK
John Bignell
London. 1725/26

25

H: 4¹⁄₁₆″ (10.3 cm); W (base): 2⅝″ (6.7 cm). Wt: 3 oz. 15 dwt.

PROVENANCE: Garrard & Co. Ltd., London (purchased from C. J. Vander Ltd., London, 1954)

Tapersticks, which first appeared in the late seventeenth century, follow· closely the design of larger contemporary candlesticks. Used primarily for the melting of sealing wax, they formed an important part of a gentleman's writing equipage. Although popular during the first half of the eighteenth century, their function was soon usurped by the taper stand or wax jack and the taper box or bougie box.

William Fitzhugh of Stafford County, Virginia, would appear to have owned a silver taperstick at an early date. "3 pair silver Candlesticks 1 small writing Do." are listed with the plate in the 1701 inventory of his estate.[1] The latter was most likely a taperstick. "2 Taper Candlesticks" appear with the plate in the 1770 inventory of the estate of Lord Botetourt, who had served for the previous two years as governor of Virginia.[2]

1954-550

1. Davis, R. B., p. 382.
2. Botetourt Inventory.

26 TAPERSTICK
Probably David Green
London. 1725/26

H: 4⁵⁄₁₆″ (11 cm); W (base): 2⅝″ (6.7 cm). Wt: 3 oz. 7 dwt. 7 gr.

26

Fully marked on underside of base.

PROVENANCE: Crichton Bros., London

PUBLISHED: Williamsburg (b), p. 257, ill.

1936-448

27

27 TAPERSTICK
James Gould
London. 1731/32

Fully marked on underside of base.

H: 4¼″ (10.8 cm); W (base): 2²¹⁄₃₂″ (6.8 cm). Wt: 2 oz. 16 dwt. 18 gr.

PROVENANCE: Crichton Bros., London

1936-449

28 TAPERSTICK
John Cafe
London. 1746/47

28

Fully marked on underside of base.

H: 4⅝" (11.8 cm); W (base): 2¹⁵⁄₁₆" (7.5 cm). Wt: 4 oz. 9 dwt.

PROVENANCE: William Randolph Hearst (sold by Parish-Watson & Co., New York, 1938)

PUBLISHED: Williamsburg (b), p. 251, ill.

This was acquired with a later removable nozzle of 1850/51.

1938-27

29 BOUGIE OR TAPER BOX
Samuel Wood
London. 1744/45

29

Fully marked on underside of cover and base.

H: 3⅜" (8.6 cm); Diam (base): 2⅞" (7.3 cm). Wt: 8 oz. 5 dwt. 6 gr.

Unidentified crest engraved on face of body opposite handle.

PROVENANCE: Crichton Bros., London

PUBLISHED: Williamsburg (b), p. 257, ill.; Clayton, p. 296

This is a particularly early and large example.

1936-446

30 SNUFFER TRAY
Simon Jouet
London. 1749/50

Fully marked on underside.

Arms of the Lightfoot family of Virginia engraved in center.

H: 2⅛" (5.4 cm); H (rim): ⅞" (2.2 cm); L: 8" (20.3 cm); W: 4" (10.2 cm). Wt: 10 oz. 7 dwt. 23 gr.

PROVENANCE: Miss Elise H. Bolling, Richmond, Virginia

This snuffer tray, as well as the pair of candlesticks of 1748/49, probably by William Gould of London (No. 16), are both engraved with the arms of the Lightfoot family of Virginia. They are believed to

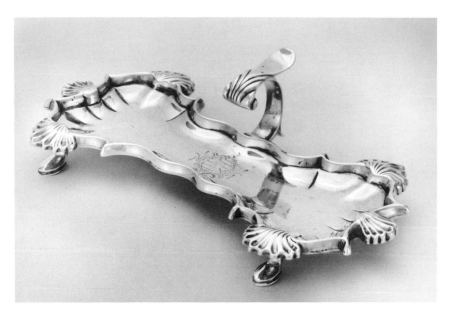

30

have been originally owned by William Lightfoot (1722–before 1771) of Teddington, Charles City County, and Yorktown, and to have descended in the Lightfoot, Minge, and Bolling families. Acquired with them were snuffers of about 1785 by William and George Richardson of Richmond, Virginia (1955-164).

1955-163

Vessels and Accessories for Alcoholic Beverages

31 WINE FOUNTAIN
Silver-gilt
Joseph Ward
London. 1702/3

Fully marked on face of neck; maker's mark and lion's head erased on bezel of cover; lion's head erased on exterior of base.

Arms of John Holles (1662–1711), earl of Clare and duke of Newcastle, engraved on face of body. Arms of Holles impaling Eastley, Scopham, Hanham, Denzell, Gilbert, Clare, Sergeaux, Bulbeck, Vere, Sandford, and Baldesmere, enclosed within Garter motto, flanked by supporters, and surmounted by ducal coronet.

H: 24⅝″ (62.6 cm); W: 14½″ (36.8 cm); Diam (base): 7″ (17.8 cm). Wt: 308 oz. 6 dwt.

PROVENANCE: The dukes of Newcastle (sold at Christie, Manson & Woods, London, 1921); H. H. Mulliner (sold at Christie, Manson & Woods, London, 1924); William Randolph Hearst (sold by Parish-Watson & Co., New York, 1938)

EXHIBITED: Loan Collection in Aid of the Children's Hospital, St. James's Court, London, 1902

PUBLISHED: J. Starkie Gardner, Old Silver-work, *Chiefly English, from the XVth to the XVIIIth Centuries* (London: B. T. Batsford Ltd., 1903), pl. LXXXVI, fig. 1; ———, "Silver Plate in the Collection of the Duke of Newcastle at Clumber," *Burlington Magazine* 8 (November 1905): 127, pl. 1, fig. 2; Christie's (July 7, 1921), lot 70; Mulliner, fig. 95; H. Avray Tipping, "The Mulliner Col-

31

lection—II: English Silver Plate," *Country Life* 55 (June 28, 1924):1037–39, fig. 3A; Christie's (July 9, 1924), lot 42, ill.; Williamsburg (b), p. 250, ill.; Clayton, p. 342.

Among the most lavish productions of the late seventeenth and early eighteenth centuries are forms used in the service of wine, such as the wine cistern and wine fountain, monteith, and ice pail. Wine cisterns of various materials have a much earlier history than wine fountains. Appearing in Continental prints and paintings from the late fifteenth century on, their use in England can be documented from the following century.[1] The 1574 inventory of the plate of Elizabeth I contains "Item oone great Sesterne of siluer to serue for a Cupbourde poiz" with a weight of 525½ ounces.[2] The wine fountain in the form of a large urn fitted with a tap does not appear to have been used in England before the reign of Charles II. Although sometimes made *en suite* with a wine cistern, fountains appear to have been less common than cisterns then, and they have survived in fewer numbers to this day.[3] There is no recorded companion cistern for this fountain.

Even though the large wine cistern was intended to rest on the floor and house chilling bottles of wine, and the wine fountain to rest on a side table and dispense the wine, such vessels, even in royal circumstances, were sometimes used for the more mundane task of washing dishes. The Treasury copy of the 1721 inventory of royal plate lists one fountain and small cistern, which are described in the lord chamberlain's copy of the same document as a "fountain and washer."[4]

Such vessels were not unknown, or at least not unthought of, in Williamsburg. When the Council drafted in 1710 a proposed list of furnishings for the Governor's Palace "for rendering the new House Convenient as well as Ornamental," they included "one Marble Buffette or sideboard with a Cistern & fountain."[5] There is no indication whether these were to be of silver or some lesser metal, or whether they were actually acquired.

This splendid example of elegant baluster form is less ornate than most examples. It is enriched with bands of chased flutes, a form of decoration especially popular during the first decade of the eighteenth century. They act as an effective foil for its bold architectural form and the handsome lions' masks with pendant handles. Such masks were frequently employed as attachments for handles on large vessels. They represent some of the finest examples of cast work during this period (see No. 23).

1938-44

---

1. N. M. Penzer, "The Great Wine-Coolers—I," *Apollo* 66 (August 1957):3–7; "The Great Wine-Coolers—II," *Apollo* 66 (September 1957):39–46.
2. Penzer, "The Great Wine-Coolers—II, p. 39; Oman (a), pp. 45–46. Penzer notes that that cistern also appears in the 1559 inventory made after the death of Mary, Queen of Scots. The earliest surviving English wine cistern is from the Rosebery collection and dates from 1667/68. Penzer records thirteen seventeenth-century examples and twenty-four dating from 1700 to 1735 ("The Great Wine-Coolers—II," pp. 41–46).
3. Oman (a), p. 46. The earliest surviving English wine fountain dates from about 1670. It and its companion wine cistern bear only the maker's mark. They are engraved with the arms of Philip Stanhope, 2nd earl of Chesterfield (ibid., p. 46, plates 37A and 38;

Penzer, "The Great Wine-Coolers—II," p. 41, fig. II, p. 40).
4. Hayward, p. 35.
5. H. R. McIlwaine, ed., *Legislative Journals of the Council of Colonial Virginia* (Richmond: Colonial Press, 1919), 3:1557.

32 MONTEITH
London. 1688/89

Fully marked on underside of base.

Arms and crest of Duckenfield, Cheshire, engraved on face of body. Owner's initials, probably those of a member of the Duckenfield family, engraved on underside of base.

H: 5¾″ (14.6 cm); Diam (rim): 10¾″ (27.3 cm); Diam (base): 6¼″ (15.9 cm). Wt: 31 oz. 10 dwt. ½ gr.

PROVENANCE: Mallett & Son, London (purchased at Christie, Manson & Woods, London, 1908); Garrard & Co. Ltd., London

PUBLISHED: Christie's (July 15, 1908), lot 147; "Accessions of American and Canadian Museums, January–March, 1962," *Art Quarterly* 25 (Summer 1962): 180, ill. p. 171

The monteith first appears in English silver in the late seventeenth century. The earliest literary mention of this form is by Anthony à Wood, the Oxford diarist, who noted in December, 1683:

This yeare in the summer time came up a vessel or bason notched at the brims to let drinking glasses hang there by the foot so that the body or drinking place might hang in the water to coole them. Such a bason was called a 'Monteigh' from a fantastical Scot called 'Monsieur Monteigh,' who at that time

32

or a little before wore the bottome of his cloake or coate so notched UUUU.[1]

Nathaniel Bailey, in his *Dictionary Britannicum* (London, 1730), ascribes the same function to the form as Wood. He defines a monteith as "a scallopped Bason to coole Glasses in." Perhaps reflecting a change in use by which time monteiths had declined in favor, Samuel Johnson, in his *Dictionary of the English Language* (London, 1775), describes a monteith as "A vessel in which glasses are washed." He includes the following couplet from William King's *Art of Cookery, In Imitation of Horace's Art of Poetry* (London, 1708):

New things produce new words, and thus
Monteth
has by one vessel sav'd his Name from Death.

He inaccurately adds that its name is "from the inventor."

The earliest surviving monteiths date from 1684, the year after Wood's passage.[2] This example is characteristic of the earliest type, having a straight notched rim on a simple hemispherical body supported on a broad, spool-form foot. It is distinguished, as are a number of examples of this type, with a repeat of flat-chased chinoiserie scenes. Such decoration appears on a broad range of forms, bearing the marks of a number of makers and dating mainly from the late 1670s and 1680s. The close similarity of this decoration has prompted Dauterman and Oman to suggest that perhaps a single shop of specialist chasers executed the decoration on most of these pieces.[3] Clayton further suggests that perhaps a retailer handled most of these pieces and that he had plain wares by a number of makers decorated by a specialist chaser for his stock.[4] The flat-chased foliate wreath enclosing the engraved armorials on this monteith is very similar to that on a monteith of the same year by George Garthorne of London, reinforcing the notion that these fanciful chinoiseries were the work of a single or small group of specialist chasers.[5] William Fitzhugh of Stafford County, Virginia, willed "one Large Silver Salver Jappan" in 1700 to one of his sons. It was probably the salver he ordered through his London agent in 1688/89, and "Jappan" probably denotes that it was enriched with this form of flat-chased chinoiserie

decoration. A small London mug of 1688/89 with a reeded neck and a globular body flat-chased with similar chinoiserie decoration was presented in 1728 to St. Michael's Parish, Talbot County, Maryland.[6]

Monteiths were owned by several Virginia families. William Fitzhugh, in the second codicil of 1701 to his will of the previous year, wrote, "I Give to my son Henry Fitzhugh my Silver Moonteeth Bason which I brought out of England."[7] In the 1714 inventory of the estate of William Churchill of Middlesex County, there is listed among "The Plate: 1 Munteth" and "In the Kitchin: 12 Pewter Basons 2 Large D? with Brims."[8] The latter two are possibly monteiths of the type with detachable rims. Also entered as "In the Kitchin" in the 1728 inventory of the estate of Nathaniel Harrison of Surry County and as "In the Kitchin" in the 1742 inventory of the estate of Henry Hacker of Williamsburg are "1 Monteth" and "1 Monteth 10/," respectively.[9] The 1741 inventory of the estate of Alexander Spotswood of Orange County, who served as governor of Virginia (1710–1722), includes "1 munteth 1."[10] The 1744 inventory of the estate of James Geddy of Williamsburg, father of the silversmith of the same name, contains "1 Pewter Monteith 5/."[11]

Two English silver monteiths with traditions of Virginia ownership from an early date are known. The earlier of the two, made by Joseph Sheene of London in 1699/1700, has descended in the Fitzhugh family and may in fact be the one mentioned in William Fitzhugh's will. It is presently on loan by a descendant to the M. H. de Young Memorial Museum. The other, made by Francis Spilsbury of London in 1733/34, is engraved with the arms and crest of the Garlick family of Virginia.[12]

1960-581

1. Andrew Clarke, ed., *The Life and Times of Anthony Wood, Antiquary, of Oxford, 1632–1695, Described by Himself, Collected from His Diaries and Other Papers* (Oxford: Clarendon Press, 1894), 3:84.

2. These include a monteith at King's College, Cambridge, with flat-chased chinoiserie decoration and the same maker's mark as the Williamsburg example (Oman [a], pl. 36A); one by George Garthorne of London (Clayton, pp. 180–81, fig. 356); and one at the Worcester Museum (Jessie McNab, "The Legacy of a Fantastical Scot," *Metropolitan Museum of Art Bulletin* 19 [February 1961]: 174; Arthur Hayden, *Chats on Old Silver*, rev. edn. [New York: Dover Publications, Inc., 1969], p. 98, ill. p. 100).

3. Carl C. Dauterman, "Dream-Pictures of Cathay: Chinoiserie on Restoration Silver," *Metropolitan Museum of Art Bulletin* 23 (Summer 1964):24–25; Oman (a), p. 16.

4. Clayton, p. 62.

5. W. W. Watts, "Silver at the Antique Dealers' Fair," *Apollo* 24 (September 1936):163, fig. v; advertisement, Mallett & Son Ltd., London, *Connoisseur Year Book, 1951*, p. xv, ill.; advertisement, Spink & Son Ltd., London, *Connoisseur* 175 (June 1970): clxxx, ill.

6. Jones (d), pp. xiix, 412, pl. cxxiv, fig. 2.

7. Davis, R. B., p. 382.

8. Middlesex County, Will Book (B) (1713–34), p. 17 (microfilm copy, Department of Research, Colonial Williamsburg Foundation).

9. "Harrison of James River," *Virginia Magazine of History and Biography* 31 (October 1923):368; York County, Wills and Inventories, no. 19 (1740–46), p. 164 (microfilm copy, Department of Research, Colonial Williamsburg Foundation).

10. Orange County, Wills, no. 1 (1735–43), p. 181 (microfilm copy, Virginia State Library, Richmond).

11. York County, Wills and Inventories, no. 19 (1740–46), p. 321 (microfilm copy, Department of Research, Colonial Williamsburg Foundation).

12. Virginia Museum (a), p. 19, no. 82; Davis, E. M., pp. 112–13, pl. II.

33 MONTEITH
Silver-gilt
Robert Cooper
London. 1710/11

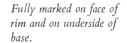
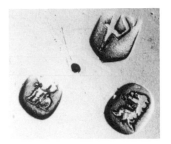

Fully marked on face of rim and on underside of base.

H: 10⅞″ (27.6 cm); W: 14¼″ (35.9 cm); Diam (base): 8⅛″ (20.6 cm). Wt: 94 oz. 6 dwt. ("96= 15=" engraved on underside of base).

PROVENANCE: Stowe, Buckinghamshire (sold by Christie, Manson & Woods, London, 1848); Sir Samuel Montagu (Lord Swaythling) (offered anonymously and bought in by Montagu at Christie, Manson & Woods, London, 1906; sold at Christie, Manson & Woods, London, 1924; purchased by Crichton Bros., London); William Randolph Hearst (sold by Parish-Watson & Co., New York, 1938)

PUBLISHED: Christie's (September 4, 1848), lot 444; Christie's (March 22, 1906), lot 120; Christie's (May 6–7, 1924), lot 40; Williamsburg (b), p. 251, ill.

33

Arms of matrimonial achievement of Richard Grenville (1797–1861), commonly called the marquess of Buckingham, and Lady Mary Campbell with coronet of a marquess, supporters, and motto engraved and repeated on opposing sides of bodies. Crests of Temple, Nugent, Brydges, Chandos, and Grenville engraved at intervals and each repeated on face of rim. He succeeded his father as duke of Buckingham and Chandos in 1839.

The simplicity and restraint of the earliest monteiths gradually gave way to a taller and more complex type with baroque scrollwork and cherubs' heads at the rim and greater chased enrichment of the body. The rims or collars on such monteiths are usually detachable for easy conversion into a punch bowl. Here the rim, originally detachable, has been soldered in place. Relatively few English silver monteiths date much later than this example. The form was revived late in the century, notably in creamware and fused silverplate.

The design source for the cast lion-mask attachments for the handles may be the illustrated detail for an iron screen at Hampton Court from Jean Tijou's

A New Booke of Drawings (London, 1693). That influential volume was the earliest English design book for ironwork.[1]

This monteith was acquired with a stand of nineteenth-century date.

1938-50

1. The detail has been reproduced here from a facsimile edition of Tijou (London, B. T. Batsford Ltd., 1896) in the Kocher collection, Colonial Williamsburg Research Department. Tijou's drawings, including this one, may also be seen in John Harris, *English Decorative Ironwork from Contemporary Source Books,* 1610–1836 (London: Alec Tiranti, 1960).

34 PUNCH BOWL
George Wickes
London. 1726/27

H: 6⅝″ (16.8 cm); Diam (rim): 9¼″ (23.5 cm); Diam (base): 7″ (17.8 cm). Wt: 46 oz. 10 dwt. 5 gr.

34

*Fully marked on
underside of base.*

PROVENANCE: Garrard & Co. Ltd., London (purchased
from C. J. Vander Ltd., London, 1954)

Large bowls intended for punch are part of the pro-
liferation of new forms in the late seventeenth century. The earliest surviving examples date from the
1680s.[1] One of these is a magnificient silver-gilt
example with cover, scrolled handles, and feet by
Philip Rollos, which was presented to the borough of
Stamford in 1685. It has a matching ladle with a
tubular silver handle.[2]

The Colonial Williamsburg collection includes a
large group of early silversmiths' tools that descended
in the succession of firms ultimately known as Garrard & Co. Some of the earlier tools may have belonged to George Wickes, the founder of this line and
the maker of this bowl, while others may have be-

*Arms of the Portal family of Ash Park,
Hampshire, engraved on face of body.*

longed to his partners and successors, Edward
Wakelin, John Parker, John Wakelin, William Taylor, and Robert Garrard.[3]

1954-586

---

1. Michael Clayton cites examples of 1680 in the Drapers' Company and the Irwin Untermyer collection and a pair of 1685 in the
Skinners' Company (Clayton, p. 208). See also Hackenbroch, p. 26,
no. 40, pl. 46; rev. edn., pp. 34–35, no. 60.
2. Oman (a), p. 45, pl. 36B; Clayton, pp. 208–09, fig. 412.
3. These firms and their surviving business accounts are discussed
in Grimwade, pp. 1–12.

35 BOWL
Richard Gurney and Thomas Cooke
London. 1746/47

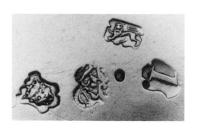

*Fully marked on
underside of base.*

35

H: 3″ (7.6 cm); Diam (rim): 7¹⁄₁₆″ (17.9 cm); Diam
(base): 3⅝″ (9.2 cm). Wt: 17 oz. 1 dwt. 3½ gr.
("17=7" engraved on underside of base).

PROVENANCE: Peter Guille Ltd., New York

1953-800

36

36 PUNCH BOWL
Richard Gurney and Thomas Cooke
London. 1750/51

H: 5¾″ (14.6 cm); Diam (rim): 12″ (30.5 cm);
Diam (base): 5¾″ (14.6 cm). Wt: 62 oz. 7 dwt.
12½ gr.

PROVENANCE: Garrard & Co. Ltd., London

*Fully marked on
underside of base.*

EXHIBITED: Art Treasures 1952, Christie, Manson &
Woods, London, 1952

Owner's motto engraved on interior of bowl at base. "Sprezzo Bassezze" is probably a personal name.

PUBLISHED: The British Antique Dealers Association, *Art Treasures 1952* (London, 1952), p. 77, no. 550, ill.

The finely executed scrolled and diapered border on this commodious punch bowl is deeply chased, and its registration is clearly visible on the interior. The waterfall effect, which can be seen on the lower C-scrolls flanking the central device, is more common in Continental than in English rococo silver.

The 1769 listing of the mortgaged silver of William Byrd III of Westover, Charles City County, Virginia, includes "2 Large Punch Bowls" with a value of £30.[1] One of these bowls was sold in 1788 by his widow, Maria Byrd, to John Brown of Providence along with seven other pieces of family silver.[2]

1955-258

1. Westover Plate.
2. Cooper, pp. 737–38. Maria was the familiar name of Mary Willing Byrd.

37 BEAKER
London. 1601/2

H: 5¹⁵⁄₁₆″ (15.1 cm); Diam (rim): 3½″ (8.9 cm); Diam (base): 3⅛″ (7.9 cm). Wt: 8 oz. 4 dwt.

PROVENANCE: Sir Samuel Montagu (Lord Swaythling) (sold at Christie, Manson & Woods, London, 1924; purchased by Crichton Bros., London); William Randolph Hearst (sold by Parish-Watson & Co., New York, 1938)

EXHIBITED: Exhibition of a Collection of Silversmiths'

Work of European Origin, Burlington Fine Arts Club, London, 1901

PUBLISHED: J. Starkie Gardner, *Exhibition of a Collection of Silversmiths' Work of European Origin* (London: Burlington Fine Arts Club, 1901), p. 27, no. 26; Charles James Jackson, *English Goldsmiths and Their Marks* (London, 1905), p. 110; 2nd edn. (London: Macmillan and Co. Ltd., 1921 and subsequent printings), p. 108; Christie's (May 6 and 7, 1924), lot 105; Edward Wenham, *Domestic Silver of Great Britain and Ireland* (Oxford: Oxford University Press, 1931), p. 170; Williamsburg (b), p. 251, ill.

37

Fully marked on underside of base.

Owner's initials engraved on underside of base.

Tall beakers, such as this, engraved with interlaced strapwork enclosing scrolled foliage with depending clusters of leaves and flowers, are of Dutch derivation. Beakers were widely used in Holland after the Reformation for both secular and ecclesiastical purposes. Their use in England, however, has always been primarily secular. They are found only occasionally in English churches, mainly in East Anglia, especially in the Norwich area. Likewise, a number of beakers have survived in the churches of northeast Scotland, where strong commercial ties with Holland also existed.[1] Beakers were popular as communion vessels in the Congregational churches of New England and the Dutch Reformed churches of New York.

A similar beaker of 1602/3 from St. Giles Without Cripplegate, London, is also engraved with a foliate midband with addorsed fleur-de-lis at intervals.[2]

1938-26

1. N. M. Penzer, "Notes on the History of the Beaker," *Antique Collector* 27 (December 1956):237–40.

2. Ibid., p. 240, fig. 8; Goldsmiths' Hall, *Catalogue of the Historic Plate of the City of London* (London, 1951), p. 29, no. 66, pl. XXVII.

38 BEAKER
Probably Fuller White
London. 1752/53 or 1753/54

38

Fully marked on face of body below rim.

Engraved with arms and crest of the Randolph family of Virginia on face of body.

H: 5¹⁄₃₂″ (12.2 cm); Diam (rim): 4³⁄₁₆″ (10.6 cm); Diam (base): 2¹⁵⁄₁₆″ (7.5 cm). Wt: 7 oz. 17 dwt. 4 gr. ("8:14" engraved on underside of base).

PROVENANCE: Children of Richard S. Ely, Alexandria, Virginia: Mrs. Nancy E. Starnes, McLean, Virginia; Mr. Richard E. M. Ely, Annandale, Virginia; and Mr. Adair A. Ely, Alexandria, Virginia

EXHIBITED: Virginia Museum of Fine Arts, Richmond, 1940

PUBLISHED: Virginia Museum (a), p. 21, no. 100; Davis, E. M., p. 115, pl. III

This beaker, engraved with the arms of the Randolph family, has a tradition of ownership at Tuckahoe, Goochland County, Virginia. It descended through the Randolph, Pleasants, Minor, and Ely families of Virginia. A pair of similar gilt-lined beakers of 1770/71, possibly by Francis Crump of London, are engraved with arms, crest, and motto of the Carter family and form part of the family silver at Shirley, Charles City County, Virginia.

1972-335

39 PAIR OF BEAKERS
Gilt-lined
Henry Haynes
London. 1771/72

H (no. 1): 5³⁄₈″ (13.7 cm); H (no. 2): 5½″ (14 cm); Diam (rim): 3¹⁵⁄₁₆″ (10 cm); Diam (base): 3″ (7.6 cm). Total wt: 30 oz. 14 dwt. 1 gr.

PROVENANCE: Garrard & Co. Ltd., London (purchased from Christie, Manson & Woods, London, 1954)

39

Fully marked on edge of each base.

PUBLISHED: Christie's (July 9, 1954), lot 98

The footed beaker or goblet was a popular form in the late eighteenth and early nineteenth centuries. The substantial bodies of this handsome pair are embellished with applied ornament in the neoclassical taste, such as the repeat of acanthus leaves, tied reeding, and beading.

Robert Carter of Nomini Hall, Westmoreland County, Virginia, imported in 1774 through his London agents, John Hyndman & Co., two silver pint goblets, which were probably of this form.[1] They are described in another account as "gilt inside."[2]

While in Paris, Jefferson commissioned Odiot in 1788 or 1789 to fashion a pair of footed beakers for him. Of similar form, they are perfectly plain and elevated on a square plinth or base. Jefferson's design for these is in the Coolidge Papers at the Mas-

sachusetts Historical Society. The beakers are privately owned.[3]

A set of six very similar silver-gilt beakers with classical medallions and two matching covered jugs or ewers, all of 1780/81 by Andrew Fogelberg and Stephen Gilbert of London, were sold at auction in 1972.[4]

1954-553, 1–2

1. "Invoice of sundry Goods, transmitted to Messers John Hyndman & Co merchants in London, the goods to be Shipped for this Place, which are to be debeted to the Acct of Robert Carter," dated March 28, 1774, Robert Carter Letter Book, no. 1 (1772–74), p. 190, Manuscript Division, Duke University Library (microfilm copy, Department of Research, Colonial Williamsburg Foundation). These were apparently ordered by Robert Carter for his wife. Philip Vickers Fithian, the Carter children's tutor, records in his journal for September 12: "In the same Ship Mrs Carter imports about 30£ value in plate in a pair of fashionable Goblets; Pair of beautiful Sauce-Cups; & a Pair of elegant Decanter-holders" (Hunter Dickinson Farish, ed., *Journal & Letters of Philip Vickers Fithian, 1773–1774: A Plantation Tutor of the Old Dominion* [Williamsburg: Colonial Williamsburg, 1957], p. 189).
2. Robert Carter Day Book, no. 13 (1773–76), p. 42, Manuscript Division, Duke University Library (microfilm copy, Department of Research, Colonial Williamsburg Foundation).
3. James A. Bear, Jr., "Thomas Jefferson's Silver," *Antiques* 124 (September 1958):234–35, figs. 4–5.
4. Sotheby's (November 30, 1972), lot 165, ill.

40 SIX NESTED TUMBLERS AND COVER
Silver-gilt
London. About 1680

Maker's mark only on bottom of each (twice on largest); cover unmarked.

H (with cover): 3″ (7.6 cm); H (tumblers): 2 3/16″–2 1/2″ (5.6 cm–6.4 cm); Diam (rims): 2 3/4″–3 3/16″ (7 cm–8.1 cm); Diam (cover): 3 5/16″ (8.4 cm). Total wt: 12 oz. 18 dwt. 18 gr.

PROVENANCE: Earl of Home (sold at Christie, Manson & Woods, London, 1919; purchased by Harman); H. H. Mulliner (sold at Christie, Manson & Woods, London, 1924; purchased by Permain); William Randolph Hearst (sold by Parish-Watson & Co., New York, 1938)

PUBLISHED: Christie's (June 17, 1919), lot 18; Mulliner, fig. 128; H. Avray Tipping, "The Mulliner Collection—II:

40

English Silver Plate," *Country Life* 55 (June 28, 1924): 1037; Christie's (July 9, 1924), lot 54; Hackenbroch, rev. edn. only, p. 41; Oman (a), p. 15, pl. 22B; Clayton, pp. 331–32, fig. 704

Modest tumblers with rounded bottoms appear during the reign of Charles I, but few surviving examples date from before the Restoration.[1] They remained popular until the latter part of the eighteenth century. Like small beakers, they are sometimes associated with traveling equipage, either nested, as in this instance, or forming part of a canteen with eating utensils. Oman cites a 1633 reference to "a neste of tumbling bowles containing three and four joynted spoons."[2] The only other recorded set of English nested tumblers, one of 1688/89 in the Untermyer collection, retains its original shagreen case.[3] The cover on the Williamsburg example can be inverted to form a stand.

These tumblers are flat-chased with broad bands of matting. Achieved by the massing of small circular punch marks, matting, like all forms of chasing, involves the manipulation of the surface without the

removal of any metal. It was used as a ground for decoration from the reign of Elizabeth I onward (see No. 51). Its broad use as primary decoration is of German derivation, and it is limited to the period from the reign of Charles I to that of William III (see No. 45). The earliest known English use of matting in this manner is the Barber Cup of 1632/33 at Winchester College.[4]

Silver tumblers appear frequently in Virginia wills and inventories of the late seventeenth and eighteenth centuries. Early mentions are the "1 Ditto [silver] Tumbler markt. with the Armes" in the 1674 inventory of the estate of Ambrose Fielding of Northumberland County[5] and the "one silver tumbler marked I I [presumably engraved for John Jennings]" in the 1678 inventory of the estate of the planter John Jennings of Isle of Wight County.[6] An unusual reference to a gilt example, "1 Silver tumbler Gilt," appears in the 1700 inventory of Turtulian Sehut of Henrico County.[7]

1938-22, 1–7

1. G. Bernard Hughes cites an unusually early London example of 1625/26, formerly in the Riley Smith collection, in "Silver Tumblers and Travelling Sets," *Country Life* 118 (November 10, 1955): 1084.

2. Oman (b), p. 146; Oman (a), p. 42.

3. Hackenbroch, rev. edn. only, no. 74, pp. 40–41, ill.

4. Oman (a), p. 15, pl. 1A.

5. "Historical and Genealogical Notes and Queries," *Virginia Magazine of History and Biography* 14 (October 1906):204.

6. "Isle of Wight County Records," *William and Mary Quarterly*, 1st ser., 7 (April 1899):241.

7. Henrico County, Deeds and Wills (1697–1704), p. 244 (microfilm copy, Virginia State Library, Richmond).

41 TUMBLER
Gilt-lined
John Payne
London. 1751/52

41

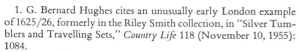

Fully marked on face of body below rim.

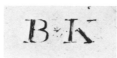

Owner's initials engraved on bottom.

H: 2⁵⁄₁₆″ (5.9 cm); Diam (rim): 2¾″ (7 cm). Wt: 4 oz. 12½ gr.

PROVENANCE: Garrard & Co. Ltd., London

1955-105

42 WINE CUP
London. 1641/42

42

H: 6⁷⁄₁₆″ (16.4 cm); Diam (rim): 3¾″ (9.5 cm); Diam (base): 3⁹⁄₁₆″ (9.1 cm). Wt: 9 oz. 10 dwt.

PROVENANCE: Lady Currie (sold at Christie, Manson & Woods, London, 1906; purchased by Garrard & Co. Ltd., London); Dr. Wilfred Harris (sold at Christie, Man-

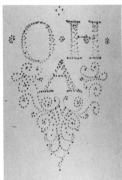

Fully marked on face of body below rim; lion passant on underside of base.

Pounced owners' initials on face of body below rim.

son & Woods, London, 1927); Garrard & Co. Ltd., London (purchased from W. P. Dobson, Milnthorpe, Westmoreland, 1954)

PUBLISHED: Christie's (June 28, 1906), lot 45; Christie's (July 5, 1927), lot 49; Comstock, p. VII, ill.

1954-587

43 WINE CUP
London. 1667/68

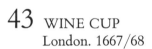

Fully marked on face of bowl below rim; lion passant on underside of base.

Arms of Southcott impaling Sotwell, as well as two sets of owners' initials, engraved on face of bowl.

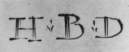

43

H: 5⅞" (15 cm); Diam (rim): 3½" (8.9 cm); Diam (base): 3⁹⁄₁₆" (9.1 cm). Wt: 8 oz. 13 dwt.

PROVENANCE: Christie, Manson & Woods, London (1929; purchased by Permain); William Randolph Hearst (sold by Parish-Watson & Co., New York, 1938)

PUBLISHED: Christie's (November 13, 1929), lot 128; Williamsburg (b), p. 251, ill.

1938-25

44 TWO-HANDLED COVERED CUP
Silver-gilt
"The hound sejant maker"
London. 1649/50

H: 8" (20.3 cm); W: 7¾" (19.7 cm); W (base): 3⅞" (9.8 cm). Wt: 28 oz. 17 dwt. 21½ gr.

PROVENANCE: Sir George Buller (sold at Christie, Manson & Woods, London, 1883; purchased by Phillips, London); Sir Samuel Montagu (Lord Swaythling) (sold at Christie, Manson & Woods, London, 1924; purchased by Crichton Bros., London); William Randolph Hearst (sold by Parish-Watson & Co., New York, 1938)

44

Fully marked on underside of base; cover unmarked.

EXHIBITED: Exhibition of a Collection of Silversmiths' Work of European Origin, Burlington Fine Arts Club, London, 1901

PUBLISHED: Christie's (April 11, 1883), lot 80; J. Starkie Gardner, *Exhibition of a Collection of Silversmiths' Work of European Origin* (London: Burlington Fine Arts Club, 1901), pp. 93–94, no. 78; Charles James Jackson, *English Goldsmiths and Their Marks* (London, 1905), p. 123; 2nd edn. (London: Macmillan & Co. Ltd., 1921 and subsequent printings), p. 123; Percy Macquoid, *The Plate Collector's Guide* (New York: Charles Scribners Sons, 1908), p. 95, fig. 35; Jackson, 2:709–10, fig. 928; H. P. Mitchell, "The Early English Silver of the Swaythling Collection—II," *Country Life* 46 (August 16, 1919): 206–7, ill.; "The Swaythling Collection of Silver Plate," *Country Life* 55 (April 5, 1924):527–28, fig. 4; Christie's (May 6–7, 1924), lot 89, ill.; Edward Wenham, *Domestic Silver of Great Britain and Ireland* (London: Oxford University Press, 1931), p. 171, pl. VII; F. Gordon Roe, "Austerity in Art: The Puritan Influence," *Connoisseur* 111 (March 1943): ill. p. 18; Edward Wenham, "Evolution of the Trophy Cup," *Antique Collector* 25 (June 1954):116, fig. 1; Sotheby's (March 16, 1961), p. 45; Oman (a), p. 39, pl. 8; Clayton, p. 94

This magnificent twelve-sided cup is by the most important English silversmith of the middle seventeenth century. Unknown by name but referred to as "the hound sejant maker," because he used a seated hound for his maker's mark, he produced a rich and varied body of work between 1646 and 1666. He secured many important commissions, both for domestic and ecclesiastical plate, during the lean years of the Civil War and the Commonwealth. Considering that he made a conspicuous quantity of plate for Royalist private chapels during the Commonwealth, it is surprising that he did not benefit more from the greatly enlarged patronage of silversmiths after the Restoration.[1]

This cup retains elements of English Renaissance two-handled cups. In its bulbous body with vertically paneled sides, each having a concave face, and its decorative cast handles of scrolled outline, it is related to matching cups of 1555/56 and 1570/71 at Corpus Christi College, Cambridge.[2] These cups, in turn, are quite similar to one of 1533/34 at Corpus Christi College, Oxford, the earliest recorded English silver two-handled cup.[3]

Similar twelve-sided cups include a greatly restored example of 1652/53 by "the hound sejant maker" at Temple Newsam House, Leeds;[4] one of 1652/53 by an unidentified London maker (ES), formerly owned by Sir Ernest Cassel and Lady Louis Mountbatten;[5] one of 1655/56 by an unidentified London maker (WH) in the Archibald A. Hutchinson collection, Fogg Art Museum, Harvard University;[6] and one of 1661/62 by an unidentified London maker (IN).[7]

The base of this cup is inscribed "Purchased/AT/Strawbery Hill/Horace Walpole." The calculated crudity and lack of subtlety, both in concept and execution, tend to discredit the veracity of the inscription. The inscription would appear to date before 1883, for in that year the cup was described in an auction catalog as "From Strawberry Hill."[8] It does not appear in Walpole's *A Description of the Villa of Mr. Horace Walpole, Youngest Son of Sir*

Later inscription engraved on underside of base.

Robert Walpole, Earl of Orford, at Strawberry-Hill near Twickenham, Middlesex. With an Inventory of the Furniture, Pictures, Curiosities, &c. (Strawberry Hill, 1784), or in *A Catalogue of the Classic Contents of Strawberry Hill Collected by Horace Walpole* (London, 1842).

1938-32

1. Charles Oman, *English Church Plate, 597–1830* (London: Oxford University Press, 1957), pp. 206–07, 210, 218, 221, 242–43; Oman (a), pp. 27–28.
2. Jones (c), pp. xx, 43, pl. LII; Clayton, pp. 94–95, fig. 194.
3. Harold Charles Moffatt, *Old Oxford Plate* (London: Archibald Constable & Co. Ltd., 1906), p. 142, pl. LXIX; Jackson, 1:165–66, ill.
4. G. E. P. How, *With Intent to Deceive: A Supplement to "Restoration and the Law,"* Published by Messrs. How in 1951 (London, 1953), pp. 7–8, figs. 3, 3A, and 3B.
5. E. Alfred Jones, "The Late Ernest Cassel's Collection of Old English Plate—II," *Country Life* 55 (January 19, 1924):85, fig. 2; Royal Northern Hospital, no. 233, pl. XII; Seaford House, pp. xxii–xxiii, 17, no. 137, pl. XLA.
6. Minneapolis Institute of Arts, *French, English and American Silver* (Minneapolis, 1956), p. 66, no. 88, fig. 19.
7. Seaford House, p. 16, no. 128; Sotheby's (June 8, 1972), lot 85, frontispiece.
8. Christie's (April 11, 1883), lot 80.

45 TWO-HANDLED COVERED CUP
London. 1655/56

Fully marked on top of cover and on face of body below rim.

H: 7¼" (18.4 cm); W: 9⅛" (23.2 cm); Diam (base): 7⅜" (18.7 cm). Wt: 41 oz. 3 dwt. 3 gr.

PROVENANCE: Christie, Manson & Woods, London, 1905 (purchased by S. J. Phillips, London); Sir Samuel Montagu (Lord Swaythling) (sold at Christie, Manson & Woods, London, 1924; purchased by Crichton Bros., London); William Randolph Hearst (sold by Parish-Watson & Co, New York, 1938)

PUBLISHED: Christie's (June 28, 1905), lot 93; Percy Macquoid, *The Plate Collector's Guide* (New York: Charles Scribners Sons, 1908), p. 97, fig. 41; Jones (c), p. xix; "The Swaythling Collection of Silver Plate," *Country Life* 55 (April 5, 1924):527–28, fig. 4; Christie's (May 5–6, 1924), lot 88, ill.; Edward Wenham, *Domestic Silver of Great Britain and Ireland* (London: Oxford University

45

Press, 1931), p. 171, pl. VII; ———, "Evolution of the Trophy Cup," *Antique Collector* 25 (June 1954):116, fig. 1; Oman (a), p. 41, pl. 13A

This important cup of imposing size and stance is closely associated in form with the principal type of contemporary tankard. Both share a flat-topped cover raised a single step above a flanged edge and a straight-sided cylindrical body supported on a broad, skirted base.[1] Such a close correspondence between cup and tankard design is rare, for these forms followed for the most part independent courses of development with only general stylistic similarities.

Three other cups of this type are known. All are by the same maker as the Williamsburg example. One of virtually identical design and size of 1657/58 is at Peterhouse College, Cambridge.[2] It has the same bold cast caryatid handles terminating in birds' heads, but its body is flat-chased with scrolled and foliate decoration. The other two both have straight-sided bodies and similar covers, plain handles of scrolled

outline, but no base or base moldings. They may represent a preliminary type for the later and more developed Williamsburg and Peterhouse College examples. One of 1651/52 is part of the Rothermere silver at the Middle Temple.[3] Its body, like that of the Williamsburg example, is decorated with a broad band of matting. The body of the other example of 1653/54, formerly in the collection of Philip Ar-

Unidentified arms engraved on face of body about 1710.

genti, is flat-chased with an encircling arcade enclosing floral decoration.[4]

1938-31

1. A tankard of this type, of 1653/54 with similar matted decoration by the maker of this cup, is among the Abingdon Corporation plate (Gerald Taylor, *Silver* [Hammondsworth, Middlesex: Penguin Books, 1956], pl. 10b; Arthur Preston, *The Abingdon Corporation Plate; Some Notes on the Abingdon Plate and Kindred Treasures and on the Donors and the Occasions of the Gifts* [Oxford: Oxford University Press, 1958], no. 17, pp. 26–28, pl. VIII; N. M. Penzer, "The Early English Silver Tankard: Part II," *Antique Collector* 31 [August 1960]:144–45, fig. 8).
2. Jones (c), pp. xix, pl. III.
3. Laird Clowes, "The Rothermere Silver at the Middle Temple," *Connoisseur* 139 (March 1957):31–32, fig. 13.
4. Seaford House, p. 19, no. 153, pl. XL.

46 TWO-HANDLED COVERED CUP
Probably John How of Salisbury
About 1670

Maker's mark and repeated secondary mark on face of body below rim; cover unmarked.

H: 6⅛″ (15.6 cm); W: 7⅞″ (20 cm). Wt: 17 oz. 17 dwt. 10 gr.

PROVENANCE: Mrs. P. E. H. Kirwan (sold at Sotheby & Co., London, 1971; purchased by How [of Edinburgh], London)

PUBLISHED: Sotheby's (October 21, 1971), lot 210, pl. XXI; Margaret Holland, "Looking at Museums, Part II: One Thought Leads to Another," *Magazine Silver* 7 (May-June 1974): 14, ill.

The dominant type of two-handled cup from the late Commonwealth until the reign of William III is of this broad pear form with cast caryatid handles. The paneling of the body of the 1649/50 example by "the hound sejant maker" (No. 44) is a rare feature and not representative. When decorated, the thin-walled bodies of such cups, as in this example, are usually high-chased with large floral designs of Dutch and German derivation. Although floral and animal forms are found separately in Continental print sources, their combination in this manner, as Oman has pointed out, is characteristically English.[1] It is

Owners' initials engraved on face of finial.

especially apt that the lion and unicorn, the royal supporters, appear on opposing sides of the body and cover, as they do on a number of cups of this type in the period shortly after the restoration of the Stuart monarchy. The imbricated ellipses encircling the bottom, providing a base for the lush vegetation and the animals, is a most unusual feature, reminiscent of and probably deriving from its more common use in embroidered designs.

This cup is one of relatively few provincial examples with this type of decoration. It is attributed to John How of Salisbury.[2] The attribution is supported, in part, by a similar, although uncovered, cup with high-chased floral decoration in the Salisbury and South Wiltshire Museum.[3] It bears the same maker's and secondary mark of four addorsed fleurs-de-lis within a shaped lozenge, as well as a black-letter "R," in apparent imitation of a date letter. It has an inscribed date of 1676 and is associated with the Eyre family of Salisbury. The presence of several

46

pieces by this maker in Wiltshire churches, a communion cup and paten with the inscribed date 1674 in the church in Durnford and a paten in the church at Wilsford With Woodford,[4] helps strengthen the attribution of this cup to Salisbury. A small un-

covered two-handled cup by this same maker with conventional chased alternate palm and acanthus leaves and pounced owners' initials and the date 1683 was sold at auction in 1972.[5]

Even though Salisbury was designated in 1423 as

one of seven provincial towns to have its own distinctive mark, there would appear never to have been an effectual assay office there. The secondary mark on this piece was applied by and at the discretion of the maker.

1972-43

1. Oman (a), p. 17.
2. The attribution of this piece was made by Mrs. G. E. P. How of How (of Edinburgh), London.
3. Salisbury and South Wiltshire Museum, *Annual Report, 1960–1961* (Salisbury, 1961), p. 17, pl. IIIB.
4. J. E. Nightengale, *The Church Plate of the County of Wilts.* (Salisbury: Bennett Brothers, 1891), pp. 38–39, 43.
5. Sotheby's (July 27, 1972), lot 136, pl. V; advertisement, D. S. Lavender, London, *Apollo* 96 (December 1972):131, ill.

47 TWO-HANDLED COVERED CUP
Silver-gilt
London. 1678/79

H: 7 3/16″ (18.3 cm); W: 10 9/16″ (26.8 cm); Diam (base): 3 13/16″ (8.1 cm). Wt: 32 oz. 12 dwt. 22 gr.

PROVENANCE: Lord Braye (sold at Sotheby, Wilkinson & Hodge, London, 1920); H. H. Mulliner (sold at Christie, Manson & Woods, London, 1924; purchased by Permain); William Randolph Hearst (sold by Parish-Watson & Co., New York, 1938)

PUBLISHED: Sotheby's (March 26, 1920), lot 155, pl. XXIII; Mulliner, fig. 92; H. Avray Tipping, "The Mulliner Collection—II: English Silver Plate," *Country Life* 55 (June 28, 1924):1037, fig. 16; Christie's (July 9, 1924), lot 52, ill.; Williamsburg (b), p. 250, ill.

Fully marked on top of cover and on face of body below rim.

The two-handled cup advanced rapidly in size and importance in the late seventeenth century. A cup, such as this, with a broad body with nearly straight sides and substantial scrolled handles, represents an intermediate type between cups of bulbous pear form (Nos. 44, 46) and those of more imposing inverted-bell form (Nos. 48–50).

The lower part of the body is high-chased with alternate acanthus and palm leaves, a form of conventionalized decoration especially popular on the

47

Arms of an unmarried lady and patrilineal member of Lucy of Charlecot, Warwickshire, engraved on face of body. Owner's initials engraved on underside of base.

bodies of cups and other drinking vessels of the 1670s and 1680s. The swirled acanthus leaves of the cover and the acanthus-wrapped fruit finial are features commonly found on cups of this type.

1938-30

48 TWO-HANDLED COVERED CUP
Robert Timbrell and Benjamin Bentley
London. 1715/16

Fully marked on face of body below rim and on bezel of cover.

H: 10⅝" (27 cm); W: 10¹³⁄₁₆" (26.4 cm); Diam (base): 4¹³⁄₁₆" (12.2 cm). Wt: 45 oz. 2 dwt. 18½ gr.

PROVENANCE: Probably Sir John Randolph (1693–1737) and his wife, Susannah Beverley; probably their son, Beverley Randolph (ca. 1720–living 1756), and his wife, Agatha Wormeley; his brother, Peyton Randolph (ca. 1721–1775), and his wife, Betty Harrison (ca. 1723–1783); their nephew, Edmund Randolph (1753–1812), and his wife, Elizabeth Nicholas (1753–1810); their daughter, Lucy Randolph (1790–1847), and her husband, Peter Vivian Daniel (1784–1860); their daughter,

48

Elizabeth Randolph Daniel (1810–1879); her niece, Lucy Randolph Moncure (b. 1861), and her husband, William Grymes; their son, William Randolph Grymes (b. 1899), and his wife (sold by them through Young's Art Shop, Richmond, Virginia, 1942)

PUBLISHED: Davis, J. D., p. 135, ill.

Arms and crest of the Randolph family of Virginia engraved on opposite sides of body, with crest repeated on cover, added with decoration in the nineteenth century.

This cup was originally severely plain. It received its profusion of repoussé decoration in the rococo taste, as well as compatible flat-chased decoration on the face of the handles, a new finial, and engraved armorials, in the nineteenth century. This was accomplished before 1857, for it is described as "my large ornamented silver Cup or Goblet, with the Cover . . . bearing the Randolph coat of arms" in the will of Peter Vivian Daniel of that year.[1]

Even though this cup has been greatly altered, it remains important as one of the few surviving pieces of silver with a documented history of ownership in Williamsburg in the eighteenth century. Listed as "the Silver Cup" in the 1780 will of Betty Randolph of Williamsburg, it was presumably owned by Peyton Randolph, her husband, whom she survived.[2] The earlier history of the cup, however, is less certain. This is probably "the great silver cup" that Beverley Randolph, Peyton's older brother, was bequeathed in a 1736 codicil to the will of their father, Sir John Randolph.[3] Unfortunately, the will and inventory of Beverley Randolph, about whom little is known, have not survived.

This cup was acquired with two salvers (No. 136)

and an unmarked punch ladle of probable American origin.

1942-37

1. Richmond City Circuit Court, Wills, no. 1 (1852–61), p. 595 (microfilm copy, Virginia State Library, Richmond).
2. York County, Wills and Inventories, no. 23 (1783–1811), p. 4 (microfilm copy, Department of Research, Colonial Williamsburg Foundation). Peyton Randolph's silver is not itemized in either his will of 1774 or the inventory of his estate in 1776. It is lumped in his inventory as "492 oz. plate @ 7/6 184/10/0." (York County, Wills and Inventories, no. 22 [1771–83], p. 337 [microfilm copy, Department of Research, Colonial Williamsburg Foundation]).
3. "Copy of Will of Sir John Randolph, Dated December 23, 1735," *Virginia Magazine of History and Biography* 36 (October 1928):379.

49 TWO-HANDLED CUP
Thomas Tearle
London. 1729/30

Fully marked on face of body below rim; maker's mark on face of each handle.

Engraved owners' initials repeated on face of each handle.

H: 5⅝" (14.3 cm); W: 8⅝" (21.1 cm); Diam (base): 3½" (8.9 cm). Wt: 16 oz. 10 dwt.

PROVENANCE: Garrard & Co. Ltd., London (purchased from C. J. Vander Ltd., London, 1951)

1954-579

50 TWO-HANDLED COVERED CUP
Peter Archambo, Sr.
London. 1738/39

H: 10³⁄₁₆" (25.9 cm); W: 9½" (24.1 cm); Diam (base): 4⁵⁄₁₆" (10.9 cm). Wt: 59 oz. 13 dwt. 13 gr. ("60=5" engraved on underside of base).

49

50

PROVENANCE: Peter G. Hildyard (sold at Sotheby & Co., London, 1954; purchased by Garrard & Co., London)

PUBLISHED: Sotheby's (October 14, 1954), lot 134

Fully marked on underside of base and on bezel of cover.

Arms and crest of the Whichote family of Aswarby Park, Lincolnshire, engraved on face of body and cover, respectively.

The two-handled covered cup replaced the standing cup as the principal article of presentation silver in the latter half of the seventeenth century, and it has served as such ever since. Christopher Whichote, who was baptized on March 15, 1738, may have received this cup as a christening present.

The Huguenot makers were primarily responsible for the development of the large two-handled covered cup of inverted bell form. They also introduced and favored the use of vertical straps, both cast and cut from sheet, in formal arrangement on hollow-ware forms. The overlapping, sinuous, foliate straps on this cup are less formal and more plastic than those of intricate trellis design on the caster by Paul Crespin

of London (No. 154). They are an indication of the emerging rococo taste.

Paul de Lamerie made similar use of straps of identical design on cups of 1732/33 and 1736/37,[1] as well as on a number of other forms. Such elements may have been supplied to both makers by specialist casters; Archambo may also have merely patterned his straps after those of de Lamerie. Archambo was undoubtedly familiar with de Lamerie's productions. His son Peter began his apprenticeship with de Lamerie on December 5, 1738, about the time this cup was made.

1954-632

1. Advertisement, S. J. Phillips, London, *Connoisseur* 182 (December 1969):xvii, ill.; Museum of Fine Arts of Houston, *Silver by Paul de Lamerie in America* (Houston, 1956), no. 28, ill.

51 TANKARD
Silver-gilt
London. 1577/78

51

H: 7⅝″ (19.4 cm); Diam (base): 4⅜″ (11.1 cm).
Wt: 18 oz. 13 dwt. 15 gr.

PROVENANCE: Earl of Harrington (sold at Christie, Manson & Woods, London, 1887; purchased by Garrard, London); Christie, Manson & Woods, London (1896); Lord Cunliffe (sold at Christie, Manson & Woods, London, 1927; purchased by Permain); William Randolph Hearst (sold by Parish-Watson & Co., New York, 1938)

PUBLISHED: Christie's (July 20, 1887), lot 108; Christie's (April 21, 1896), lot 160; Christie's (December 12, 1927), lot 76; Williamsburg (b), p. 250, ill.

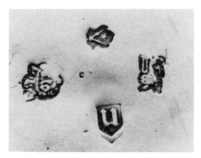

Fully marked on underside of base and on cover below finial.

Pounced owner's initials on underside of base. Monogram with coronet above engraved on interior face of each hinge plate (probably eighteenth century).

This is the earliest piece of silver in the Colonial Williamsburg collection and is a very early tankard of cylindrical form. In 1572, just five years before it was made, Archbishop Matthew Parker presented three silver-gilt tankards as New Year's presents to three Cambridge colleges. The earlier two, a matched pair, bear London marks for 1570/71. One is at Gonville and Caius College, the other at Trinity Hall College. The third, at Corpus Christie College, bears London marks for the following year. These are the earliest

recorded English tankards with silver bodies of cylindrical form.[1] A horn tankard with silver-gilt mounts, formerly in Lord Swaythling's collection, bears London marks for 1561/62.[2]

Even at that period, the basic form of the tankard was established: elevated cover with flanged edge, tapered straight-sided body with molded rim and base, and hollow scroll handle of D-shaped section with thumbpiece and terminal. This tankard, like most Elizabethan examples, is chased, stamped, and engraved with a profusion of Renaissance decoration, transmitted to England primarily through printed designs from Germany and the Low Countries. Its body is encircled by two bold bands, deriving from the medieval bound wooden water-carrying vessel of similar form and the same name. Gilding, which appears on much Elizabethan silver, heightens the rich effect.

A small triangular pouring spout was at one time added at the rim of the body opposite the handle. The tankard was described as "with spout" when it was sold in 1896. The removal of the spout before its sale in 1927 caused a partial loss of the gilding on the body.

1938-28

1. Jackson, 1:178, ill.; 2:751, fig. 979; Jones (c), pp. xx, xxi, 28, 33, 44, plates XXXI, XXXVII, LIV; N. M. Penzer, "The Early English Silver Tankard: Part I," *Antique Collector* 31 (June 1960):106–7, figs. 6–7.
2. Jackson, 2:750, fig. 978.

52 TANKARD
Dublin. 1680/81

Fully marked on top of cover and on face of body to right of handle.

H: 7¼″ (18.4 cm); Diam (base): 5½″ (14 cm).
Wt: 28 oz. 10 dwt. 16 gr.

PROVENANCE: Sir Samuel Montagu (Lord Swaythling) (sold at Christie, Manson & Woods, London, 1924;

52

53

Fully marked on interior of cover and on underside of base; maker's mark on face of handle.

Unidentified crest engraved on face of body opposite handle. Owners' initials engraved on face of handle and on underside of base.

purchased by Crichton Bros., London): William Randolph Hearst (sold by Parish-Watson & Co., New York, 1938)

PUBLISHED: Christie's (May 6–7, 1924), lot 49; Williamsburg (b), p. 251, ill.

1938-33

Unidentified crest engraved on face of body opposite handle.

PROVENANCE: Garrard & Co. Ltd., London (purchased from C. J. Vander Ltd., London, 1953)

1954-539

53 TANKARD
Fuller White
London. 1760/61

H: 8¼″ (21 cm); Diam (base): 4¾″ (12.1 cm).
Wt: 26 oz. 10 dwt. 8½ gr.

54 TANKARD
Sebastian and James Crespell
London. 1767/68

H: 4³¹⁄₃₂″ (12.6 cm); Diam (base): 3⅝″ (9.2 cm).
Wt: 17 oz. 16 dwt.

54

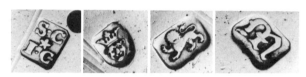

Fully marked on underside of base; maker's mark and lion passant on underside of cover.

Arms and crest of probable arbitrary assumption engraved on face of cover.

PROVENANCE: Garrard & Co. Ltd., London (purchased from Mrs. Cornwall, Virginia Water, Kent, 1953)

This type of tankard contrasts sharply with the more popular eighteenth-century forms with straight-sided or baluster-shaped bodies (Nos. 53, 55). Its flat cover with pointed lip and lack of base moldings recalls English tankards of the second quarter of the seventeenth century. Its solid handle of rectangular section without lower scroll and terminal differs from the conventional hollow tankard handle of D-shaped section and S-scroll outline. This tankard probably had originally an openwork thumbpiece. A London tankard of 1649/50 at Winchester College shows the earlier use of the hooped body and handle of related design.[1]

1954-538

_____

1. Oman (a), p. 43, pl. 25B.

55 TANKARD
John Swift
London. 1774/75

55

Fully marked on interior of cover and on face of body to right of handle.

H: 7$\frac{15}{16}$" (20.2 cm); Diam (base): 5$\frac{3}{16}$" (12.6 cm). Wt: 27 oz. 15 dwt. $\frac{1}{2}$ gr.

PROVENANCE: Museum of Fine Arts, Boston

1954-344

56 MUG
London. 1695/96

56

Fully marked on underside of base.

*Owners' initials engraved
on underside of base.*

H: 3″ (7.6 cm); Diam (base): 2¹¹⁄₁₆″ (6.8 cm). Wt:
8 oz. 3 dwt. 5½ gr.

PROVENANCE: Garrard & Co. Ltd., London (purchased
from J. C. Lowe, London, 1963)

1963-136

57 MUG
Robert Timbrell and Benjamin Bentley
London. 1716/17

H: 4⁷⁄₁₆″ (11.3 cm); Diam (base): 4″ (10.2 cm). Wt:
10 oz. 6 dwt. 2 gr.

PROVENANCE: Museum of Fine Arts, Boston

57

*Fully marked on face of body
to right of handle; maker's
mark on face of handle.*

*Owners' initials engraved and
partially obliterated on underside of base.*

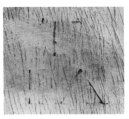

The similarities of most mugs to tankards of the same
date is readily apparent. Except in rare instances, the
mug, unlike the tankard, is uncovered. Straight-
sided mugs, such as this, with hollow scrolled handles
and applied base moldings came into use at the close
of the seventeenth century. About 1715 the bodies of
mugs begin to curve inward at the base, and they
are supported on a narrow splayed foot, as in the following example. Scrolled handles cast in halves replace hollow wrought ones of conventional tankard
type. From about 1725, the bodies of mugs assume a
fuller baluster form (Nos. 59–60). Such mugs, some-

times referred to as canns, remained popular until about 1770, when straight-sided tankards and mugs with hooped bodies appeared (see No. 54).

1954-315

58 MUG
Paul de Lamerie
London. 1719/20

58

Fully marked on underside of base.

Arms of Montgomery quartered with Eglinton and impaling Percy engraved on face of body opposite handle.

H: 3¾″ (9.5 cm); Diam (base): 3¹/₁₆″ (7.9 cm). Wt:

10 oz. 12 dwt. 5 gr. ("10 11 17" engraved on underside of base).

PROVENANCE: Garrard & Co. Ltd., London (purchased from C. J. Vander Ltd., London, 1953)

A similar mug of 1720/21 by Paul de Lamerie with the same engraved armorials was exhibited in Houston in 1956.[1] Similar mugs of 1728/29 by Thomas Tearle of London and of 1729/30 by George Boothby of London are also in the collection (1969-259; 1954-546).

1954-537

———

1. Museum of Fine Arts of Houston, *Silver by Paul de Lamerie in America* (Houston, 1956), no. 3.

59 MUG
Paul de Lamerie
London. 1734/35

59

H: 4⅞″ (12.4 cm); Diam (base): 3¾″ (9.5 cm). Wt: 15 oz. 8 dwt. 5½ gr.

PROVENANCE: Mrs. Anne Brooke Harold, Lynchburg, Virginia

PUBLISHED: John D. Davis, "Domestic Silver of the Colonial United States," in *Spanish, French, and English Traditions of the Colonial Silver of North America* (Winterthur: Henry Francis du Pont Winterthur Museum, 1969), p. 70 and fig. 2, p. 72; Davis, J. D., p. 136, ill.

Inscribed for John Randolph of Roanoke over an area of former engraving on face of body opposite handle.

Fully marked on underside of base.

John Randolph of Roanoke (1773–1833) owned this substantial mug of broad baluster form. His widowed mother, Frances Bland Randolph, married St. George Tucker of Williamsburg in 1778. It probably did not descend to him in the Randolph family, for, in order to have it inscribed, he had an area of former engraving removed, probably the arms of a former and unrelated owner. The present inscription dates from 1810 or later, since not until then did John Randolph add to his own name that of Roanoke, his home in Charlotte County, Virginia.[1] He did not take up permanent residence there until that year. This piece would appear to have passed from him to his half-brother, Henry St. George Tucker (1780–1848), who married Ann Evelina Hunter; to their daughter, Virginia Tucker (1817–1858), who married Henry Laurens Brooke (1808–1874); to their son, St. George Tucker Brooke (b. 1844), who married Mary H. Brown; and to their daughter, the last owner, Anne Washington Brooke, who married Edward B. Harold.

The mug is of interest as a piece of de Lamerie silver with a history of Virginia ownership extending from at least the early nineteenth century. A salver of 1742/43 in the Donald S. Morrison collection, a kettle on stand and a bread basket of 1744/45 in the Metropolitan Museum of Art, and a waste bowl of 1744/45 in the Irwin Untermyer collection, all fashioned by de Lamerie in his elaborate rococo manner, are engraved with the arms of David Franks, the prominent Philadelphia merchant, impaling those of his wife, Margaret Evans, whom he married in 1743.[2]

De Lamerie had a penchant for inventive detail. The distinctive scrolled and ribbed handle of this mug has an unusual grip in the form of a grotesque

mask. An identical cann of 1736/37 by de Lamerie is recorded.[3]

John Randolph of Roanoke also owned a mug of 1769/70 by Jacob Marsh of London, which is privately owned by a descendant in Williamsburg. Engraved with the Randolph family crest and his initials, it is quite similar in form to but larger than the following example.[4]

1964-434

1. William Cabell Bruce, *John Randolph of Roanoke, 1773–1833* (New York: G. P. Putnam's Sons, 1933), 2:737. The first instance of his use of name with epithet is believed to be in a letter to Dr. George Logan, dated January 24, 1810.

2. Jessie McNab Dennis, "London Silver in a Colonial Household," *Metropolitan Museum of Art Bulletin* 26 (December 1967): 174–79, ill.; ———, "Franks Family Silver by Lamerie," *Antiques* 93 (May 1968):638–41, figs. 1–5; Hackenbroch, pp. 55–56, no. 97, plates 112–13; rev. edn., pp. 94–95, no. 184, ill.; Marvin D. Schwartz, "More English Silver in the Morrison Collection," *Antiques* 91 (February 1967):232, ill. A pair of tea canisters of 1742/43 by de Lamerie are engraved with the arms of David's brother, Naphtali Franks, impaling those of his wife, the former Phila Franks, who lived in London and may have assisted in supplying David and his wife with their de Lamerie silver (Dennis, "London Silver in a Colonial Household," pp. 177–78, fig. 4; ———, "Franks Family Silver by Lamerie," pp. 638–40, fig. 7; Sotheby's [May 2, 1963], lot 138, pl. xx).

3. Advertisement, Wartski Ltd., London, *Antique Dealers' Fair & Exhibition, 1964* (London, 1964), p. 93, fig. 5.

4. Davis, E. M., p. 115, pl. I.

60 MUG
John White
London. 1752/53

H: 4 3/16″ (10.6 cm); Diam (base): 3 1/8″ (7.9 cm). Wt: 8 oz. 4 dwt. 18 gr.

PROVENANCE: Henry Philip Strause, Richmond, Virginia (sold by Thalhimer Brothers, Richmond, 1945)

60

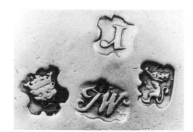

Fully marked on underside of base.

A pair of similar mugs of 1753/54 by Richard Gurney and Thomas Cooke of London, engraved with the arms and motto of the Byrd family of Westover, Charles City County, Virginia, were sold by Maria Byrd in 1788 along with six other pieces of family silver to John Brown of Providence. They are privately owned.[1]

1945-2

---

1. Cooper, pp. 737–39, fig. 8.

61 JUG

David Willaume, Jr.
London. 1744/45

H: 9¼″ (23.5 cm); Diam (base): 5¾″ (14.6 cm).
Wt: 45 oz. 8 dwt. 7 gr.

PROVENANCE: S. J. Shrubsole Corp., New York

Large baluster-shaped jugs, such as this and the following example, are generally associated with the service of beer. In its exacting proportions and bold

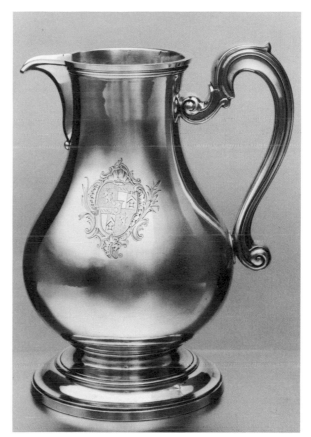

61

Fully marked on underside of base.

curvilinear form, this extremely well-made example of heavy gauge typifies the best of plain English silver of the first half of the eighteenth century. Huguenot makers favored complex scroll handles of this form. Willaume used a handle of similar design on his pair of chamber pots of the previous year (No. 212).

1972-158

Fully marked on underside of base.

Arms of Edwardes of Rhyd-y-Gors, Carmarthenshire, with those of Mallet borne in pretense, engraved on face of body.

62 JUG
Thomas Moore
London. 1758/59

Arms of Clifford impaling Bagge engraved on face of body opposite handle.

H: 9″ (22.9 cm); Diam (base): 4⁹⁄₁₆″ (11.6 cm). Wt: 32 oz. 11 dwt. 6½ gr.

PROVENANCE: Wartski Ltd., London (1954); Garrard & Co. Ltd., London

PUBLISHED: Advertisement, Wartski Ltd., London, *Apollo* 60 (July 1954):v, ill.

1955-236

63 PUNCH LADLE
London. 1729/30

Fully marked on interior of bowl.

Owner's initials engraved on underside of bowl.

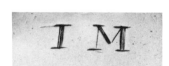

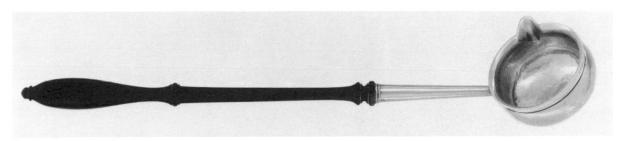

63

L: 14″ (35.6 cm); Diam (bowl): 2¹³⁄₁₆″ (7.2 cm).

PROVENANCE: Henry Philip Strause, Richmond, Virginia (sold by Thalhimer Brothers, Richmond, 1945)
1945-10

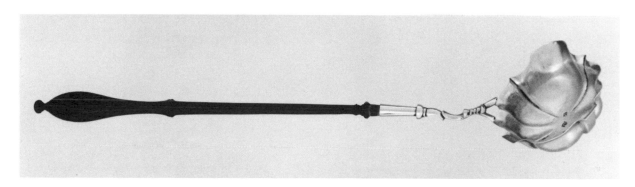

64 PUNCH LADLE
Robert Innes
London. 1751/52

L: 13½″ (34.3 cm); W (bowl): 2⅝″ (6.7 cm).

PROVENANCE: Garrard & Co. Ltd., London (purchased from Walter H. Willson Ltd., London, 1954)
1954-544

Fully marked on interior of bowl.

Owners' initials on underside of bowl.

65 STRAINER
London. 1725/26

65

Fully marked on interior of bowl; leopard's head crowned on underside of one handle and lion passant on underside of other.

L: 7″ (17.8 cm); Diam (bowl): 3⅜″ (8.6 cm). Wt: 2 oz. 14 dwt. 6 gr.

PROVENANCE: Garrard & Co. Ltd., London (purchased from Sotheby & Co., London, 1954)

PUBLISHED: Sotheby's (August 4, 1954)

1954-529

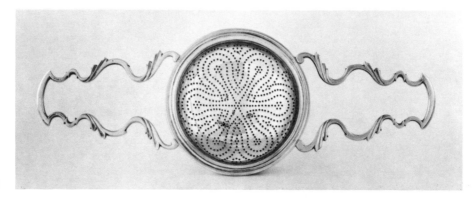

66

66 STRAINER
Edward Aldridge and John Stamper
London. 1753/54

Fully marked on interior of bowl (leopard's head crowned and date letter indistinct); maker's mark and lion passant on underside of each handle at end.

L: 11⁹⁄₁₆″ (29.4 cm); Diam (bowl): 4⁵⁄₁₆″ (11 cm). Wt: 5 oz. 2 dwt. 7 gr.

PROVENANCE: Peter Guille Ltd., New York

A similar strainer with shorter handles of about 1750 by Edward Aldridge is part of the Carter family silver at Shirley, Charles City County, Virginia. Another strainer of similar form of 1773/74 by Charles Aldridge and Henry Green is also in the Colonial Williamsburg collection (1967-170).

1953-801

67 PAIR OF BOTTLE SLIDERS OR BOTTLE STANDS
Probably Philip Freeman
London. 1774/75

67

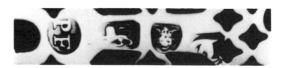

Fully marked on face of each body opposite blank reserve for engraving.

H: 1¹¹⁄₁₆″ (4.3 cm); Diam (rim and base): 4¹³⁄₁₆″ (12.2 cm). Wt: 8 oz. 17 dwt. 19 gr.

PROVENANCE: Garrard & Co. Ltd., London (purchased from R. Clapha, London, 1954)

Wine coasters were generally called bottle sliders or bottle stands in the eighteenth century. Those with pierced sides and turned wooden bases first appear in about 1760. Robert Carter of Nomini Hall, Westmoreland County, Virginia, imported in 1774 through his London agents, John Hyndman & Co., "3 Ditto [silver] bottle sliders, pierced" and engraved with the Carter family crest.[1] Charles Harris, "Working Silversmith from London," informed his Charleston clients in 1768 that he "Makes and sells all sorts of new fashioned bottle stands. . . ."[2]

1954-540, 1–2

1. "Invoice of sundry Goods, transmitted to Messers John Hyndman & Co merchants in London, the goods to be Shipped for this Place, which are to be debeted to the Acct of Robert Carter," dated March 28, 1774, Robert Carter Letter Book 1 (1772–74), p. 190, Manuscript Division, Duke University Library (microfilm copy, Department of Research, Colonial Williamsburg Foundation). These were apparently ordered by Robert Carter for his wife, and only two appear to have been sent. Philip Vickers Fithian, the Carter children's tutor, records in his journal for September 12 : "In the same Ship Mrs Carter imports about 30£ value in plate in a pair of fashionable Goblets; Pair of beautiful Sauce-Cups; & a Pair of elegant Decanter-holders" (Hunter Dickinson Farish, ed., *Journal & Letters of Philip Vickers Fithian, 1773–1774: A Plantation Tutor of the Old Dominion* [Williamsburg: Colonial Williamsburg, 1957], p. 189). Fithian's nomenclature would appear to be his own, for he describes the "2 silver Sauce Boats" in the Carter invoice as "Sauce-Cups."

2. Alfred Coxe Prime, ed., *The Arts & Crafts in Philadelphia, Maryland, and South Carolina, 1721–1785: Gleanings from Newspapers* (Topsfield, Massachusetts: Walpole Society, 1929), p. 67.

68 CORKSCREW
John Harvey
London. About 1750

Maker's mark only on end of cover.

L: 3⅜″ (8.6 cm). Wt: 1 oz. 3 dwt. 10 gr.

PROVENANCE: Berry-Hill Galleries, New York

1954-139

69 BOTTLE TICKET
Sandilands Drinkwater
London. About 1750

69

Maker's mark and lion passant on back.

L: 2¹⁄₃₂″ (5.2 cm). Wt: 8dwt. 15 gr.

PROVENANCE: Sotheby & Co., London (1971)

PUBLISHED: Sotheby's (March 4, 1971), lot 38

The earliest silver bottle tickets or wine labels, as they are commonly called, date from the second quarter of the eighteenth century. They are a function of the increased use of a variety of wines and the development of the glass decanter. They enjoyed a consider-

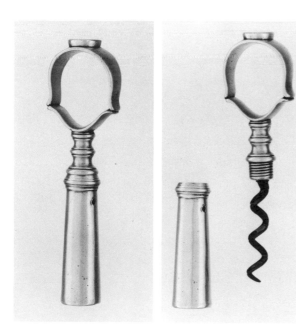

68

able popularity between 1750 and 1850.[1] Their marking was voluntary until 1790, and most examples before that date are unmarked or, as in this instance, only partially marked. The Marking Silver Plate Act of that year specified that "bottle tickets," regardless of weight, were no longer exempt from being assayed and marked.

The most prevalent early type is of escutcheon form, either chased with fruited grape vines, as in this instance, or plain, as in the following example. Six other similar bottle tickets by Sandilands Drinkwater were acquired with this example (1971-95–100). Bottle tickets of this type undoubtedly influenced the production between 1753 and 1756 of enameled ones of escutcheon form at the Battersea factory, handsomely decorated with designs by Ravenet, as well as Staffordshire examples.[2] After the Battersea factory went bankrupt in 1756, two auctions were held. Among the effects of Stephen Janssen, the founder and one of the factory's partners, were sold "a Quantity of beautiful Enamels, colour'd and uncolour'd . . . consisting of . . . Bottle Tickets with Chains for all sorts of Liquors, and of different Subjects." "A great variety of beautiful enamell'd . . . Bottle Tickets" were among the articles sold from the factory's remaining stock.[3]

"18 Silver bottle Labells" are listed with the "Plate, in the Pantry" in the Governor's Palace in Williamsburg in the 1770 inventory of the estate of Lord Botetourt, who served as governor of Virginia between 1768 and 1770.[4]

1991-94

---

1 N. M. Penzer lists nearly 500 different names appearing on bottle tickets in his *Book of the Wine-label* (London: Home & Van Thal, 1947). The term wine label is misleading, for they bear many names other than wines, such as those of spirits, sauces, flavorings, toilet waters, and medicinal compounds.

2. Ibid., pp. 45–54, pl. 1; Victoria and Albert Museum, *Bottle-tickets* (London, 1958), plates 2–3.

3. Penzer, *Book of the Wine-label*, p. 47.

4. Botetourt Inventory.

70 BOTTLE TICKET
Unmarked
England. About 1750

L: 2¹⁵⁄₃₂" (6.3 cm). Wt: 9 dwt. 19 gr.

70

Unidentified arms of an unmarried lady engraved on face.

PROVENANCE: Sotheby & Co., London (1971)

PUBLISHED: Sotheby's (March 4, 1971), lot 36, ill.

1971-93

71 BOTTLE TICKET
Sandilands Drinkwater
London. About 1750

71

Maker's mark and lion passant on back.

L: 2¼″ (5.7 cm). Wt: 12 dwt. 2 gr.

PROVENANCE: Sotheby & Co., London (1971)

PUBLISHED: Sotheby's (March 4, 1971), lot 55, ill.

Cast bottle tickets of this bacchanalian pattern were fashioned by several makers in the mid-eighteenth century. Examples of this and related patterns, however, are more common during the first quarter of the following century.

1971-101

72 BOTTLE TICKET
Probably Benjamin Bickerton
London. About 1775

72

Maker's mark and lion passant on back.

L: 1⅞″ (4.8 cm). Wt: 8 dwt. 13 gr.

PROVENANCE: Sotheby & Co., London (1971)

PUBLISHED: Sotheby's (March 4, 1971), lot 35, ill.

1971-92

73 BOTTLE TICKET
James Phipps
London. About 1780

73

Maker's mark only, twice on back.

Unidentified crest engraved on face.

L: 2³⁄₁₆″ (5.6 cm). Wt: 6 dwt. 21 gr.

PROVENANCE: Sotheby & Co., London (1971)

PUBLISHED: Sotheby's (March 4, 1971), lot 29, ill.

The Phipps family, like the Batemans, produced a large number of handsome and well-executed bottle tickets in the late eighteenth and early nineteenth centuries. Most of these are in the neoclassical taste, often, as in this instance, with bright-cut borders. This example of scroll form and the preceding example of goblet and crescent form are common late eighteenth-century types.

1971-91

Vessels and Accessories for Tea, Coffee, and Chocolate

74 TEAPOT

Pentecost Symonds of Plymouth
Hallmarked at Exeter. 1714/15

H: 6⅛″ (15.6 cm); L: 7¹⁵⁄₁₆″ (20.2 cm); Diam (base): 3⅛″ (7.9 cm). Wt: 14 oz. 17 dwt.

PROVENANCE: Christie, Manson & Woods, London (1946; purchased by the Goldsmiths & Silversmiths Company Ltd., London [presently Garrard & Co. Ltd.]); Garrard & Co., London

PUBLISHED: Christie's (May 6, 1946), lot 75; Helen Comstock, "The Connoisseur in America," *Connoisseur* 136 (September 1955): 73–74, ill.; Comstock, p. VI, ill.; Clayton, p. 301.

During the Commonwealth period, fashionable Londoners were introduced to the drinking of tea, coffee, and chocolate. These exotic beverages, especially tea, had an enormous impact on social customs and the decorative arts.[1]

The earliest surviving English silver teapot, now in the Victoria and Albert Museum, London, was made in 1670 and presented by George Berkeley to the East India Company.[2] Except for the inscription indicating its intended use, it would be readily confused with early coffeepots of similar form having tall bodies with tapered straight sides, tall conical covers, and straight spouts (see No. 80). The earliest

Fully marked on underside of base and on bezel of cover.

Owners' initials engraved on underside of base.

78

example is followed by three teapots of melon form with curved spouts, influenced by oriental wine pots. These include a plain example made before 1679 for Archbishop Sharp of St. Andrew's, probably by Robert Smythier of London;[3] a silver-gilt example with matted panels of about 1685 by Benjamin Pyne of London in the Carter collection in the Ashmolean Museum, Oxford;[4] and a similar silver-gilt example of about 1685, possibly by William Hoare of London, in the Victoria and Albert Museum, London.[5] Small so-called cordial pots of late seventeenth-century date may have also served as teapots.[6]

During the first quarter of the eighteenth century, silver teapots increased in number. In their squat pear-shaped and globular forms, they assumed the horizontal stance that distinguishes them to this day from the vertically-disposed coffee and chocolate pots. This splendid example of bold contour and pleasing detail is an important piece of early eighteenth-century provincial silver. Pentecost Symonds, the maker, worked in Plymouth. He, like a number of West Country makers, had his wares hallmarked at Exeter. An assay office had been established there in 1701.

Handsome cut-card work, a decorative appliqué cut from sheet, enriches the cover. First appearing in the 1660s and usually of foliate or strap design, the Huguenot makers favored its use. Symonds, in this instance, raised a secondary cover to fit like a cap over the main one. He then pierced it in this formal lattice and husk design of French character. After it had been soldered to the cover, he applied the attenuated gadroons.

At least three other pear-shaped teapots by Symonds have survived, a plain example of 1712/13,[7] and ones of 1712/13[8] and 1713/14,[9] both with similar cut-card work of alternate palm leaves and pierced straps on their covers. These indicate a significant provincial production of well-conceived and executed silver teapots at a relatively early date.

1954-535

1. For an excellent discussion see Rodris Roth, *Tea Drinking in 18th-Century America: Its Etiquette and Equipage* (Washington: United States Government Printing Office, 1961).

2. Jackson, 2:943–44, fig. 1258; N. M. Penzer, "The Early Silver Teapot and Its Origin," *Apollo* 64 (December 1956):209–10, fig.

II; Oman (c), p. 6, fig. 66; Oman (a), pp. 57–58, pl. 70A; Clayton, p. 301, fig. 637.

3. G. E. P. How, "Rarities," *Notes on Antique Silver* (Summer 1943):9, ill.; Royal Ontario Museum, p. 27, no. D.31, fig. 28; Christie's (November 29, 1972), lot 115, ill.

4. Jackson, 2:947, fig. 1262; Gerald Taylor, *Silver* (Harmonsworth, Middlesex: Penguin Books, 1956), p. 147, pl. 26a.

5. Penzer, "The Early Silver Teapot and Its Origin," p. 210, fig. v; Oman (b), p. 148, pl. XXIV, fig. 83; Oman (c), p. 6, pl. 89; Oman (a), p. 58, pl. 71.

6. Representative of these are a silver-gilt example of about 1685 by an unidentified London maker (F.S.S.) with fine pictorial engraving in the Museum of Fine Arts, Boston (Hughes, p. 192, fig. 234), and a silver-gilt example of about 1690 by David Willaume, Sr., of London in the British Museum (Hugh Tait, "Huguenot Silver Made in London [c. 1690–1723]: The Peter Wilding Bequest to the British Museum. Part 1," *Connoisseur* 180 [August 1972]: 269–70, fig. 4).

7. "International Saleroom," *Connoisseur* 168 (July 1968):192, fig. 15.

8. Margaret Holland, "English Silver at Tea Time," *Magazine Silver* 5 (July–August 1972):17, ill.; P. M. Inder, "Silver in the Exeter Museum," *Connoisseur* 183 (July 1973):184–85, fig. 11.

9. Christie's (December 10, 1958), lot 78B, ill.; Judith Banister, "The Silversmiths of Devonshire," *Antique Dealer and Collectors' Guide* 15 (January 1961):19–20, ill.

75 TEAPOT
Simon Pantin
London. 1726/27

H: 5⅛″ (13 cm); L: 9¹⁵⁄₁₆″ (13.5 cm); W (base): 3″ (7.6 cm). Wt: 19 oz. 11 dwt.

PROVENANCE: Firestone and Parson, Boston

PUBLISHED: Advertisement, Firestone and Parson, Boston, *Antiques* 98 (July 1970): 15, ill.

Fully marked on underside of base; maker's mark and lion passant on underside of cover.

Unidentified arms engraved on face of body.

Even though a globular teapot of transitional form of 1705/6 by Benjamin Pyne of London is re-

75

corded,[1] examples earlier than 1720 are not plentiful. But by the time Simon Pantin, the noted Huguenot maker, fashioned this stunning example, they had supplanted those of pear form. Pantin executed this piece with deft assurance, controlling the robust form of its body, subtly extending the paneling into the cover, and maintaining an exact sense of scale between the body and the well-modeled spout and foot. Much of the domestic silver of the reigns of Queen Anne and George I, with the conspicuous exception of the enriched productions in the Huguenot style, is severely plain. The polygonal paneling of hollowware, such as this, and of cast articles, especially candlesticks, provides an elegant and pleasurable variation.

1972-247

---

1. Sotheby's (November 6, 1969), lot 159, ill.; advertisement, David G. Udy, Warminster, Wiltshire, *Grosvenor House Antiques Fair* (London, 1971), p. 105, fig. 2.

76

76 TEAPOT
Thomas Farren
London. 1734/35

Fully marked on underside of base; lion passant on underside of cover.

H: 4³/₁₆″ (10.6 cm); L: 8³/₁₆″ (20.8 cm); Diam (base): 2½″ (6.3 cm). Wt: 12 oz. 6 dwt. 16 gr.

PROVENANCE: Garrard & Co. Ltd., London

Globular teapots with curved and straight spouts, and often an engraved strapwork border around the cover opening, predominate during the 1720s and 1730s. One such teapot of 1730/31 by John England of London, having a straight spout, is engraved with the arms of the Nelson family of Yorktown, Virginia. It was originally owned by Thomas Nelson (1677–1745), and is presently on loan by descendants to the National Park Service.

1955-259

77 TEAPOT
William Shaw and William Priest
London. 1759/60

Fully marked on underside of base; lion passant on leaf of finial, on nut securing finial, and on interior of cover.

H: 6⅞″ (17.5 cm); L: 10¼″ (26 cm); Diam (base): 3¾″ (9.5 cm). Wt: 23 oz. 16 dwt. 6 gr. ("24..2.." engraved on underside of base).

PROVENANCE: Mrs. Nellie Ionides (sold at Sotheby & Co., London, 1963)

PUBLISHED: Hugh Honour, "Chinoiserie Silver in the Collection of the Hon. Mrs. Ionides," *Connoisseur* 140 (January 1958):219, fig. 5; ———, "Silver Reflections of Cathay: Part II," *Antiques* 81 (March 1962):307; Sotheby's (July 4, 1963), lot 195.

During the middle decades of the eighteenth century,

77

inverted pear-shaped teapots supported on a tall circular foot, sometimes referred to then as "double bellied," displaced the less pretentious globular ones. This visually unstable form was a function of rococo fashion, and it was utilized for a number of other hollowware articles, such as coffeepots, kettles, cream pots, and casters (Nos. 84–85, 90–91, 97, 156–57). Discrete engraved borders, such as on the previ-

ous example, gave way to profuse scrolled and naturalistic high-chasing. Chinoiserie elements often appear intermingled with rococo ornament, for there was a natural affinity between the rococo and the exotic and asymmetrical features of chinoiserie

decoration. Even though examples of rococo chinoiserie decoration in silver date from the 1740s, notably those by Paul de Lamerie,[1] most examples of this rather standard chased type date from the late 1750s and 1760s. A tea canister of the same year by Shaw and Priest, likewise high-chased with chinoiserie and rococo decoration, is in the Victoria and Albert Museum, London.[2]

An inverted pear-shaped teapot of 1751/52 by an unidentified London maker with a tradition of ownership by Elizabeth Nelson of Yorktown, Virginia, who married in 1738 and lived until 1793, was exhibited in 1940 at the Virginia Museum of Fine Arts, Richmond.[3]

1963-138

---

1. A silver-gilt tea canister of 1744/45 is in the Metropolitan Museum of Art (Hugh Honour, "Silver Reflections of Cathay: Part II," *Antiques* 81 [March 1962]:306–7, fig. 2). A similar pair of the same year was sold at auction in Geneva in 1972 (Christie's [International] [November 14, 1972], lot 270, pl. 44). A later pair of 1747/48 is in the Goldsmiths' Company, London (Jackson, 2:966, fig. 1297; John B. Carrington and George R. Hughes, *The Plate of the Worshipful Company of Goldsmiths* [Oxford: Oxford University Press, 1926], p. 98, pl. 64; Philips, p. 110, pl. CLIV).

2. Gerald Taylor, *Silver* (Harmonsworth, Middlesex: Penguin Books, 1956), pl. 31a; Oman (c), pl. 139.

3. Virginia Museum (a), p. 21, no. 98; Davis, E. M., p. 116.

78 TEAPOT
John Denziloe
London. 1774/75

H: 4³¹⁄₃₂″ (12.6 cm); L: 8⁹⁄₁₆″ (21.8 cm); Diam (base): 3³¹⁄₃₂″ (10.1 cm). Wt: 12 oz. 7 dwt. 12 gr.

PROVENANCE: Garrard & Co. Ltd., London (purchased from C. J. Vander Ltd., London, 1954)

Fully marked on under-side of base; lion pas-sant on bezel of cover.

Two tea services by John Denziloe, purchased by George Mason of Fairfax County, Virginia, are exhibited at his home, Gunston Hall. One consists of a tea canister and sugar basket of 1783/84 and a cream pot of the following year, the other of a teapot, tea canister, sugar basket, and cream pot, all of 1784/85. Both are of oval plan with engraved decoration and the Mason family crest and motto. Tradition asserts that Mason acquired four silver tea services for his four daughters.[1]

1954-554

———

1. "In Virginia," *Arts in Virginia* 1 (Winter 1961):31, fig. 3.

79 TEAPOT
William Plummer
London. 1790/91

H: 6⅜" (16.2 cm); L: 10¾" (27.3 cm); L (base): 5¹⁵⁄₁₆" (15.1 cm); W (base): 3³¹⁄₃₂" (10.1 cm). Wt: 17 oz. 7 dwt. 12 gr.

PROVENANCE: Garrard & Co. Ltd., London

From the early 1770s teapots in the neoclassical taste are usually of circular or oval plan with straight sides and spouts and without a supporting foot or base.

Fully marked on underside of base; lion passant on interior of cover.

Crest of the Piggot family engraved on face of cover. "Piggot/Russel Sqr" scratched on underside of base.

During the 1780s and 1790s, forms tended to be plain and flatly decorated. The preference for chased or applied sculptural ornament, much in evidence on earlier Adamite silver (No. 87), shifted to an emphasis on decorative engraving, such as the repetitive formal borders of scrolls and paterae, as in this example, or in conjunction with drapery and floral swags and oval enclosures for paterae and armorials, as in the hot water urn (No. 92). Interest is lent to the body of this piece by its division into gently shaped and

79

reeded panels. This teapot was acquired along with a coffeepot, cream pot, and sugar basket, all of the same year (Nos. 86, 98, 103). Although fashioned by different makers, they are all engraved with similar decorative borders and the Piggot family crest. A pair of plain oval teapots with matching stands of 1786/87 by William Plummer of London, engraved with the Carter family arms and crest, forms part of the Carter family silver at Shirley, Charles City County, Virginia.[1]

1958-458

———————

1. Barbara Snow, "Living with Antiques: Shirley, Charles City County, Virginia," *Antiques* 83 (May 1963):545, ill.

80 CHOCOLATE POT
John Wisdom
London. 1708/9

80

H: 9¼″ (23.5 cm); Diam (base): 3¹⁵⁄₁₆″ (10 cm.)
Wt: 20 oz. 16 dwt. 1 gr.

PROVENANCE: Miss L. Coats, Fornethy House, Perthshire (sold at Christie, Manson & Woods, London, 1954); Garrard & Co. Ltd., London

PUBLISHED: Christie's (July 21, 1954), lot 79, ill.

Fully marked on body below rim to right of handle; maker's mark and lion's head erased on bezel of cover; lion's head erased on underside of finial.

Owner's cypher engraved on face of body opposite handle.

Chocolate pots for the most part closely correspond in design to contemporary coffeepots. The position of the handle at right angles to the spout does not serve to distinguish between the two, for this occurs on coffeepots of the late seventeenth century and the first half of the eighteenth century. Usually, the only difference is the presence of a circular hole in the top of the cover of the chocolate pot to accommodate the stirring rod or mill. For this purpose, the finial is either hinged at the side, as in this instance, pivoted, or removable. The spout on this example is wrought from sheet and not cast, as are spouts on most coffee and chocolate pots before 1710.

Stirring rods were consistently referred to as "chocolate mills" in the seventeenth and eighteenth centuries.[1] This term, as Hughes and Pinto have pointed out, has often been understandably confused with a hand machine to grind or pulverize chocolate.[2] Chocolate mills usually consist of a turned wooden handle with a cluster of plain or pierced flanges of wood or metal at one end. Very few chocolate pots retain their mills. A rare example is that of 1738/39 by Paul Crespin of London in the Farrer collection at the Ashmolean Museum, Oxford.[3] Clayton cites, but does not describe or illustrate, an example of 1774.[4] Wenham illustrates a chocolate pot with lamp and stand of 1807/8 by John Parker of London with a mill having pierced silver flanges.[5] Mills are most frequently encountered with miniature chocolate pots, and, in that instance, they are rendered entirely in silver. Full-sized mills were produced by turners in the seventeenth and eighteenth centuries,[6] who sold them separately and probably supplied the wooden parts to silversmiths for mounting. Modest examples entirely of wood were probably intended for use with chocolate pots of base metal.[7] Two examples of extreme size with handsomely shaped and pierced silver flanges and partial silver handles of 1739/40, both fashioned by John Hugh Le Sage of London, would appear too large for use in chocolate pots and may have served as punch whisks.[8] An unmarked example of similar date sold at auction in 1973.[9]

John Worlidge described in 1675 the preparation of chocolate and the necessary role played by the mill:

[Some] boil it [the chocolate 'sliced or scraped fine'] in water and sugar; others mix half water and half milk and boil it, then add powdered chocolate to it and boil them together; others add wine and water. Be sure whilst it is boiling to keep it stirring, and when it is off the fire, whir it with your hand mill. That is, it must be mixed in a deep pot of Tin, copper or stone, with a cover with a hole in the middle of it, for the handle of the mill to come out at, or without a cover. The mill is only a knop at the end of a slender handle or stick, turned in a turner's lathe, and cut in notches, or rough at the end. They are sold at turners for that purpose. This being whirled between your hands, whilst the pot is over the fire, and the rough end in the liquor causes an equal mixture of the liquor with the chocolate and raises a head of froth over it. Then pour it out for use in small dishes for that purpose. You must add a convenient quantity of sugar to the mixture.[10]

This procedure had changed very little when Elizabeth Raffald, in her Experienced English Housekeeper (London, 1769), wrote:

Scrape four ounces of chocolate and pour a quart of boiling water upon it, mill it well with a chocolate mill, and sweeten it to your taste, give it a boil and let it stand all night, then mill it again very well, boil it two minutes, then mill it till it will leave a froth upon the top of your cups.[11]

As late as 1861, Mrs. Isabella Beeton, in her Book of Household Management, illustrates a conventional chocolate mill with a turned handle and pierced flanges and instructs: "Chocolate prepared with in a mill, as shown in the engraving, is made by putting in the scraped chocolate, pouring over it the boiling milk-and-water, and milling it over the fire until hot and frothy."

William Fitzhugh of Stafford County, Virginia, in a 1701 codicil to his will bequeathed "to my son Thomas Fitzhugh my Silver Chocolate Pott which I brought out of England." His estate's inventory of 1703 included "1 Copper. Chocolate Pott" with the "Household Furniture."[12] Interestingly enough, there are no articles listed for tea or coffee in his will or inventory. Thomas Lee, on the other hand, a resident of nearby Westmoreland County, owned a considerable quantity of silver, including a chocolate pot, coffeepot and teapot.[13] The 1770 inventory of the estate of Lord Botetourt listed among the goods and furnishings of the Governor's Palace in Williamsburg "3 chocolate pots with four mills," as well as "24 lb of chocolate."[14]

1954-577

1. Molinet was a less-used term.
2. G. Bernard Hughes, "Silver Pots for Chocolate," Country Life 125 (October 20, 1960):856–57; Edward H. Pinto, Treen and Other Wooden Bygones: An Encyclopedia and Social History (London: G. Bell & Sons, 1969), pp. 291–92.
3. Jones (a), pp. xv, 144, pl. LXXVII; Banister, p. 192, pl. 78.
4. Clayton, p. 63.
5. Edward Wenham, "Silver Chocolate-Pots," Antique Collector 17 (September–October 1946):172–73, figs. 9–10.
6. Chocolate mills are listed in the trade cards of John Alexander, "Ivory and Hard Wood Turner" (ca. 1770), and Thorn's "Cricket Bat, Turnery, and Patten Warehouse" (ca. 1765) (Ambrose Heal, The London Furniture Makers from the Restoration to the Victorian Era, 1660–1840 [London: B. T. Batsford Ltd., 1953], pp. 2, 181). See Worlidge quote in text.
7. Pinto, Treen, pl. 312.
8. Advertisement, How (of Edinburgh), London, Connoisseur 170 (February 1969):LII, ill.; Hackenbroch, rev. edn. only, p. 82 no. 159, ill.
9. John Herbert, ed., Christie's Review of the Season 1973 (London: Hutchinson & Co. [Publishers] Ltd., 1973), p. 457, ill.
10. Quoted by Hughes, "Silver Pots for Chocolate," p. 856.
11. Mrs. Raffald recommended in the making of lemon syllabubs to "mill them with a chocolate mill to raise the froth."
12. Davis, R. B., pp. 382, 384.
13. Ethel Armes, Stratford Hall, The Great House of the Lees (Richmond: Garret Massie, 1936), p. 54. These and other silver

articles were advertised as stolen in the *Maryland Gazette* of March 4, 1729.

14. Botetourt Inventory. These probably included the "2 chocolate pots" listed with copper or, at least base-metal objects among the "Goods sold his Excellency Lord Botetourt" in 1768 from the estate of Francis Fauquier, who preceded Botetourt as governor of Virginia.

81 COFFEEPOT
Peter Archambo, Sr.
London. 1734/35

81

H: 8⅞″ (22.5 cm); L: 7⅝″ (19.4 cm); Diam (base): 4⁷⁄₁₆″ (11.3 cm). Wt: 30 oz. 1 dwt. 4 gr.

PROVENANCE: Garrard & Co. Ltd., London

The general drinking of coffee began in 1652 with the opening of the Pasqua Rosee, the first of many London coffeehouses.[1] The earliest English silver coffeepot, however, is that of 1681/82, probably by George Garthorne of London, in the Victoria and Albert Museum, London.[2] It resembles the earliest silver teapot of eleven years earlier (see No. 74), as

well as other early coffeepots. These include examples of 1689/90, ascribed by Jackson to Francis Garthorne of London, in the royal collections;[3] of 1690/91, probably by George Garthorne of London, in the Assheton Bennett collection in the City of Manchester Art Gallery;[4] of 1692/93 with later rococo chasing;[5] of 1700/1701 by Andrew Raven of London

Fully marked on underside of base; lion passant on interior of cover.

Owner's crest engraved on opposite sides of body.

in the Farrer collection in the Ashmolean Museum, Oxford;[6] of 1700/1701 by Andrew Raven, formerly part of the Sneyd family silver;[7] and of 1701/2 by William Gibson of London.[8] These all have a tall circular body with tapered straight sides and a tall conical cover with a finial. Except for the earliest one of 1681/82, the handles are placed at right angles to (rather than opposite) the spout. Beginning with that of 1690/91, all have thumbpieces and, except for that of 1700/1701 in the Ashmolean Museum, spouts of early curved (rather than straight) form with a hinged flap at the pouring end. A mature example of this form of wrought spout can be seen in the chocolate pot of 1708/9 (No. 80).

This coffeepot and the following two examples evidence the persistence of the tapered straight-sided body, even though coffeepots of baluster and other curved forms had been made intermittently from the close of the seventeenth century. Cast curved spouts had replaced wrought ones by about 1710, by which time, also, the thumbpiece had been discarded. Tall domed covers, first appearing in the late seventeenth century, tend to diminish in height after about 1725, with the covers of many coffeepots of the 1730s and 1740s, as in this and the following two examples, having a flattened top and short contracted sides. This handsome example is chased and engraved with unusually broad borders of foliated scrolls, shells, faces, and diapering.

A plain coffeepot of similar form of 1732/33 by Joseph Smith of London with a tradition of ownership in the family of Edward Jacquelin (1668–1739) of Jamestown, Virginia, was exhibited in 1940 at the Virginia Museum of Fine Arts, Richmond.[9]

1955-260

82

PROVENANCE: Garrard & Co. Ltd., London

Coffeepots of this small size are uncommon. The lozenge enclosure for the arms indicates an unmarried lady.

1956-295

1. The earliest known coffeehouse in England was established in Oxford in 1650. Anthony à Wood, the diarist, noted in that year that "Jacob, a Jew, opened a Coffey house at the Angel, in the Parish of S. Peter in the East, Oxon, and there it was by some, who delighted in Noveltie, drank" (Bryant Lillywhite, *London Coffee Houses; A Reference Book of Coffee Houses of the Seventeenth, Eighteenth, and Nineteenth Centuries* [London: George Allen and Unwin Ltd., 1963], p. 17).

2. Jackson, 2:944–45, fig. 1259; Oman (c), p. 6, fig. 74; Oman (a), pp. 57–58, pl. 70B; Clayton, p. 69, fig. 134.

3. Jackson, 2:946, fig. 1261.

4. Hayward, pl. 49A; City of Manchester Art Gallery, *Catalogue of Silver from the Assheton Bennett Collection* (Manchester, 1965), p. 20, no. 75, pl. XVI.

5. Jackson, 2:947, fig. 1263.

6. Jones (a), pp. xix, 34, pl. XIX, no. 3; Hayward, p. 47, pl. 49B; Banister, p. 159, pl. 41.

7. Christie's (June 24, 1924), lot 45, ill.

8. Parke-Bernet Galleries, *Art Treasures Exhibition* (New York, 1955), no. 209, ill.

9. Virginia Museum (a), p. 19, no. 80; Davis, E. M., pp. 109–10, pl. I.

82 COFFEEPOT
Aymé Vedeau
London. 1740/41

H: 5½″ (14 cm); L: 5⅜″ (13.7 cm); Diam (base): 3¹⁄₁₆″ (7.9 cm). Wt: 11 oz. 2 dwt. 20 gr. ("10–12" engraved on underside of base).

Fully marked on face of body to right of handle.

Arms of an unmarried lady of the Cartwright family, Nottinghamshire, engraved on face of body.

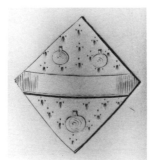

83 COFFEEPOT
Jonathan Fossy
London. 1740/41

H: 9⅛″ (23.2 cm); L: 7¹³⁄₁₆″ (19.8 cm); Diam (base): 4⁹⁄₁₆″ (11.6 cm). Wt: 26 oz. 13 dwt. 3 gr. ("oz/25 17" engraved on underside of base).

Fully marked on face of body to right of handle; lion passant on interior of cover.

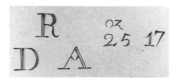

Owners' initials and weight engraved on underside of base.

83

PROVENANCE: Garrard & Co. Ltd., London (purchased from C. J. Vander Ltd., London, 1953)

PUBLISHED: Davis, J. D., p. 134, ill.

1954-520

84 COFFEEPOT
Francis Crump
London. 1756/57

Fully marked on underside of base; lion passant on interior of cover.

H: 13⅝″ (34.6 cm); L: 10″ (25.4 cm); Diam (base): 5⁷⁄₁₆″ (13.8 cm). Wt: 56 oz. 11 dwt. 23 gr.

PROVENANCE: Sotheby & Co., London (1962); purchased by How (of Edinburgh), London; Firestone and Parson, Boston

PUBLISHED: Sotheby's (March 15, 1962), lot 139, pl. XIII; "Accessions of American and Canadian Museums, January–March, 1967," *Art Quarterly* 30 (Summer 1967): 164; Judith Banister, "Three Centuries of Silver Coffee Pots," *Antique Dealer and Collectors Guide* 25 (July 1972): 70

84

Owners' cypher engraved on face of body.

This coffeepot is of unusual size and good weight. It is of fully developed rococo form, having a tall, double-bellied, baluster-shaped body with a double-domed cover and a tall circular base. The body, like most examples of this date, is plain, providing an effective contrast to the highly decorative spout and handle sockets. A coffeepot of similar size and identical design of the same year by Crump was sold at auction in New York in 1959.[1]

1967-93

1. Parke-Bernet (March 19–21, 1959), lot 497, ill.

Owner's initials engraved on underside of base.

85 COFFEEPOT
Daniel Smith and Robert Sharp
London. 1771/72

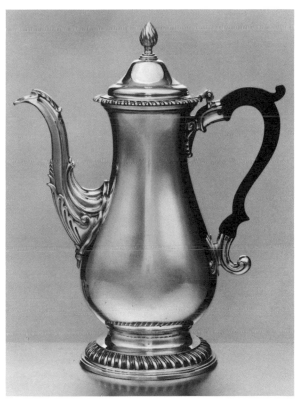

85

Fully marked on face of body to right of handle; maker's mark and lion passant on bezel of cover.

H: 10⅞″ (27.6 cm); L: 8¹³⁄₁₆″ (22.4 cm); Diam (base): 4½″ (11.4 cm). Wt: 29 oz. 13 dwt. 5 gr.

PROVENANCE: Garrard & Co. Ltd., London (purchased from Jaffe Rose Ltd., London, 1950)

A coffeepot of 1765/66 by Thomas Whipham and Charles Wright of London with the engraved crest of the Byrd family of Westover, Charles City County, is in the Virginia Historical Society, Richmond.[1] It is of this conventional elongated pear form with similar spout, handle sockets, and gadrooned base.

1954-521

1. Virginia Museum (a), p. 23, no. 125; Davis, E. M., p. 117.

86 COFFEEPOT
John Robins
London. 1790/91

86

Fully marked on underside of base; maker's mark, lion passant, and sovereign's head on bezel of cover.

Crest of the Piggot family engraved on face of cover.

H: 11¹⁵⁄₁₆″ (30.3 cm); L: 10⅝″ (27 cm); L (base): 5¼″ (13.3 cm); W (base): 3⅞″ (8.6 cm). Wt: 32 oz. 1 dwt. 12 gr.

PROVENANCE: Garrard & Co. Ltd., London

This coffeepot of representative urn form was acquired with a matching sugar dish of the same year by John Robins (No. 103), as well as a teapot and cream pot of the same year by different makers (Nos. 79, 98). The latter two are engraved with the same decorative borders and the Piggot family crest.

1958-456

87 HOT WATER OR COFFEE JUG
Silver-gilt
Henry Greenway
London. 1775/76

H: 13½″ (34.3 cm); Diam (base): 5¹⁄₁₆″ (12.9 cm). Wt: 46 oz. 4 dwt.

PROVENANCE: Private collector, Scarsdale, New York (sold at Parke-Bernet Galleries, New York, 1968; purchased by Hartman Galleries, New York); de Havilland (Antiques) Ltd., London (purchased from Sotheby & Co., London, 1971); S. J. Phillips Ltd., London

Fully marked on face of body below rim to right of handle; lion passant on underside of cover.

EXHIBITED: English Silver of Four Centuries, 1585–1835, Hartman Galleries, New York, 1969

PUBLISHED: Parke-Bernet (October 18, 1968), lot 39, ill.; Hartman Galleries, *English Silver of Four Centuries, 1585–1835* (New York, 1969), no. 65, ill.; Sotheby's (October 21, 1971), lot 183, ill.

This jug is an extremely fine example of early neo-classical silver. Its striking visual presence derives not only from its elegant and sophisticated form of classical inspiration, but also from its unusually rich sculptural quality. Bold satyrs' masks and swag-and-scroll-framed paterae provide strong focal points. The sculptural quality, evident in finer early neo-classical silver, dissipated with the increasing reli-

87

ance on linear engraving during the last quarter of the century. The chasing of the cover, body, and base (the masks and legs and the inset central patera of the base are cast) is superbly executed. Under the sponsorship of James Stuart and Robert Adam, the tripod became emblematic of the classical past, and it was adapted to a variety of domestic articles, especially lighting devices.[1] Notable among these is a set of four candelabra of 1774/75, fashioned by John Carter of London for Sir Watkin Wynn after a design by Robert Adam.[2] John Winter of Sheffield made modified use of the tripod in his candlesticks of about 1774 (No. 21).

Two very similar tripod jugs by Greenway, one of 1776/77 in a private collection[3] and the other of the following year in the Victoria and Albert Museum, London,[4] differ mainly from this example in having bands of alternate paterae and husks within beaded moldings at the tops of the lower sections of their bodies with ribbon-tied drapery swags below. Both are supported on triangular bases with inward-curved sides and squared corners.

The wicker wrapping of the handle is a replacement.

1973-373

1. Nicholas Goodison, "Mr. Stuart's Tripod," *Burlington Magazine* 114 (October 1972):695–704.
2. Rowe, pp. 37–38, plates 12–13.
3. David Udy, "Neo-classical Silver," *Discovering Antiques*, no. 46 (1971):1102–3, fig. 6.
4. Jackson, 1:315–16, fig. 342; Oman (c), pl. 163; Rowe, pp. 41–42, pl. 25.

88 KETTLE ON STAND
William Shaw
London. 1727/28

Fully marked on underside of kettle and lamp; leopard's head crowned, lion passant, and date letter on ring holding lamp; lion passant on cover of kettle and lamp.

H: 13″ (33 cm); L (kettle): 8⁹⁄₁₆″ (21.8 cm); Diam (base of kettle): 3¾″ (9.6 cm); H (stand): 4″ (10.2 cm). Wt (kettle): 31 oz. 8 dwt. 6 gr. ("38=10" en-

graved on underside of base); (stand): 16 oz. 4 dwt. 19 gr. ("16=10" engraved on underside of lamp).

PROVENANCE: Garrard & Co. Ltd., London (purchased at Christie, Manson & Woods, London, 1954)

PUBLISHED: Christie's (June 30, 1954), lot 91; Comstock, p. V, ill.

88

It is only reasonable that the introduction of the kettle should soon follow that of the teapot. Although the form of kettles closely corresponds to that of contemporary teapots, they can be distinguished from the latter by their greater size and a broad bail handle placed over the cover and attached with pivots at the shoulder of the body. Usually set on stands fitted with lamps, they housed the hot water to replenish the smaller teapot, in which the tea was infused. They rarely stood on the tea table but rather on a small stand nearby. Occasionally silver tripod stands were fashioned for this purpose.[1]

Arms of Knightly of Northamptonshire and War-wickshire quartering Wightwick of Berkshire and Staffordshire with those of Marow of Middlesex and Warwickshire borne in pretense engraved on face of body. Crest of the Knightly family engraved on cover of lamp.

This is a comparatively modest example of the globular type. It is finely engraved at the shoulder with a conventional strapwork border incorporating foliated scrolls and winged cherubs' faces. The wicker wrapping of the handle is a replacement.

1954-570

1. A silver tripod stand which retains its original kettle of 1724/25 by Simon Pantin of London is in the Untermyer collection (Hackenbroch, pp. 43–44, no. 72, plates 84–85 and frontispiece; rev. edn., pp. 72–73, no. 138, ill.). Silver tripod stands without their original kettles include examples of 1717/18 by David Willaume, Sr., of London (with a later kettle of 1724/25) in the collection of the duke of Buccleuch; of 1719/20 by John White of London (with a later kettle of 1846/47); of 1725/26 by John Corporon of London in the collection of the duke of Northumberland; and an unmarked example of about 1725, formerly in the collection of the marquess of Exeter and Colonel H. H. Mulliner, in the Victoria and Albert Museum, London (E. Alfred Jones, "Old Silver in the Possession of the Duke of Buccleuch, K.T.—III," *Old Furniture, A Magazine of Domestic Ornament* 7 [July 1929]:133–35, fig. 9; Christie's [December 14, 1966], lot 45, ill.; *Illustrated Catalogue of the Loan Exhibition of English Decorative Art at Lansdowne House* [London: "The Collector," 1929], no. 164, pl. 34; Oman [c], pl. 116). A silver tea table with a tripod base of about 1715, possibly by Ambrose Stevenson of London, is fitted with a later octagonal salver top of 1758/59 by Francis Crump of London (Sotheby's [July 4, 1968], lot 135, ill.). Occasionally the circular tops of mahogany tripod stands are notched to receive the feet of silver salvers, such as the pair with salvers of 1741/42 at Dunham Massey, Cheshire, which are recorded in a house inventory of 1752 as "2 Mahogany stands to set the silver Tea and Coffee Tables on" (Macquoid and Edwards, 3: 163–64, figs. 1–2). Two rectangular tea tables covered with silver plates are recorded, one of about 1725 from the collection of the duke of Portland and the other of 1742/43 by Augustin Courtauld of London in the Kremlin (E. Alfred Jones, *Catalogue of Plate Belonging to the Duke of Portland, K.G., G.C.V.O. at Welbeck Abbey* [London: St. Catherine Press, 1935], pp. xvii, 124, pl. xviii; ———, *The Old English Plate of the Emperor of Russia* [Letchworth: Arden Press, 1909], pp. li–lii, 58, pl. xxix).

89 KETTLE ON STAND
George Boothby
London. 1731/32

89

Fully marked on underside of kettle and lamp; lion passant on cover of kettle and lamp.

H: 14¾" (37.5 cm); L (kettle): 9¹³⁄₁₆" (24.9 cm); Diam (base of kettle): 4⅜" (11.1 cm); H (stand): 4¼" (10.8 cm). Wt: 97 oz. 18 dwt. 3½ gr.

PROVENANCE: Sotheby & Co., London (1964; purchased by Thomas Lumley Ltd., London); Firestone and Parson, Boston, Massachusetts

Arms of Boothby impaling Worthington engraved on face of body with Boothby family crest engraved on cover of lamp and rim of stand.

PUBLISHED: Sotheby's (March 19, 1964), lot 88, pl. III; advertisement, Firestone and Parson, Boston, *Antiques* 97 (January 1970):30, ill.

This kettle is one of the finest examples of the globular type. Its bold design is especially well integrated. There is a proper visual relationship between the height and character of the kettle and stand. The strength of its broad body of compressed spherical form is matched by the generous detailing of its other elements, such as the moldings above and the attachments below the large handle pivots and its stocky spout with its forcefully paneled lower sides ending in deep scallops. With its upward-curving shaped rim and its well-articulated legs and feet, the stand both securely receives and supports the kettle. It avoids the compromising features, found in some examples of this type, of an overly mannered handle, a pierced apron, and excessive splay to the legs. The body is hinged below the spout to the stand with a removable pin to permit tilting the body for pouring. The leather wrapping of the handle, as in the following example, appears to be original. Like the previous example, this kettle is handsomely engraved at the shoulder with a conventional strapwork border incorporating foliated scrolls and masks and arms below. Fashioned for a member of the Boothby family, one wonders whether the client was indeed related to the maker.

The kettle is extraordinarily heavy for its type. Its weight more closely approximates that of pearshaped kettles and stands from earlier in the century. Some of these are even of greater size and weight, such as the 1708/9 example by Lewis Mettayer of London of 128 ounces in the Untermyer collection,[1] the 1709/10 example by Anthony Nelme of London of 118 ounces 14 pennyweight in the duke of Portland's collection,[2] and the 1713/14 example by Paul de Lamerie of London of 113 ounces in the Farrer collection in the Ashmolean Museum, Oxford.[3] Henry Wetherburn, the Williamsburg tavern-keeper, owned an immense silver kettle, probably of this earlier type, which was listed in the 1760 inventory of his estate as "1 Tea Kettle 130 [oz.] 4 [dwt] @ 7/6 49.0.7½."[4]

A similar kettle of 1727/28 by Peter Archambo, Sr., of London, reputed to have been part of the furnishings of Tryon Palace, New Bern, North Carolina, is recorded.[5]

1972-246

1. Hackenbroch, p. 42, no. 70, pl. 82; rev. edn., pp. xxi, 67–68, no. 129, ill.

2. E. Alfred Jones, *Catalogue of Plate Belonging to the Duke of Portland, K.G., G.C.V.O. at Welbeck Abbey* (London: St. Catherine Press, 1935), p. 96, pl. x.

3. Jones (a), pp. xvi, 42, pl. XXII.

4. York County, Wills and Inventories, no. 21 (1760–71), pp. 36–43 (microfilm copy, Department of Research, Colonial Williamsburg Foundation).

5. E. Alfred Jones, "Some Old English Plate in America," *Connoisseur* 55 (December 1919):205–6, fig. 1.

90 KETTLE ON STAND, WITH CASE
Thomas Whipham
London. 1747/48

H: 14¾" (37.5 cm); L (kettle): 9⅝" (24.5 cm); Diam (base of kettle): 3⅜" (8.6 cm); H (stand): 4⅛" (10.5 cm); H (case): 16¾" (42.5 cm). Wt: 63 oz. 19 dwt. 18 gr.

PROVENANCE: Windsor White, Duxbury, Massachusetts

PUBLISHED: Davis, J. D., p. 137, ill.

This kettle of representative rococo form and decoration retains its original fitted case, made of deal covered with tooled leather and lined with green baize over marbled paper. Few such cases survive with their original contents. Two similar but empty cases, one for a coffeepot and the other for a breadbasket, are also in the Colonial Williamsburg collection (L1970-225, 226).

The wicker wrapping of the handle appears to be original. In most instances, silversmiths probably had

tion of this example was exhibited in 1940 at the Museum of Fine Arts, Richmond. Made by William Grundy of London in 1749/50, it is believed to have been originally owned by Anne Carter, daughter of

Arms of Kelly, Devonshire, impaling Drew, Wiltshire, engraved within a cartouche on one side of body and the Kelly family crest on the other.

90

Fully marked on underside of body and lamp.

Charles Carter (1707–1764) of Cleve, King George County, who married Col. Lewis Willis (1734–1813) of Fredericksburg, and to have descended through their son, Byrd Charles Willis (1781–1846) to the present owner.[3]

1962-264

this work done by basketmakers. Judith Banister has found in her examination of the accounts of the Scott family of basketmakers of London that they "wickered" the handles, mainly of kettles and coffeepots, for about a dozen different silversmiths during the eighteenth century.[1] They charged Paul de Lamerie six shillings for "laping" six silver handles in 1727.[2]

A fully developed rococo kettle on stand of this form but without the elaborate high-chased decora-

---

1. Judith Banister, "A Basketmaker's Accounts with Some 18th Century Silversmiths," *The Proceedings of the Society of Silver Collectors*, no. 9 (Spring 1967):21–24.
2. Ibid., p. 21; ———, "A Link with Paul de Lamerie," *Apollo* 123 (March 1961):67–68.
3. Virginia Museum (a), p. 20, no. 20; Davis, E. M., p. 114, pl. II.

91 KETTLE ON STAND
Thomas Whipham
London. 1747/48

91

Fully marked on underside of kettle and lamp.

Arms of Whitmore, Shropshire, impaling those of an unidentified family on face of kettle.

H: 13¾″ (34.9 cm); L (kettle): 9¼″ (23.5 cm); Diam (base of kettle): 3¼″ (8.3 cm); H (stand): 4³⁄₁₆″ (10.6 cm). Wt (kettle): 40 oz. 12 dwt. 4 gr.; (stand): 23 oz. 7 dwt. 14 gr.

PROVENANCE: James Robinson, Inc., New York

This kettle and stand was produced in the same shop and in the same year as the previous example. Although they share many cast elements, the plain body of this example indicates the options, involving both fashion and expense, that were open to clients.

1937-152

92 HOT WATER URN
James Young
London. 1788/89

92

Fully marked on underside of base; maker's mark, lion passant, and sovereign's head on bezel of cover.

Unidentified arms and crest engraved on opposite sides of body; crest repeated on cover.

H: 16¼″ (41.3 cm); L: 7⅝″ (19.4 cm); W (base and feet): 4¹³⁄₁₆″ (12.2 cm). Wt: 34 oz. 7 dwt. 6 gr.

PROVENANCE: Garrard & Co. Ltd., London

By 1760 the kettle with stand and lamp had declined in favor. The hot water or tea urn assumed its function as a dispensing storage vessel for hot water to replenish the teapot. Early ovoid urns in the rococo taste (No. 248) gave place in the 1770s to the elegant neoclassical form. A characteristic late eighteenth-century decorative engraving scheme enhances this fine example. It was acquired with a larger matching urn measuring 24½″ in height (1958-461).

1958-462

93 HOT WATER JUG AND STAND
Rebecca Emes and Edward Barnard
London. 1810/11

H: 12⅛″ (30.8 cm); L: 6⅞″ (17.5 cm); Diam (base of jug): 3⁹⁄₁₆″ (9.1 cm); H (stand): 4²¹⁄₃₂″ (11.8 cm); Diam (rim of stand): 5¾″ (14.6 cm). Wt: 49 oz. 13 dwt. 5 gr. ("29ıı3ıı" engraved on underside of jug).

PROVENANCE: Anonymous gift

PUBLISHED: Williamsburg (a), p. 8, ill.

93

Fully marked on underside of base of jug; maker's mark, lion passant, date letter, and sovereign's head on edge of base of stand; maker's mark, lion passant, and date letter on underside of lip of cover of jug and on bezel of lamp; lion passant, date letter, and sovereign's head on face of body of lamp.

This was a popular form of jug during the first two decades of the nineteenth century. A large number of similar examples were made primarily by Paul Storr, among other makers. Some of them have the same form of ivory handle with a grooved face and a full loop in the lower part. A number of four-piece tea services by Storr include a jug of this type, as well as a teapot, sugar bowl, and cream jug. This would tend to indicate that such jugs, invariably fitted with lamps, were intended for hot water. N. M. Penzer has noted that the lack of a strainer in a jug of this type is a further indication of its use for hot water.[1] The name "FS Darwin" is scratched in script letters on the underside of the Williamsburg jug.

G1971-3013

_____

1. N. M. Penzer, *Paul Storr, 1771–1844, Silversmith and Goldsmith* (London: B. T. Batsford Ltd., 1954), p. 118, pl. xx.

94 CREAM POT
George Jones
London. 1725/26

94

Fully marked on underside of base.

H: 2⅝″ (6.7 cm); Diam (base): 1⅝″ (4.1 cm). Wt: 2 oz. 7 dwt. 3 gr.

PROVENANCE: Garrard & Co. Ltd., London (purchased from C. J. Vander Ltd., London, 1954)

Small jugs for milk or cream were late in joining the tea equipage, and it has been questioned whether the English at first added milk or cream to their tea. The earliest examples date from the reign of Queen Anne, but they are scarce before 1720. Early cream pots, such as this example, are small in size and of broad baluster form with a small triangular pouring spout and a short foot. A similar London example of 1726/27 probably by William Matthew or William Spackman (maker's mark is indistinct) is also in the Colonial Williamsburg collection (1954-323).

1954-560

95 CREAM POT
John Gamon
London. 1736/37

95

Fully marked on underside of body.

H: 3²⁷⁄₃₂″ (9.8 cm). Wt: 3 oz. 4 dwt. 16 gr. ("oz/ 3 ÷ 5" engraved on underside of foot).

PROVENANCE: Firestone and Parson, Boston

Unidentified arms engraved on face of body.

Three short cabriole legs were applied to cream pots from about 1725. This example is of standard mid-century conformation with an elongated pear-shaped body with a flaring serrated rim, broad pouring lip, and slender double-scroll handle. A similar cream pot of 1755/56 by an unidentified London maker ("I·W" with a mullet above and a rosette below) is also in the Colonial Williamsburg collection (1964-456).

1966-166

96 CREAM POT
London. 1737/38

Fully marked on underside of body (maker's mark indistinct).

Owners' initials engraved on underside of foot.

H: 4¹⁄₁₆″ (10.3 cm). Wt: 4 oz. 12 dwt. ("4=15" engraved on underside of foot).

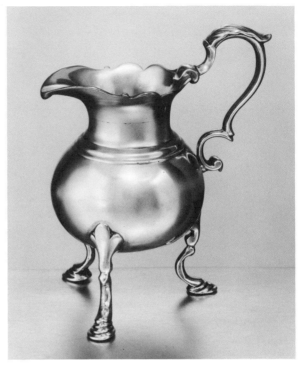

96

PROVENANCE: Garrard & Co. Ltd., London (purchased from W. A. Shakman, Chalfont St. Giles, Buckinghamshire, 1951)

Cream pots of this compressed baluster or pear form with a molding at the contraflexure of neck and body, dating mainly from the 1730s and early 1740s, tend to be of heavier gauge and have a fuller handle treatment than those of more standard pear form, such as the previous example.

1954-548

97 CREAM POT
London. 1763/64

Fully marked on face of body to right of handle.

H: 4″ (10.2 cm); Diam (base): 1³¹⁄₃₂″ (5 cm). Wt: 3 oz. 9 dwt. 19 gr.

PROVENANCE: Museum of Fine Arts, Boston

97

During the third quarter of the century, many cream pots assumed the inverted-pear or double-bellied body of teapots and coffeepots in the rococo taste. Although some examples of this type continued to be supported on three cabriole legs, many have a more stable splayed circular foot, such as this modest example with gadrooned rim and base moldings.

1954-324

98 CREAM POT
Gilt-lined
Henry Chawner
London. 1790/91

Fully marked on underside of base.

Crest of the Piggot family engraved on exterior of base.

H: 6⅜₆″ (15.7 cm); L (base): 3⅛″ (7.9 cm); W (base): 2⅛″ (5.4 cm). Wt: 7 oz. 1 dwt. 20 gr.

PROVENANCE: Garrard & Co. Ltd., London

98

From about 1775, most cream pots or jugs in the Adam taste are of this tall helmet form with a high-arched loop handle. This example matches in shape and decorative engraving—and was acquired with—the teapot, coffeepot, and sugar basket (Nos. 79, 86, 103), all of the same year and engraved with the Piggot family crest.

1958-459

99 CREAM PAIL
Samuel Herbert
London. 1752/53

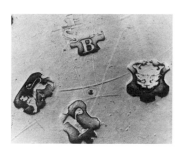

Fully marked on underside of base.

H: 3⁷⁄₁₆″ (8.7 cm); H (rim): 1²⁷⁄₃₂″ (4.7 cm); Diam (rim): 2⁵⁄₈″ (6.7 cm); Diam (base): 1¹¹⁄₁₆″ (4.3 cm). Wt: 2 oz. 5 dwt. 3 gr.

PROVENANCE: Garrard & Co. Ltd., London (purchased from C. J. Vander Ltd., London, 1954)

99

Owner's crest engraved on face of body.

Although first appearing about 1730, most cream pails date from between 1760 and 1780. Many examples from the second half of the century are pierced and fitted with blue glass liners. James Geddy, the Williamsburg silversmith, advertised in the *Virginia Gazette* of June 4, 1772, that he had just imported for sale, among other small silver articles and a considerable listing of jewelry, "chased Cream Buckets." The 1777 inventory of the estate of William Pearson, a Williamsburg tanner, listed "1 silver Cream bucket & Ladle 70/."[1] An example with similar banded sides and interlaced handle of 1761/62 by Alexander Johnston of London is in the Virginia Historical Society, Richmond. It was originally owned by John Robinson (1704–1766) of King and Queen County, Virginia, who served as speaker of the House of Burgesses and treasurer of the colony.

1954-556

———

1. York County, Wills and Inventories, no. 22 (1771–83), p. 387 (microfilm copy, Department of Research, Colonial Williamsburg Foundation).

100 CREAM BOAT
Probably Thomas Smith or Thomas Satchwell
London. 1777/78

100

Fully marked on underside of body.

H: 3½″ (8.9 cm); L: 4⁵⁄₈″ (11.8 cm). Wt: 2 oz. 16 dwt. 6 gr.

PROVENANCE: Garrard & Co. Ltd., London (purchased from C. J. Vander Ltd., London, 1954)

Diminutive sauceboats are generally considered to have been used for milk or cream. Clayton cites a late pair of 1797 with an inscription linking them to a coffeehouse, which tends to confirm that use.[1] The beading of the rim of this modest example is punched to simulate a more elaborate applied rim.

1954-557

———

1. Clayton, p. 81.

101 COVERED SUGAR BOWL
Richard Bayley
London. 1726/27

a low domed cover. Perhaps the earliest example is that of 1691/92 by Francis Garthorne of London in the Assheton Bennett collection in the City of Manchester Art Gallery.[1] Its cover, like most early examples, is surmounted by a finial of turned design. An alternative to a finial after about 1715 is a short reel-shaped ring, as in this fine representative example, so that the cover could be inverted to form a shallow saucerlike dish, perhaps used as a spoon tray.

1965-97

1. Hayward, p. 48, pl. 56A; City of Manchester Art Gallery, *Catalogue of Silver from the Assheton Bennett Collection* (Manchester, 1965), p. 16, no. 54, pl. VIII; Clayton, p. 287, fig. 579.

102 COVERED SUGAR BOWL
Samuel Taylor
London. 1754/55

101

Fully marked on underside of base; leopard's head crowned, lion passant, and date letter on top of cover

Owners' initials engraved on underside of cover and base.

H: 2¹¹⁄₁₆″ (6.2 cm); Diam (cover): 4⁷⁄₁₆″ (11.3 cm); Diam (base): 2⅞″ (7.3 cm). Wt: 9 oz. 10 dwt. 20 gr. ("9=12=0" engraved on underside of base).

PROVENANCE: Norman C. Hurst (sold at Christie, Manson & Woods, London, 1965)

PUBLISHED: Christie's (March 10, 1965), lot 50, pl. 18.

Early sugar bowls, extremely rare before 1700, have a hemispherical body supported on a short foot and

102

Fully marked on underside of base; maker's mark and lion passant on interior of cover.

Arms engraved on face of body and crest on top of cover. Those of the first quarter are unidentified, but would appear to be of Irish or Scottish provenance. Those of the third quarter (excluding the impalement) are of Peirse, Yorkshire and Kent.

H: 4¹⁵⁄₁₆″ (12.5 cm); Diam (cover): 4⅜″ (11.1 cm); Diam (base): 2¹³⁄₁₆″ (7.1 cm). Wt: 9 oz. 5 dwt. 12½ gr.

PROVENANCE: Garrard & Co. Ltd., London (purchased from S. G. Schwersee, Finchingfield, Essex, 1954)

This is a relatively late sugar bowl to have this type of invertible cover with a reel-shaped handle and foot. Most double-bellied rococo examples have a finial on their double-domed covers.

1954-566

103

103 SUGAR BASKET
Gilt-lined
John Robins
London. 1790/91

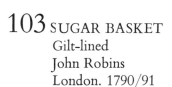

Fully marked on underside of base; lion passant on face of handle.

H: 5⅞″ (14.9 cm); L: 4¾″ (12.1 cm); W: 3⅝″ (9.2 cm); L (base): 3⁷⁄₁₆″ (8.7 cm); W (base): 2⁷⁄₁₆″ (5.9 cm). Wt: 6 oz. 1 dwt. 9 gr.

PROVENANCE: Garrard & Co. Ltd., London

Footed vase and boat-shaped sugar bowls, sometimes pierced and glass-lined, predominate during the last three decades of the century. A bail handle is often fitted with pivots at the rim to form a sugar basket, as in this instance. It was acquired with a matching coffeepot of 1790/91, also by John Robins (No. 86),

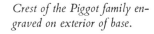

Crest of the Piggot family engraved on exterior of base.

as well as a teapot and cream pot of 1790/91 by different makers (Nos. 79, 98), the latter two engraved with the same decorative borders and the Piggot family crest. An unengraved sugar basket of 1790/91 by Robert Hennell of London is part of the Carter family silver at Shirley, Charles City County, Virginia.

1958-457

104 TEA CANISTER
John Gibbon
London. 1719/20

H: 4¹³⁄₁₆″ (12.2 cm); L (base): 3⅜″ (8.6 cm); W (base): 2¼″ (5.7 cm). Wt: 6 oz. 14 dwt.

PROVENANCE: Museum of Fine Arts, Boston

104

Fully marked on face of body above base; maker's mark and and lion's head erased on face of sliding cover; cap unmarked.

Owners' initials engraved on underside of base.

Tea canisters, which joined the tea equipage in the late seventeenth century, vary greatly in design. Early types tend to be of polygonal form, with this being the most common pattern between 1710 and 1730. Canisters of this type are usually fitted with sliding covers to facilitate filling. Their domed, pull-off caps may have been used to measure the tea.

1954-330

105 SET OF TWO TEA CANISTERS AND SUGAR BOX, WITH CHEST
Elizabeth Godfrey
London. 1741/42

Fully marked on underside of each base and on underside of cover of sugar box; leopard's head crowned, lion passant, and date letter on body of both tea canisters (because of removable base plates); maker's mark and lion passant on underside of both tea canister covers.

Arms of an unmarried lady of the Gregory family, Nottinghamshire and Lincolnshire, engraved on front of body and on either end of sugar box and on one end of both tea canisters; arms erased at an early date from within chased cartouche on bodies of both tea canisters and beneath present arms on front of sugar box.

H (sugar box): 4⅜" (11.1 cm); L: 4½" (11.4 cm); W:3⅜" (8.6 cm); H (tea canisters): 4⅜" (11.1 cm); L (base): 3⅛" (7.9 cm); W (base): 2⅜" (6 cm); H (chest without handle): 6⅜" (16.2 cm); L (base): 11¼" (28.6 cm); W (base): 5⅛" (13 cm). Wt (sugar box): 20 oz. 8 dwt. 11 gr. ("20–7" engraved on underside of body); tea canisters: 12 oz. 4 dwt. 12 gr. ("12=7" engraved on underside of base) and 12 oz. 7 dwt. 21½ gr. ("12=10" engraved on underside of base).

PROVENANCE: James Robinson Inc., New York

PUBLISHED: Williamsburg (b), p. 252, ill.

Tea canisters were often made in pairs with a larger and matching sugar box and fitted in a lined chest, usually of finished wood or covered with shagreen. George Washington, writing to Lafayette in 1783, ordered, along with numerous plated articles, "1 Tea-chest, such as usually appertains to tea or breakfast tables, the inner part of which, to have three departments, two for tea's of different kinds, the other for

105

Sugar."[1] The term "tea caddy" is commonly used today for both the "tea canister" and the "tea chest," as they were generally referred to in the eighteenth century. George Hepplewhite, in his *Cabinet-Maker and Upholsterer's Guide* (London, 1788), illustrates three "Tea Chests" and three "Tea Caddies." His is one of the earliest uses of the latter term, by which he distinguished small tea chests with only one or two compartments from larger examples. Thomas Sheraton, in his *Cabinet Dictionary* (London, 1803), states that "This word ['Cady'] is now applied to various kinds

of tea chests, of square, octagon and circular shapes," again alluding to the smaller type, sometimes lined with sheet lead and not fitted with separate canisters.

This set is handsomely flat-chased with rococo scroll, shell, and floral ornament framing cartouches on some of their sides. The protective chest is undoubtedly largely responsible for their crisp condition. The pieces exemplify the fine work produced in the shop of Elizabeth Godfrey, who deserves to be considered the preeminent woman silversmith of the eighteenth century. Twice she registered marks at Goldsmiths' Hall, first in 1731 after the death of her first husband, the silversmith Abraham Buteux, and again in 1741, the year this set was made, when she continued after his death the business of her second husband, Benjamin Godfrey, whom she had married in 1734. She maintained the firm until the mid-1750s.

1937-153, 1–4

---

1. Buhler, p. 41.

106 SET OF TWO TEA CANISTERS AND A SUGAR BOX
London. 1756/57

Fully marked on underside of each base; maker's mark and lion passant on underside of each cover; lion passant below engraved crest on body of both tea canisters (because of removable base plates).

Owner's crest engraved on face of each body.

H (sugar box): 4⅞″ (11.3 cm); L (base): 3⅜″ (5.9 cm); W (base): 3⁵⁄₁₆″ (8.4 cm); H (tea canisters): 4⅞″ (11.3 cm); L (base): 3⁵⁄₁₆″ (8.4 cm); W (base): 2⅝″ (6.7 cm). Wt (sugar box): 11 oz. 15 dwt. 10 gr.; (tea canisters): 12 oz. 17 dwt. 12 gr. and 12 oz. 18 dwt. 17 gr.

PROVENANCE: Garrard & Co. Ltd., London (purchased from T. W. F. Bullock, Fen Ditton, Cambridgeshire, 1953)

The canisters of this set, like the preceding ones, have sliding covers and base plates (but the sugar boxes do not). All three members are high-chased at their shoulders with scrolled floral garlands on a matted ground in the rococo taste. The tops of their covers, flat-chased with scrolls and shells, are fitted with hinged flap handles of curling shell form as in the previous set. The interiors of the tea canisters, as is occasionally found, are lined with sheets of lead. A very similar set of the same year and by the same unidentified maker retains its original shagreen-covered case with silver mounts.[1] William McCaa of Norfolk advertised for sale in the *Virginia Gazette* of January 18, 1770, among other silver articles, "A set of chased silver tea canisters in a neat case, covered with fish skin, and lined with crimson, &c." It is not known, of course, whether they were of this rectangular form or of circular or bombé form.

1954-522, 1–3

1. Advertisement, Harvey & Gore Ltd., London, *Connoisseur* 141 (June 1958):i, ill.

107 TEA CANISTER
Probably William Cripps
London. 1757/58

107

*Fully marked on underside
of base; cover unmarked.*

H: 4¾″ (12.1 cm); Diam (base): 2¹⁄₁₆″ (5.2 cm).
Wt: 5 oz. 10 dwt. 3 gr.

PROVENANCE: Garrard & Co. Ltd., London (purchased
from C. J. Vander Ltd., London, 1954)

1954-555

108 BOWL
Humphrey Payne
London. 1712/13

Fully marked on face of body below rim.

108

H: 2¹¹⁄₁₆″ (6.2 cm); Diam (rim): 5¼″ (13.3 cm);
Diam (base): 3¼″ (8.3 cm). Wt: 6 oz. 13 dwt.
19½ gr.

PROVENANCE: Garrard & Co. Ltd., London (purchased
from W. P. Dobson, Milnthorpe, Westmoreland, 1954)

This small bowl and the following example may have
been slop or waste bowls with tea or coffee services.
Small bowls of this sort served as repositories for the
dregs from the pot and cup.

1954-512

109 BOWL
Alexander Johnston
London. 1755/56

109

Fully marked on underside of base.

H: 3¹⁵⁄₁₆″ (10 cm); Diam (rim): 5¹¹⁄₁₆″ (14.5 cm); Diam (base): 3⁹⁄₁₆″ (9.1 cm). Wt: 15 oz. 17 dwt.

PROVENANCE: Museum of Fine Arts, Boston

1954-325

110 SPOON TRAY
John Tuite
London. 1734/35

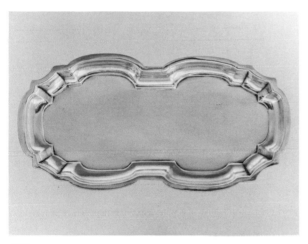

110

Fully marked on underside.

D

E G

Owners' initials engraved on underside.

L: 6⅜″ (16.2 cm); W: 3¼″ (8.3 cm). Wt: 2 oz. 17 dwt. 2 gr.

PROVENANCE: Garrard & Co. Ltd., London (purchased from C. J. Vander Ltd., London, 1954)

Small oval and oblong trays in silver for holding teaspoons, dating mainly from the first half of the eighteenth century, form part of the considerable equipage used in serving tea. The covers of sugar bowls fitted with reel tops were perhaps also inverted for this purpose (Nos. 101–2). John Tuite, a specialist salver-maker, fashioned this modest example.

1954-561

111 SUGAR TONGS
Hugh Arnett and Edward Pocock
London. About 1720

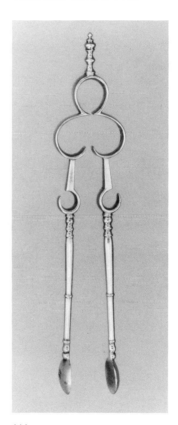

111

Maker's mark and lion passant on grips.

L: 4⅞″ (11.3 cm). Wt: 12 dwt. 17 gr.

PROVENANCE: A. C. D. Pain (sold at Christie, Manson & Woods, London, 1972); How (of Edinburgh), London

PUBLISHED: Christie's (March 15, 1972), lot 21.

The earliest sugar tongs are of fire-tong form, either of spring type, as here, or with pivoting arms, as in an actual pair of fire tongs. This handsome example, with well articulated handle and moldings, can be dated shortly after the reintroduction of the sterling standard in 1719, in which year Arnett and Pocock entered their mark. Heal records their partnership as active between 1719 and 1724.[1]

1972-395

———————

1. Sir Ambrose Heal, *The London Goldsmiths, 1200–1800* (Cambridge: University Press, 1935), p. 97.

112 SUGAR TONGS
John Wirgman
London. About 1755

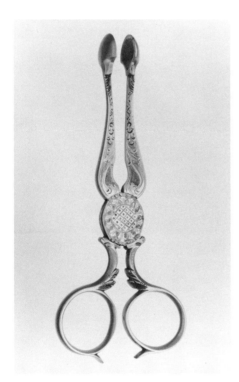

112

L: 4⁹⁄₁₆″ (11.6 cm). Wt: 1 oz. 3 dwt. 8 gr.

PROVENANCE: Garrard & Co. Ltd., London (purchased from C. J. Vander Ltd., London, 1954)

Sugar tongs of this scissor type with scrolled arms

and shell-shaped grips were the most popular form during the middle decades of the eighteenth century. Relatively few are fully marked. This finely chased

Maker's mark and lion passant on interior of each grip.

pair is part of a set with six teaspoons and their original shagreen-covered case (No. 188). Sugar tongs and teaspoons, as well as other tea accessories, were sometimes housed with the tea canisters and sugar box in tea chests. Three other partially marked tongs of this type, two by Richard Mills and the third by an unidentified maker ("T·W"), are also in the Colonial Williamsburg collection (1954-337, 559; 1963-188).

1954-563

113 STRAINER SPOON
London. About 1760

Maker's mark and lion passant on underside of handle.

L: 5⁹⁄₁₆″ (14.1 cm); W (bowl): 1⁵⁄₁₆″ (2.4 cm). Wt: 10 dwt. 3 gr.

PROVENANCE: Garrard & Co. Ltd., London

A large number of eighteenth-century spoons of this distinctive form—with a pierced oval bowl and a slender stalk-like handle tapering gradually to a pointed terminal—survive. It is generally agreed that they were used in the service of tea, the bowl to skim tea leaves and other matter from tea bowls and cups and the pointed end to clear the obstruction by tea leaves of the strainer within the teapot at the entrance to the spout. The *London Gazette* in 1697 referred to "long or strainer tea-spoons with narrow pointed ends."[1] Strainer spoons appear in conjunction with teaspoons in contemporary silversmiths' advertisements and accounts,[2] and they are often included as part of the accessories in a fully outfitted tea chest.

From the reign of James I, spoons have also been used for removing impurities from the communion wine, although if made for that purpose they do not have pointed ends. Such spoons, which usually follow the design of contemporary domestic spoons, sometimes have pierced bowls. Occasionally a tea-strainer spoon is found with church plate.[3] Strainer spoons, such as this example, are rarely fully marked, and they usually bear only the maker's and fineness marks. The underside of the bowl of this example has a raised swage design of a shell and scrolls, a type of decoration more often found on contemporary tea-spoons (see No. 188).

1971-394

1. G. Bernard and Therle Hughes, *Three Centuries of English Domestic Silver, 1500–1800* (London: Lutterworth Press, 1952), p. 160; Hughes, p. 46.

2. Oman (a), p. 154; Clayton, p. 278.

3. Charles C. Oman, *English Church Plate, 597–1830* (London: Oxford University Press, 1957), pp. 252–53.

Articles and Accessories for Dining

114 EPERGNE
William Cripps
London. 1759/60

Fully marked on underside of central basket and on neck of body; maker's mark and lion passant on underside of each saucer and on interior end of each arm.

H: 15¾" (40 cm); L: 26¼" (66.7 cm); W: 26" (66 cm). Wt: 260 oz. 2 dwt. 12 gr.

PROVENANCE: Crichton Bros., London

The epergne, one of the large centerpiece forms of French development,[1] was introduced into England in the first quarter of the eighteenth century. Even though references to their use in England date from the early 1720s,[2] no examples have survived from that decade. Early examples tend to be of heavy baroque form and more complex and varied than subsequent rococo examples.[3] They also appear to have been used throughout the dinner, for they often include such dining accessories as casters, cruets, salts, and sauceboats. Rococo examples, on the other hand, were dressed primarily for the dessert course.

Owner's crest engraved on interior of central basket, on face of each saucer, and on face of each leg; owner's cypher engraved at a later date on underside of each saucer.

During the third quarter of the century, epergnes in the rococo taste were produced in large numbers, and most of them assume a rather standard appearance. The cast chinoiserie heads on the scrolled ends of the central basket and the phoenixes that dominate the cast apron sections, though not peculiar to this epergne or maker, lend interest to this example. The piercing of the basket and body, as well as the high chasing of the body, are less perfunctory than that on most examples of this period.

Occasional references to the use of silver epergnes in eighteenth-century Virginia are encountered. "An Epergne" valued at £50 heads the 1769 listing of silver belonging to William Byrd III of Westover, Charles City County.[4] A "Silver Epern weighing 92:19" is listed with the "New plate in the House" in the 1789 inventory of the estate of General Thomas Nelson of Yorktown.[5] Richard Corbin of Laneville, King and Queen County, purchased in 1794 from Richard Davies, a London jeweler and goldsmith, a large silver service, which included "an Elegant Epergne w^h Branches and Large Bason at Top, [£]59.17.8/2 setts of Rich Cut Glasses for Do, 7.0.0."[6]

1936-453

---

1. The other major centerpiece form is that of a tureen elevated on a large base, usually embellished with sculptural detail. These vary in design, and they were not produced in the same number as epergnes. An early and magnificent French example is that by Thomas Germain, made between 1729 and 1731, in the Museum of Ancient Art, Lisbon (*French Master Goldsmiths and Silversmiths from the Seventeenth to the Nineteenth Century* [New York: French & European Publications, 1966], ill. pp. 116–17). A sampling of English examples includes one of 1740/41 by Paul Crespin of London, formerly in the collection of Mrs. James de Rothschild (Christie's [May 13, 1964], lot 104, pl. 13; Banister, p. 192, pl. 77); one of 1741/42 probably by Nicholas Sprimont of London, though marked by Crespin, in the English royal collections (Clayton, p. 122, pl. 20); one of 1747/48 by Nicholas Sprimont in the Victoria and Albert Museum, London (*Burlington Magazine* 114 [September 1972]:645, fig. 55); one of about 1760 by John Parker and Edward Wakelin of London in the Museum of Fine Arts, Boston (Clayton, p. 122, fig. 264); one of 1780/81, based on the Sprimont example in the royal collections, from the collection of the duke of Rutland (Jackson, 1:316, fig. 343); and one of 1786/87 by James Young of London, also derived from the Sprimont example (Sotheby's [October 22, 1970], lot 157, frontispiece).
2. "One Aparn 783.0.0" is listed in the 1721 inventory of royal plate ("An Account of all His Majesty's Plate in any of his Majestys Palaces or elsewhere together with the respective denominacions and weights of each piece or Parcell, as also of all Plate, now remain^g in his Maties Jewell Office," dated September 1721 (MS, Public Records Office, London, L.C. 5/114; photostat copy, Department of Collections, Colonial Williamsburg Foundation). It was described in 1725 as an "Aparn containing one Table Basket and Cover, one foote, four Salt Boxes, 4 Small Salts, four Branches,

6 Casters, 4 Sauceboats" (Oman [b], p. 114). In 1721, the Hon. George Treby purchased from Paul de Lamerie "a fyne polished Surtout Cruette frames Casters Branches & Saucers weighing together oz/505=dwt/10" and "2 Double Salts for the Surtout oz/27=dwt/10" (Phillips, pp. 45–46, figs. 12–13). Lady Grisell Baillie, when she visited Twickenham in 1721 as the guest of Sir Robert Walpole, commented on the use of a silver epergne in the center of the dining table on formal occasions (G. Bernard Hughes, "Georgian Silver Epergnes," *Canadian Antiques Collector* 4 [March 1969]:8).
3. Representative of these is one of 1731/32 by David Willaume, Sr., and Ann Tanqueray of London (Sotheby's [June 27, 1963], lot 47, frontispiece), and one of 1734/35 by Paul de Lamerie of London (Phillips, p. 97, plates XCV–XCVI).
4. Westover Plate. This epergne was sold in 1788 by Maria Byrd of Westover to John Brown of Providence along with seven other pieces of family silver (Cooper, pp. 737–38).
5. York County, Wills and Inventories, no. 23 (1783–1811), p. 183 (microfilm copy, Department of Research, Colonial Williamsburg Foundation).
6. "A Service of Plate, 1794," *Virginia Magazine of History and Biography* 7 (October 1899):186–87.

115 EPERGNE
Thomas Pitts
London. 1762/63

Fully marked on face of canopy, on underside of central basket, and on neck of body. Maker's mark and lion passant on underside of each saucer, on interior end of each scrolled plug on legs, and with varying completeness on the interior end of each arm.

H: 26½" (67.3 cm); L: 28" (71.1 cm); W: 27½" (69.9 cm). Wt. 232 oz.

PROVENANCE: Christie, Manson & Woods, London (1902; purchased by Davis); Carrington & Co., London (prior to 1911); Garrard & Co. Ltd., London

PUBLISHED: Christie's (May 14, 1902), lot 117; Jackson, 2: 927–28, fig. 1237; Edith Gaines, "Powell? Potts? Pitts!—the T·P Epergnes," *Antiques* 87 (April 1965):462–63, fig. 3

Blank cartouche engraved within central basket on base.

115

This epergne is an excellent example of the harmonious blending of chinoiserie and rococo elements. To my knowledge it is the only recorded English epergne with a double pagoda canopy, although a number of single–pagoda examples, principally by Pitts, are known. The use of a central canopy did not originate with Pitts. It had been previously employed by Charles Ballin of Paris in his epergne of 1727/28 in the Hermitage Museum;[1] by George Wickes of London in his epergne of 1745/46 after a design by William Kent in the English royal collections;[2] and by Thomas Heming of London in his epergne of 1753/54.[3] The latter example has a small canopy of pagoda form. Heming also fashioned an epergne for George III in the same year as the Williamsburg example with a canopy based on that of the previously mentioned epergne by Wickes after a design by Kent, also made for royal use.[4]

Thomas Pitts, like his son, William, who succeeded him, specialized in the production of epergnes and pierced basketwork.[5] Until Arthur Grimwade published his study of the Garrard ledgers in 1961, Pitts's mark had long been attributed to Thomas Powell, Jackson having made a tentative attribution of the mark to that maker in 1905. Grimwade discovered in the "Workmens" ledger for 1766 to 1775 that Pitts supplied Parker and Wakelin with a number of epergnes.[6]

This is but an instance of the substantial traffic in goods produced by specialist makers and supplied within the trade for retailing.[7] It is only reasonable that Parker and Wakelin would rely on Pitts for epergnes, considering the extensive amount of piercing and the necessary pattern work for cast elements, such as aprons, legs and feet, arms for saucers and baskets, as well as the applied rims for these, and the flower-wrapped, columnar canopy supports and finials.

Pitts may have fitted the epergne originally with a lower set of arms, supporting four additional saucers or, more likely, sweetmeat baskets. The slots for these on the shoulders of the legs are fitted with contemporary removable plugs with scrolled ends, marked by Pitts. It was sold in 1902 and illustrated by Jackson in 1911 having but a single set of arms.

An apparent shop number "470" is precisely engraved on the underside of the central basket. "N⁰ 369" is scratched in the same location.

1960-580

---

1. *French Master Goldsmiths and Silversmiths from the Seventeenth to the Nineteenth Century* (New York: French & European Publications, 1966), ill. pp. 96–97. A sketch of the epergne, probably by Ballin, is also illustrated with the central dish dressed with fruit. William Kent's design for an epergne or "surtoute," published by John Vardy in 1744, also shows the central dish dressed with fruit (John F. Hayward, "A 'Surtoute' Designed by William Kent," *Connoisseur* 143 [April 1959]:83, fig. 1). The epergne depicted in one of George Wickes's trade cards also shows the central dish and saucers dressed with fruit. An impression of this trade card is in the possession of Garrard & Co. Ltd., London.

2. E. Alfred Jones, *The Gold and Silver of Windsor Castle* (Letchworth: Arden Press, 1911), pp. xliii, 78, pl. xxxix; Hayward, "A 'Surtoute' Designed by William Kent," p. 83, figs. 1 and 3.

3. Christie's (May 13, 1964), lot 99, pl. 12; Clayton, pp. 122, 127, fig. 266.

4. Jones, *The Gold and Silver of Windsor Castle*, pp. xliii, 88, pl. xlv.

5. See Edith Gaines, "Powell? Potts? Pitts!—the T·P Epergnes," *Antiques* 87 (April 1965):462–65; ———, "More by—and about—Pitts of the Epergnes," *Antiques* 91 (June 1967):748–53.

6. Grimwade, p. 6.

7. Other instances concerning this partnership and its successor are cited by Grimwade (ibid., pp. 5–6).

116 EPERGNE
Thomas Pitts
London. 1763/64

Fully marked on foot ring of central basket and on rim of body; maker's mark and lion passant on foot ring of each saucer and on interior end of three arms (fourth arm unmarked).

H: 12¾" (32.4 cm); L: 19⅜" (49.2 cm); W: 18⅛" (46 cm). Wt: 118 oz. 2 dwt. 5 gr.

PROVENANCE: Gift of Mr. Vanderbilt Webb, New York

PUBLISHED: Edith Gaines, "Powell? Potts? Pitts!—the T·P Epergnes," *Antiques* 87 (April 1965): 462, 465, fig. 7

G1938-191

116

117 EPERGNE
Emick Romer
London. 1775/76

Fully marked on face of foot of central basket and on face of rim of body; maker's mark and lion passant on underside of each small basket and saucer and on underside of each small basket handle; maker's mark on interior end of arms for baskets and saucers.

Unidentified crest engraved within oval reserve on one side of basket, on underside of rim of each small basket and saucer, and on reverse of one urn medallion of apron.

H: 15⅞″ (40.3 cm); L: 24½″ (62.2 cm); W: 24″ (61 cm). Wt: 133 oz. 3 dwt. 16 gr.

PROVENANCE: Anonymous gift

PUBLISHED: Williamsburg (a), p. 8, ill.

This example is representative of a group of transi-

tional epergnes from the mid-1770s, in which neo-classical decoration has been added to their basic rococo form. It, like others in the group, has a tall neck, chased with paterae and husk swags on a reeded ground. Cast paterae and husk swags are applied at the rims of the central basket, smaller baskets, and saucers. The paterae, swags, and oval reserves on the bodies of these elements are chased. The oval urn medallions and husk swags of the apron are cast.

G1971-2058

118 BREADBASKET
William Kidney
London. 1736/37

Fully marked on underside of base.

H: 9⅜″ (23.8 cm); L: 12½″ (31.8 cm); W (handle): 12⁹⁄₁₆″ (31.9 cm); L (base): 9¹³⁄₁₆″ (24.9 cm); W (base): 8″ (20.3 cm). Wt: 57 oz. 12 dwt. 9 gr. ("59=5=0" engraved on underside of base).

118

Unidentified owner's crest engraved on face of handle.

the handle is formed from two wrought strips, and the side members, pivots, and rim attachments are composed of cast parts. The asymmetrical shells with pendent scrolls, repeated at even intervals around the rim, and the ruffled scrolls and cartouche on the handle face are early rococo decorative elements. Small cast masks of a bearded man are applied to the side members of the handle. These members on subsequent rococo examples often incorporate a three-dimensional demifigure, as in the following two examples.

1954-576

1. Clayton, pp. 18, 22, fig. 8. An example of 1602/03 is illustrated in G. E. P. How, " 'Per Ounce' and 'All At,' " *Notes on Antique Silver,* 1 (Summer 1941):14 and in Royal Ontario Museum, pp. 15–16, no. B.21, fig. 15.

2. Hayward, p. 54, pl. 58B.

3. E. Alfred Jones, "Welsh Goldsmiths," *Connoisseur* 109 (July 1942):116, fig. VII.

4. Advertisement, Thomas Lumley Ltd., London, *Connoisseur* 148 (December 1961):xiii, ill.; Victoria and Albert Museum, *Third International Art Treasures Exhibition* (London, 1962), pp. 36–37, no. 280, pl. 175; Sotheby's (May 30, 1963), lot 14, frontispiece; Banister, p. 182, pl. 68.

5. Clayton, pp. 18, 22, fig. 12; Phillips, pp. 92, 99, plates LXXIII–LXXVI, CVII.

PROVENANCE: Garrard & Co. Ltd., London (purchased from C. J. Vander Ltd., London, 1954)

Circular baskets with steep pierced sides and flared pierced foot date from as early as 1597.[1] A single example of 1711/12 by Thomas Folkingham of London in the Victoria and Albert Museum, London,[2] another of 1731/32 by John Edwards of London from the collection of the marquess of Exeter,[3] and a pair of 1734/35 by Paul de Lamerie of London,[4] although fitted with side handles, are late expressions of this early form. By the time de Lamerie fashioned the latter pair, the large oval basket with handles at either end or a large central bail handle, as in this instance, had become the standard form. Breadbaskets with interlaced sides, appropriately simulating wickerwork, were especially popular during the 1730s, even though earlier and later examples are known. De Lamerie fashioned a number of such handsome baskets during that decade.[5]

The sides of this basket are wrought, pierced, and chased with a narrow cast molding applied to the upper edge and an inset base. The center section of

119 PAIR OF BREADBASKETS
Silver-gilt
Paul de Lamerie
London. 1747/48

Fully marked on underside of each body.

H: 10¾″ (27.3 cm); L: 15⅞″ (38.4 cm); W: 13⅛″ (33.3 cm). Wt (no. 1): 81 oz. 14 dwt. 4 gr. ("83=16" engraved on underside of base); (no. 2): 82 oz. 4 dwt. 14½ gr. ("84=14" engraved on underside of base).

PROVENANCE: Sneyd family, Keele Hall, Staffordshire (sold at Christie, Manson & Woods, London, 1924); William Randolph Hearst (sold by Parish-Watson & Co., New York, 1938)

PUBLISHED: Christie's (June 24, 1924), lot 64, ill.; Williamsburg (b), p. 250, ill.

119

The most important example of English rococo silver in the collection is this pair of silver-gilt breadbaskets of 1747/48 by Paul de Lamerie, the most celebrated of eighteenth-century English silversmiths. He, more than any other English silversmith, realized the rich potentialities of this decorative style. He had an unusual ability, stemming from his extreme inventiveness, to integrate form and varied ornament with rich overall decorative effect and a rhythmic play of textures.

The complex composition of these baskets is carefully orchestrated with skillful modulations from one section to the next based primarily upon differing decorative means. The rim is formed by an elaborate cast overlay, bound by broad sinuous curves, inviting the eye to move from cherubs with wheat sheaves and sickles to male and female lions peering out from groups of flowers. The lower edge of the rim is of very irregular outline, which helps it blend in with the bold surrounding piercing of the sides, which are engraved to give them added fullness. The sides are further strengthened visually by their division into shaped panels of varied widths, which relate to the placement of the cherubs and lions above. The eye then moves from the engraved openwork of the sides to the deep-set flat-chased border of the base, composed of bold paired C-scrolls and relieved by delicate floral garlands within, which frame and form a transition to the even more delicate engraved arms in the center. The rhythm of the rim is echoed in that of the apron and outward curling leaf feet. The handle aids in the successful distribution of these cast sculptural elements.

These baskets were probably made for Ralph Sneyd (1723–1793) of Keele Hall, Staffordshire, whose family arms they bear. They are referred to as

"2 Chased Bread Baskets" with the "Silver Gilt Plate" in the "List of Plate At Keele Hall April 1854."[1] They remained in the family until the sale of Sneyd family heirlooms at Christie's on June 24, 1924, at which time William Randolph Hearst purchased them, as well as the chandelier and two sets of sconces (Nos. 1–3).

A de Lamerie breadbasket of 1744/45 in the Metropolitan Museum of Art, also in his rich and inventive rococo style, is one of a small group of pieces by this maker engraved with the arms of David Franks, the prominent Philadelphia merchant, impaled with those of his wife, Margaret Evans, whom

Arms of the Sneyd family of Keele Hall, Staffordshire, engraved in center of each base.

he married the previous year (see No. 59). A more modest London rococo breadbasket of 1752/53 in a private collection was originally owned by and is engraved with the arms of the Byrd family of Westover, Charles City County, Virginia. Maria Byrd sold it along with seven other pieces of family silver to John Brown of Providence in 1788.[2]

1938-45, 1–2

---

1. Sneyd Plate.
2. Cooper, pp. 737–38, 740, fig. 10.

120 BREADBASKET
Samuel Herbert
London. 1759/60

120

Fully marked on exterior of body amidst piercing; maker's mark and lion passant on underside of handle.

H: 13 13/16″ (35 cm); L: 13 5/8″ (34.6 cm); W: 11 1/4″ (29.6 cm). Wt: 47 oz. 3 dwt. 1/2 gr.

PROVENANCE: The earls of Harewood, Harewood House, Leeds (sold at Christie, Manson & Woods, London, 1957); Wing Cdr. Ronald B. Guy, Norfolk, Virginia (purchased from John Westley Antiques, Uxbridge, Middlesex)

Arms of Lascelles impaling Chaloner engraved in center of base for Edward Lascelles of Harewood House, Gouldsborough, Stank, and North Allerton, all of Yorkshire, who married Anne Chaloner of Guisborough, Yorkshire, in 1761. He was created Baron Harewood in 1796 and Viscount Lascelles and earl of Harewood in 1812.

PUBLISHED: Christie's (March 13, 1957), lot 70

A large number of rococo breadbaskets were produced during the third quarter of the eighteenth century. Many, of lightened form and construction, like this and the following example, were made to a standard formula by specialist firms in basket and pierced work.

1960-3

121 BREADBASKET
William Plummer
London. 1767/68

121

Fully marked on exterior of body amidst piercing.

H: 11¹³⁄₁₆″ (30 cm); L: 14½″ (36.8 cm); W: 12⅞″ (32.7 cm). Wt: 51 oz. 4 dwt. ("52=15" engraved on underside of body).

PROVENANCE: Katherine Turner, Lexington, Kentucky

1940-222

122 TWO DESSERT BASKETS AND STANDS
Silver-gilt with eighteenth-century cut-glass basins
John Wakelin and William Taylor
London. 1787/88 and 1789/90

Fully marked on underside of each basket and stand.

H (no. 1): 8″ (20.3 cm); H (without basin): 7⁷⁄₁₆″ (18.9 cm); L (basket): 14⅜″ (36.5 cm); L (stand): 15⅜″ (39.1 cm); W (stand): 10¹³⁄₁₆″ (27.6 cm); H (no. 2): 7⅝″ (19.4 cm); H (without basin): 7¹⁄₁₆″ (17.9 cm); L (basket): 14⁵⁄₁₆″ (36.4 cm); L (stand): 15⅜″ (39 cm); W (stand): 10¹³⁄₁₆″ (27.5 cm). Wt (no. 1; basket): 48 oz. 0 dwt. 13 gr. ("47=3" engraved on underside); (stand): 53 oz. 1 dwt. 8 gr. ("53=19" engraved and "99-2" scratched on underside). Wt (no. 2; basket): 42 oz. 7 dwt. 6 gr. ("41=13" engraved on underside); (stand): 51 oz. 15 dwt. 20 gr. ("50 =13" engraved on underside).

PROVENANCE: The dukes of Newcastle (sold by Henry Francis Hope, 8th duke of Newcastle, at Christie, Manson & Woods, London, 1921); Mrs. N. Locan (sold at Christie, Manson & Woods, London, 1972; purchased by Harvey & Gore, London); Thomas Lumley Ltd., London

Arms of Henry Fiennes Pelham Clinton (1720–1794), 2nd duke of Newcastle and 9th earl of Lincoln, engraved on opposite sides of each basket and stand.

122

PUBLISHED: Christie's (July 7, 1921), lots 50 and 51; Christie's (July 5, 1972), lot 70, ill.; John Culme and John G. Strang, *Antique Silver and Silver Collecting* (London: Hamlyn, 1973), pp. 42–43, fig. 67

The firm of Wakelin and Taylor was responsible for a series of similar baskets and stands of this refined neoclassical design. An early example, practically identical to these, is that of 1777/78 engraved with the arms of George, 2nd Baron Rodney, and his wife, Anne Harley.[1] A late example of the type is a basket without a stand of 1807/8 with the mark of William Burwash and Richard Sibley of London in the Sterling and Francine Clark Art Institute, Williamstown, Massachusetts.[2] Their association with the dessert service, sharing some of the same functions as the epergne, is indicated by the references to these baskets as charged to "His Grace The Duke of Newcastle" in the Wickes-Wakelin-Garrard ledgers in the Victoria and Albert Museum, London, for December, 3, 1788:

To a fine chased fruit bason and stand 99 oz. 2 dwt. @ 10s. 6 d.	52	0	6
[To two small ditto and stands]			
To engraving 8 Coats and Supporters and 4 Crests and Garters	2	16	0
To 2 large glasses @ 27s. 0d. and 4 ditto for small basons	8	6	0

and for January 6, 1790:

To a chase'd fruit bason and stand to match	49	9	2
To double gilding etc.	15	0	0
To engraving 4 Coats, Supporters, etc.	1	4	0
2 glass basons	1	7	0

Further, when Wakelin and Taylor supplied Philip Stanhope, 5th earl of Chesterfield, with three similar baskets and stands in 1792, the largest was described in the same accounts as "a fine chased epergne bason & table 86.18 @ 10/6 35.12.6."[3] The term "epergne bason" in this instance may not only reflect their general use but also an unusual form of epergne with detachable oval baskets and an oval base, obviously derived from baskets and stands of this type, such as that of 1790/91 by William Holmes of London.[4]

These baskets are fitted with contemporary glass basins cut to complement the design of the baskets. They create a striking contrast of light and material which unfortunately cannot be appreciated in the case of many of these baskets, whose basins have not survived, or which have been subsequently fitted with metal liners. Wakelin and Taylor provided the duke of Newcastle, in this instance, as well as the earl of Chesterfield, with replacements at the time of purchase. The upper part of one of these basins is broken across the end and has been repaired with staples.

1972-438, 1–2

---

1. Advertisement, Crichton Bros., London, *Antique Collector* 19 (November–December 1948): unp., ill.

2. Sterling and Francine Clark Art Institute, *An Exhibition of Old Silver Dining Accessories: Part Two* (Williamstown, 1966), no. 55, ill.

3. Christie's (June 27, 1973), lot 9, ill. The three baskets and stands with the letter for 1791/92 and later plated liners were sold at that time.

4. Christie's (March 31, 1965), lot 109, pl. 3.

123 SOUP TUREEN
George Wickes
London. 1737/38

H: 11″ (27.9 cm); L: 18″ (45.7 cm); W: 10½″ (26.7 cm). Wt: 168 oz. 1 dwt. 11 gr. ("N 2/171= 0" engraved on underside of body).

Fully marked both on underside of body and on bezel of cover.

PROVENANCE: Thomas Watson (1693–1750), 1st marquess of Rockingham; Charles Watson-Wentworth (1730–1782), 2nd marquess of Rockingham; William Fitzwilliam (1748–1833), 4th Earl Fitzwilliam, and subsequent Earls Fitzwilliam (sold after the death of William Henry Lawrence Peter Fitzwilliam (1910–1948), 8th Earl Fitzwilliam, at Christie, Manson & Woods, London, 1948; purchased by Rayman); Louis Wine Ltd., Dublin (1965); Firestone and Parson, Boston

PUBLISHED: Christie's (June 9, 1948), lot 114; T. P. Greig, "In the Auction Rooms," *Connoisseur* 121 (June 1948): 130, ill., and (July 1948):65; advertisement, Louis

123

Wine Ltd., Dublin, *Connoisseur* 158 (March 1965):lix, ill.

George Wickes fashioned this magnificent tureen, originally one of a pair, along with a considerable quantity of other plate, for Thomas Watson (1693–1750), then earl of Malton, created 1st marquess of Rockingham in 1746. It is appropriately in the formal Palladian taste, for Watson's intention may have been to acquire furnishings of congenial character for the new east block of his Yorkshire country seat, Wentworth House. Not surprisingly, he had chosen Henry Flitcroft, architect of the Whig establishment, to design this immense addition of 606 feet in length, its center section based on Colin Campbell's Wanstead.[1]

In addition to the usual trappings of this ponderous style—the alternate floral and fruit swags of the cover, the banded reeding at the neck of the body, and the legs with lion mask attachments and ball-and-claw feet—other large sculptural elements of heraldic significance not only proclaim Watson's rank and importance but also lend great visual presence and excitement to the piece. A cast applique of his arms with an earl's coronet, supporters, and motto is repeated on either side of the body. Created a Knight of the Bath in 1725, the collar of that order surrounds the shield of arms. His crest of a griffin passant sur-

mounts the cover and, in variant form, serves as the handles for the body. In their vertical movement and outward-facing stance, the latter resemble handles of animal and human forms on wine coolers and ewers of the late seventeenth and early eighteenth centuries.[2]

This tureen and its mate are recorded in George Wickes's private client accounts, presently in the possession of Garrard & Co. Ltd., London, for July 14, 1738, as "To 2 Fine Tarreens 345.15 [weight] 10/6 [cost per ounce] 181 10 [total cost]." The high cost of fashioning per ounce is probably attributable to the large amount of individual pattern work for the cast elements, all of which are extremely well modeled and finely finished. The pair of tureens remained in related families at Wentworth House until they were sold at auction in 1948. Their second owner, Charles Watson-Wentworth (1730–1782), 2nd marquess of Rockingham, served twice as prime minister of England. He is remembered, in part, for his role in the repeal of the Stamp Act in 1766 and his later favoring of American independence in opposition to Lord North's American policies.

The inventory of the furnishings of the Governor's Palace in Williamsburg taken after the death of Lord Botetourt, who served as governor of the colony from 1768 to 1770, listed "1 Turin & Ladle" among "Plate, in the Pantry."[3]

1972-245

1. Christopher Hussey, *English Country Houses: Early Georgian, 1715–1760* (London: Country Life Ltd., 1955), pp. 150–57.
2. Representative examples of this type of handle treatment are illustrated in Hayward, plates 21–24, 34 A and B.
3. Botetourt Inventory.

124 SOUP TUREEN
Charles Frederick Kandler
London. 1769/70

Fully marked both on underside of body and on bezel of cover.

H: 9½″ (24.1 cm); L: 15⅝″ (39.7 cm); W: 7¾″ (19.7 cm). Wt: 87 oz. 15 dwt. 15½ gr.

PROVENANCE: Garrard & Co. Ltd., London

1960-239

Arms of Duane of Lincoln's Inn, London, and of Ireland impaling those of Dawson, Monaghan, engraved on one side of body with crest on cover; arms of Hutchinson, Yorkshire or Durham or of Hutchinson, earls of Donoughmore, Ireland,

quartered with those of Lawse, Forster, Bathurst, and Dawson, with those of Clarke of Knedlington, Yorkshire, quartered with those of Vavasour in pretense engraved on other side of body with crest of Hutchinson engraved on cover.

125 PAIR OF ENTRÉE DISHES
William Sumner
London. 1803/4

Fully marked on exterior of body of each below rim; maker's mark, lion passant, date letter, and sovereign's head on interior of each cover; maker's mark, lion passant, and sovereign's head on each finial.

125

Arms and crest of Cooper, Sligo, engraved respectively on face of both covers and bodies with cast finials of crest form. Modern arms (not illustrated) engraved on face of each cover.

H: 6¾″ (16.2 cm); L: 11⅜₆″ (27.4 cm); W: 8⅜₆″ (20.8 cm). Wt (no. 1): 53 oz. 2 dwt. 23 gr.; (no. 2): 52 oz. 12 dwt.

PROVENANCE: Anonymous gift

PUBLISHED: Williamsburg (a), p. 8, ill.

G1971-2057, 1–2

126 SALVER
Richard Bayley
London. 1718/19

Fully marked on face of top near edge; lion's head erased on interior of foot near edge.

H· 4″ (10.2 cm); Diam (top): 12⅞₆″ (31.6 cm); Diam (foot): 4½″ (11.4 cm). Wt: 35 oz. 1 dwt. 19½ gr.

PROVENANCE: Garrard & Co. Ltd., London

Thomas Blount in the second edition of his *Grossographia* (London, 1661) defined a salver as "a new fashioned piece of wrought plate; broad and flat, with a foot underneath, and is used in giving Beer, or other liquid thing, to save or preserve the Carpit and Cloathes from drops." From the 1650s to the early eighteenth century, most salvers are of this enlarged paten form. They were put to a number of uses in the service of food and drink, as stands for matching two-handled covered cups and other ornamental plate, and as elements, usually in pairs, in large toilet services. The lord chamberlain described as "six fruite dishes" the six large gilt salvers of

126

1663/64 of conventional form with broad chased rims and depressed flat centers, that constituted part of the plate presented to Czar Alexei of Russia by the earl of Carlisle's embassy in 1664.[1] The "3 Salvers" listed in the 1703 inventory of the estate of William Fitzhugh of Stafford County, Virginia, are referred to in his will of 1700 as "one Large Silver Salver Jappan" and twice as "one small salver or Bread Plate."[2] A London salver of this form of 1713/14 with an indistinct maker's mark, engraved with the initials of Thomas Nelson (1677–1745) of Yorktown, Virginia, and his wife, Margaret Reade, who were married in 1710, is on loan by descendants to the National Park Service. Maria Byrd of Westover,

Arms of Hastings Ingram of Walford and Earl's Court, Warwickshire, and of Worcestershire, and of Anne Mollins of West Hall, Dorset, engraved on face of top in center.

Charles City County, Virginia, sold in 1788 to John Brown of Providence two silver salvers and six other pieces of family silver. One of these salvers of this form, engraved with the Byrd family arms, is in the Herreshoff collection.[3] Another, a London example of 1723/24, engraved with the crest of the Jacquelin family of Virginia, was exhibited in 1940 at the Virginia Museum of Fine Arts, Richmond.[4]

Some church patens of the late seventeenth and early eighteenth centuries, used to serve the eucharistic bread, are of this standard form of domestic salver with a broad top and a tall central foot. The discrepancy between the date letters and engraved dedications on some of these would indicate that some may have been made originally for domestic use.[5] A salver of 1710/11 by Alice Sheene of London, similar to this example, is among the plate at Abingdon Church, Gloucester County, Virginia.[6] Three earlier London salvers, all with gadrooned rims and feet, are still owned by Virginia churches. One of 1691/92 by Benjamin Pyne of London is engraved with the arms of Edmund Andros, who served as governor of Virginia from 1692 until 1698 and presented this salver in 1694 to Bruton Parish Church in Williamsburg, then Middle Plantation.[7] The vestry records for April 7, 1694, note: "His Excellency Sir Edmund Andros, Knight, was pleased to give to Bruton Parish a large Silver Server."[8] A smaller one of 1694/95 was given by Sarah Braine in 1697 to Westover Church, Charles City County.[9] The third of 1698/99 by Richard Syng of London is among the plate of St. John's Church, Hampton.[10]

This salver, in excellent condition, is engraved with fine armorials within a forceful baroque cartouche. The engraver's scribed circular guide is clearly discernible.

1960-240

1. E. Alfred Jones, *The Old English Plate of the Emperor of Russia* (Letchworth: Arden Press, 1909), pp. xxii, xl, 48, pl. xxiv, no. 2; Charles C. Oman, *The English Silver in the Kremlin, 1557–1663* (London: Methuen & Co. Ltd., 1961), pp. 39–40, pl. 32. Oman comments that fruit dishes are indistinguishable from this early form of salver. He contends that the large salver of about 1640 attributed to Christian van Vianen in the duke of Northumberland's collection, because of its embossed badge in the center, was not intended as a stand for a cup and should be considered a fruit dish (Oman [a], p. 42, frontispiece). It should be noted that the salvers presented to Czar Alexei have flat centers and that the pair of salvers in the Calverly toilet service in the Victoria and Albert Museum, London, for instance, have chased centers. Perhaps, all of these should be termed "salvers" with the knowledge that one of their principal uses, irrespective of flat or raised centers, was as fruit dishes.

2. Davis, R. B., pp. 378, 382. Fitzhugh instructed his London agent in 1689 to send him "a Salver about 30 oz.," which he had referred to as "One Silver Salvator plate" in a letter of the previous year. This was probably the "one Large Silver Salver Jappan" mentioned in his will of 1700 with "Jappan" likely denoting that it was enriched with flat-chased chinoiserie decorations (see No. 32).

3. Cooper, pp. 737–38, 740, fig. 9.

4. Virginia Museum (a), p. 19, no. 75; Davis, E. M., p. 112.

5. Jackson illustrates a London salver of 1691/92 which was presented to the church at Durrington, Wiltshire, in 1702 (Jackson, 1:436–37, figs. 494–95).

6. Jones (d), p. 1, pl. i, fig. 1; Virginia Museum (b), p. 46, no. 17, ill.

7. Jones (d), pp. lxi, 473, pl. cxli, fig. 2; Francis Hill Bigelow, *Historic Silver of the Colonies and Its Makers* (New York: Macmillan Company, 1917), pp. 238–40, fig. 145; Virginia Museum (b), pp. 36–37, no. 11, ill.

8. William A. R. Goodwin, edited and revised by Mary F. Good win, *The Record of Bruton Parish Church* (Richmond: Dietz Press, 1941), p. 129.

9. Jones (d), pp. lxi, 488, pl. lxxxv, fig. 2; Virginia Museum (b), pp. 38–39, no. 12, ill.

10. Jones (d), pp. lxi, 205, pl. cxli, fig. 1; Bigelow, *Historic Silver of the Colonies and Its Makers*, p. 240, fig. 146; Virginia Museum (b), p. 44, no. 15, ill.

127 PAIR OF SALVERS
John Tuite
London. 1727/28

Fully marked on underside of each.

127

H: 1⅜" (3.5 cm); W: 8⁹⁄₁₆" (21.8 cm). Total wt: 36 oz. 16 dwt.

PROVENANCE: Garrard & Co. Ltd., London (purchased from C. J. Vander Ltd., London, 1954)

Arms of William Ilbert of Bowringsleigh, Devonshire, and his wife, Bridget Courtenay, Powderham Castle, Devonshire, engraved on face of each in center.

Late in the reign of Queen Anne, salvers with three or four short legs placed near the rim first appear. A magnificent pair of large circular gilt salvers of 1713/14 by Simon Pantin of London, each supported on three short scrolled legs, is perhaps the earliest example.[1] Occasional transitional examples are fitted with a detachable central trumpet foot, as well as short legs at the rim. Square or rectangular salvers with short profiled sides and indented corners, such as this pair, were especially popular during the 1720s and 1730s. John Tuite, their maker, who had been

trained and had worked in Dublin prior to entry of his mark at the London Goldsmiths' Hall in 1720, was a prolific maker of salvers before his death in 1740. His was only one of many London firms specializing in the production of salvers during the eighteenth century. Such specialization is partially explained by the skill required to set and maintain a flat bottom during fabrication. A small salver of similar design of 1729/30 by Edward Cornock of London is also in the Colonial Williamsburg collection (1954-515).

1954-513, 1–2

1. "Notable Works of Art Now on the Market," *Burlington Magazine* 113 (December 1971), plates XXXIII–XXXIV; Clayton, p. 231, fig. 460.

128 SALVER
William Darker
London. 1728/29

Fully marked on face near edge.

H: 1⁹⁄₁₆″ (4 cm); Diam 10″ (25.4 cm). Wt: 19 oz. 16 dwt. 2 gr.

PROVENANCE: Garrard & Co. Ltd., London (purchased from Christie, Manson & Woods, London, 1962)

PUBLISHED: Christie's (March 28, 1962), lot 141, pl. XXV

128

Arms of Windham of Norfolk and Somerset impaling probably those of Playse of Norfolk engraved in center.

One of the handsomest of eighteenth-century salver types—of practical utility also for wine glasses and for teacups and saucers—is this scalloped form, dating mostly from shortly before and during the 1720s. Octafoil examples, such as this, are the most common, though ones with six, ten, and twelve scallops were made. An example with twelve scallops of 1725/26, also by Darker, is in the Sterling and Francine Clark Art Institute, Williamstown, Massachusetts.[1] The Williamsburg salver, like most of the kind, has

hammered sides without an applied rim at the edge, and it is supported on four curved bracket feet. In laying out the piece, Darker, as did others on similar salvers, stamped a center punch mark on the underside for each of the scallops.

1962-135

---

1. Sterling and Francine Clark Art Institute, *Exhibit Nine: Old English Silver, Coffee Pots and Salvers* (Williamstown, Massachusetts, 1958), no. 522, ill.

129 SALVER
Silver-gilt
Thomas Farren
London. About 1730

Maker's mark only, twice on underside.

H: 2⅛″ (5.4 cm); L: 13⅜″ (34 cm); W: 9¼″ (23.5 cm). Wt: 45 oz. 14 dwt. 1 gr. ("46=0" engraved on underside).

PROVENANCE: English royal plate; Lords Brownlow, Belton House, Grantham, Lincolnshire (sold at Christie, Manson & Woods, London, 1929); Museum of Fine Arts, Boston (purchased from S. J. Phillips, London, 1960)

PUBLISHED: Christie's (March 13, 1929), lot 57, ill.; Edward Wenham, "The Dispersal of the Belton Plate," *Interna-*

English royal arms engraved in center.

tional Studio 93 (May 29, 1929):28–29, ill.; "Accessions of American and Canadian Museums, April–June, 1962," *Art Quarterly* 25 (Autumn 1962):274; Christie's (May 29, 1963), unp., forward [*sic*]; Clayton, p. 322, fig. 688

This oblong gilt salver of extremely fine workmanship is in the formal Huguenot style. As in other salvers of this general format (Nos. 135, 137), the finely chased and engraved inner border not only frames the handsomely engraved royal arms in the center, but also serves as a transition from the somewhat heavy rim and sides. The arms form the focal point, and the eye is guided to them by intersecting lengthwise and crosswise axes created by the applied masks and the inward cant of the flanking gadroons of the rim and by diagonal axes created by the pointed corner indentations of the sides, repeated in the lozenges of the inner border.

The underside bears only the mark of Thomas Farren. Like other silver made for royal or ambassadorial use, it was free of the obligation and expense of hallmarking. This salver and its mate in the Museum of Fine Arts, Boston, both of which were owned by the Lords Brownlow, may have been part of the considerable plate thinned from the royal collections in 1808, at which time a number of pieces were acquired by the 1st Earl Brownlow and others (see No. 1).

1961-1

130 SALVER
Robert Abercromby
London. 1736/37

H: 1 3/16" (3 cm); Diam: 9 9/16" (24.3 cm). Wt: 16 oz. 10 dwt. 5 gr.

130

Fully marked on underside.

PROVENANCE: Museum of Fine Arts, Boston

During the middle decades of the eighteenth century, most salvers were of circular plan and scrolled outline with short inclined sides raised from the same piece as the bottom and with a narrow, cast and applied molding at the edge for strength and appearance. This border pattern, misleadingly referred to within the trade as "Chippendale," probably because of its close similarity to that of the tops of tripod tea tables, was particularly popular during the 1730s.

Many of the standard salver types during that period were made by specialist makers, such as Robert Abercromby, the maker of this salver, William Peaston (No. 136), John Swift (No. 137), and Ebenezer Coker (Nos. 138–39), among others. A larger and less conventional salver of 1735/36 by Robert Abercromby, engraved with the arms of the Randolph family of Virginia, is privately owned in Richmond.[1]

1954-329

---

1. Virginia Museum (a), p. 20, no. 84; Davis, E. M., p. 115.

131 SALVER
Francis Spilsbury
London. 1737/38

131

Fully marked on underside.

H: 15⁄16″ (2.4 cm); Diam: 5¹⁵⁄₁₆″ (15.1 cm). Wt: 6 oz. 16 dwt.

PROVENANCE: Garrard & Co. Ltd., London (purchased from W. Comyns, London, 1954)

Unidentified arms engraved in center.

Small circular salvers often served as stands for teapots and coffeepots.

1954-516

132 SALVER
Paul Crespin
London. 1738/39

132

Fully marked on underside.

Owner's cypher en-graved in center.

H: 1⅜″ (3.5 cm); Diam 9¾″ (24.8 cm). Wt: 18 oz. 12 dwt. ("19=0" engraved on underside).

PROVENANCE: Bracher & Sydenham, Reading (1951); Garrard & Co. Ltd., London (purchased from Thomas Lumley Ltd., London, 1954)

PUBLISHED: Advertisement, Bracher & Sydenham, Reading, *Connoisseur Souvenir of the Eleventh Antique Dealers' Fair and Other Exhibitions* (June 1951), p. 56, ill.

Circular salvers of this form with broadly fluted sides and bracket feet, deriving from unfooted dessert dishes, date mainly from the 1730s. They sometimes served as stands for tea kettles, and an example of 1731/32 with kettle, also by Crespin, was exhibited in 1958 at the Royal Ontario Museum, Toronto.[1]

1954-542

1. Royal Ontario Museum, pp. 44, 47, no. G.12, ill. It is also illustrated in Wenham, p. 202, fig. 1 and in an advertisement, D. S. Lavender, London, *Apollo* 95 (January 1972):49, ill.

133 PAIR OF SALVERS
John Robinson
London. 1741/42

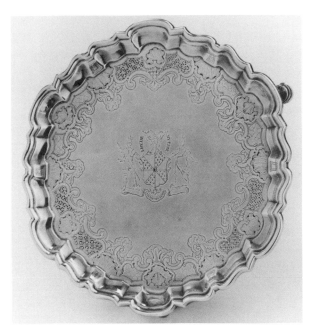

133

Fully marked on underside of each.

Arms of John Campbell (1705–1782), 4th earl of Loudoun, engraved in the center of each.

H: 1⅛″(2.9 cm); Diam: 7⅝″ (19.4 cm). Wt (no. 1): 10 oz. 14 dwt. 21 gr. ("11=6" engraved on underside); (no. 2): 11 oz. 12 dwt. 1 gr. ("12= 3½" engraved on underside).

PROVENANCE: Garrard & Co. Ltd., London (purchased from Sotheby & Co., London, 1955)

Fully marked on underside.

PUBLISHED: Sotheby's (June 16, 1955), lot 131

John Campbell, Lord Loudoun, the original owner of these salvers, was appointed governor of Virginia in 1756, and held that title until 1759, though never exercising the powers of office in Virginia, where he was served by a succession of deputies: Robert Dinwiddie, James Blair, and Francis Fauquier. He was also appointed commander-in-chief of the British forces in North America in 1756, and he did serve in American and Canada in that capacity.

1955-166, 1–2

Arms of William Turner of Whitefriars, Canterbury, Kent, and Elizabeth Scott of Lyminge, Kent, whom he married on June 3, 1718, engraved in center. The arms of the escutcheon of pretense are those of the Scott family.

134 SALVER
Thomas Rush
London. 1742/43

H: 1⅝″ (4.1 cm); Diam: 12¼″ (30.8 cm). Wt: 32 oz.

PROVENANCE: Garrard & Co. Ltd., London (purchased from Mrs. Burgess, Sutton on Sea, Lincolnshire, 1953)

1954-514

135 SALVER
Silver-gilt
Peter Archambo, Sr.
London. 1744/45

Fully marked on underside.

135

H: 2″ (5.1 cm); Diam: 17½″ (44.5 cm). Wt: 74 oz. 18 dwt. 12. gr.

PROVENANCE: John Hall & Co. Ltd., Manchester (1950–51); David Udy, Warminster, Wiltshire

PUBLISHED: Advertisement, John Hall & Co. Ltd., Manchester, *Connoisseur* 125 (March 1950):xxix, ill. and *Connoisseur Souvenir of the Eleventh Antique Dealers' Fair and Other Exhibitions* (June 1951), p. lix, ill.; W. D. John and Jacqueline Simcox, *English Decorated Trays* (Newport, Monmouthshire: Ceramic Book Company, 1964), pp. 10–11, ill.

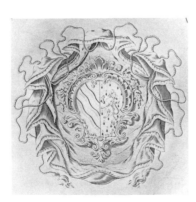

Arms of Sir Robert Godschall, who served as lord mayor of London in 1742, engraved in center.

This fine gilt salver is of a distinctive rococo type with elaborate cast rims. Most examples are by Huguenot makers and date mainly from the early 1740s. The difficulty of raising short sides and setting the bottom is eliminated by having the bottom plate merely held between the inner edge of the rim and a lower lip. The rim of this salver is cast in sections and built up with cast overlays. Even though it is smaller than most of its type, which usually measure about 24 inches in diameter, it is one of the most successful. It has an especially vigorous rim with large projecting alternate scrolled and ruffled cartouches and shells connected by scrolls framing fruited grape vines and floral swags. The bold rhythm of the rim is repeated

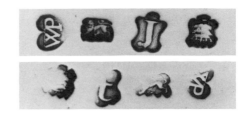

Fully marked on the underside of each.

Crest of the Randolph family of Virginia engraved in the center of each.

in the broad, flat-chased, inner border and the engraved drapery and tasseled rope surrounding the arms in the center. It is supported on three short, leaf-faced, scrolled legs with lion's feet. Salvers of this type regained favor in the first quarter of the nineteenth century.

1972–436

136 TWO SALVERS

William Peaston
London. 1753/54 and 1754/55

H: 1⅛″ (2.9 cm); Diam: 8½″ (21.6 cm). Total wt: 25 oz. 5 dwt. 9 gr.

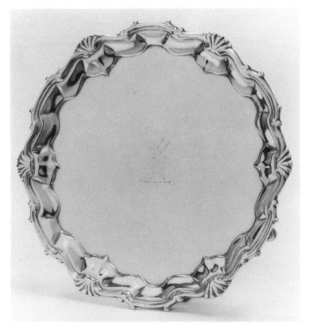

PROVENANCE: Peyton Randolph (ca. 1721–1775) and his wife, Betty Harrison (ca. 1723–1783); their nephew, Edmund Randolph (1753–1812), and his wife, Elizabeth Nicholas (1753–1810); their daughter, Lucy Randolph (1790–1847), and her husband, Peter Vivian Daniel (1784–1860); their daughter, Elizabeth Randolph Daniel (1810–1879); her niece, Lucy Randolph Moncure (b. 1861), and her husband, William Grymes; their son, William Randolph Grymes (b. 1899), and his wife (sold by them through Young's Art Shop, Richmond, Virginia, 1942)

PUBLISHED: Davis, J. D., p. 135, ill.

These matching salvers, like the two-handled covered cup (No. 48), are of importance as part of the few surviving pieces of silver with a documented history of ownership in Williamsburg in the eighteenth century. Peyton Randolph, one of Williamsburg's

most illustrious citizens, originally owned them. He served as king's attorney for Virginia, speaker of the House of Burgesses, chairman of the Virginia committee of correspondence, and first president of the Continental Congress. They are listed as "2 Silver Waiters" in the 1780 will of his wife, Betty Randolph.[1]

A similar salver of this conventional, shell-and-scroll-edge type (7¼ inches in diameter) of 1752/53 by Dorothy Mills of London is also in the Colonial Williamsburg collection (1953-803).

1945-16, 1–2

1. York County, Wills and Inventories, no. 23 (1783–1811), p. 4 (microfilm copy, Department of Research, Colonial Williamsburg Foundation).

137 PAIR OF SALVERS
John Swift
London. 1753/54

H: 1⅜″ (3.5 cm); Diam 11″ (27.9 cm). Total wt: 39 oz. 18 dwt. 15½ gr.

Fully marked on underside of each.

Arms and motto of the Spotswood family of Virginia engraved in center of each.

PROVENANCE: William Bernard of Fredericksburg, Virginia; his granddaughter, Elizabeth Bernard Pollock; her nephew, William Bernard, Naples, Florida

These salvers were acquired with a tradition of ownership by the children of Alexander Spotswood (1676–1740), who served as governor of Virginia

137

Fully marked on underside.

between 1710 and 1722. He spent his last ten years at Germanna, Spotsylvania County, about twenty miles from Fredericksburg, where the great-grandfather of the last owner bought them.

They are conventionally enriched with a broad inner border of flat-chased scrolls and flowers.

1963-115, 1–2

138 SALVER
Ebenezer Coker
London. 1771/72

Cypher of Josiah Granberry (1728–1772) and his wife, Christian Gregory, of Suffolk, Virginia, engraved in center.

H: 1⁷⁄₁₆″ (3.7 cm); Diam: 12⁵⁄₃₂″ (30.9 cm). Wt: 29 oz. 10 dwt.

PROVENANCE: Joseph A. Miller, Hallieford, Virginia

PUBLISHED: Ivor Noel Hume, *Here Lies Virginia: An Archaeologist's View of Colonial Life and History* (New York: Alfred A. Knopf, 1963), pp. 229–31, fig. 88

This salver was acquired with three smaller ones of matching design[1] and a partial cruet frame (No. 160). The articles were found buried between two pieces of roofing slate approximately twenty inches below the surface of a field on the farm of Elwood L. Boyce near Bowers Hill in Nansemond County, Virginia, on November 11, 1961. Two mugs of 1771/72 by Charles Wright of London had been previously found that year. All bear the same engraved cypher. Clustering in date between 1765 and 1771 and exhibiting little wear from use, they were probably buried in the eighteenth century, although no immediate reason is apparent. When found, care was not taken from an archaeological standpoint to determine their context.

The key to the identity of the original owners of these pieces is a tankard of conventional baluster form of 1771/72 by Charles Wright of London, the same date and maker as the pair of mugs, at St. Paul's Episcopal Church, Edenton, North Carolina.[2] It is engraved with the same ornamented cypher confirming its original inclusion in this group, but bears the important later inscription: "Presented to St. Paul's Church. EDENTON. by Mrs Mary Granby. 1833." Mary Harvey Granberry (1771–ca. 1833)[3] was the wife of James Granberry (d. 1804), son of Josiah Granberry (1728–1772) and his wife, Christian Gregory, the original owners of the tankard and the other pieces. Raised in Nansemond County, Josiah Granberry moved to Chowan County, North Carolina, in 1747 and by 1752 had established himself as a merchant. By 1768 he was living in Suffolk, Nansemond County, where he died in December of 1772. He had served as a vestryman of St. Paul's Church in 1755 and as church warden in 1756

and 1762, which perhaps prompted his daughter-in-law's gift.

1965-151

1. These include one of 9″ of 1768/69 by John Carter of London (1965-152) and two of 6⅞″ of 1765/66 and 1771/72, both by Ebenezer Coker of London (1965-53 and 54).
2. Jones (d), p. 167, pl. LX, fig. 1.
3. Her surname is misspelled phonetically on the tankard. The following genealogical information is taken from Edgar Francis Waterman, *The Granberry Family and Allied Families* (Hartford: Edgar F. Waterman, 1945). Confirming and additional information given by Mrs. Elizabeth V. Moore of Edenton, North Carolina.

139 PAIR OF SALVERS
Ebenezer Coker
London. 1768/69

139

Fully marked on underside of each.

H: ¾" (1.9 cm); W: 6" (15.2 cm). Total wt: 16 oz.

PROVENANCE: Garrard & Co. Ltd., London (purchased from C. J. Vander Ltd., London, 1954)

1954-518, 1-2

140 SALVER
Robert Makepiece and Robert Carter
London. 1776/77

140

Fully marked on underside.

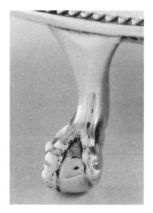

H: 1¼" (3.2 cm); L: 9" (22.9 cm); W: 7" (17.8 cm). Wt: 12 oz. 10 dwt.

PROVENANCE: Garrard & Co. Ltd., London (purchased from C. J. Vander Ltd., London, 1954)

An oval teapot stand of 1786/87 by William Plummer of London of similar design—beaded edge but without the chased husk decoration and the applied inner beaded border—is engraved with the Carter family arms and is part of the Carter family silver at Shirley, Charles City County, Virginia.[1]

1954-517

———

1. Barbara Snow, "Living with Antiques: Shirley, Charles City County, Virginia," *Antiques* 83 (May 1963):545, ill.

141 TRAY
John Crouch and Thomas Hannam
London. 1791/92

Fully marked on underside.

Unidentified arms and crest engraved in center.

L: 26¼" (66.7 cm); W: 17⅛" (36.5 cm). Wt: 117 oz ("118-8" scratched on underside).

PROVENANCE: Garrard & Co. Ltd., London

PUBLISHED: W. D. John and Jacqueline Simcox, *English Decorated Trays (1550–1850)* (Newport, Monmouthshire: Ceramic Book Company, 1964), pp. 66–67, ill.

Large rectangular and circular salvers, sometimes referred to as "tea boards" and "tea tables" in the eighteenth century, were used primarily in the service of tea and coffee. During the last quarter of the century they were generally displaced by large oval trays with a handle at either end. The firm of Crouch and Hannam specialized during this period in the production of large oval trays, usually with reeded rims and handles and often, as in this instance, with fluted

141

sides and engraved inner borders of a repetitive foliate design.

A splendid large rectangular salver of 1716/17 by Thomas Folkingham of London with incurved sides and indented corners, engraved with the Carter family arms, is part of the Carter family silver at Shirley, Charles City County, Virginia.[1] The mortgaged silver of William Byrd III of nearby Westover, also in Charles City County, included in 1769

"1 Large Waiter" with the considerable value of £20.[2] The inventory of the furnishings of the Governor's Palace in Williamsburg taken after the death of Lord Botetourt, who served as governor of the colony from 1768 to 1770, listed among "Plate, in the Pantry" "1 Large Tea Board."[3] A large oval tray, quite similar to this example, by William Sutter of London, was won by John Tayloe III's horse

Calypso at the Virginia Jockey Club races at Hanover Court House on October 6, 1796. Engraved on the face with the Tayloe family arms and on the underside with a portrait of the horse, it is still owned by the family.[4]

1958-460

1. Barbara Snow, "Living with Antiques: Shirley, Charles City County, Virginia," *Antiques* 83 (May 1963):544, ill.
2. Westover Plate.
3. Botetourt Inventory.
4. "In Virginia," *Arts in Virginia* 5 (Spring 1965):31, ill.

142 EIGHT DINNER PLATES
Peter Archambo, Jr. and Peter Meure
London. 1755/56

Fully marked on underside of each rim.

H (rim): ¾″ (1.9 cm); Diam: 8⅜″ (21.3 cm).
Total wt: 136 oz. 12 dwt.

PROVENANCE: Museum of Fine Arts, Boston

142

Unidentified arms and crest with coronet engraved on opposite sides of each rim.

Silver plates and dishes of wavy outline with cast and applied gadrooned rims, such as this set and the following example, enjoyed a long period of popularity from about 1730 until about 1820. Large eighteenth-century dinner services usually contained several dozen plates to permit the necessary removes and a considerable number of dishes for the various courses. The "2 dozn. Silver Plates" and "Six silver Dishes" in the 1703 inventory of the estate of William Fitzhugh of Stafford County[1] and the "60 Plates" and "27 Dishes" listed with the "Plate, in the Pantry"

of the Governor's Palace in Williamsburg in the 1770 inventory of the estate of Lord Botetourt,[2] are conspicuous references to the use of silver plates and dishes in Virginia. Botetourt's "27 Dishes" are further mentioned in a 1771 packing list as "15 Round Dish-

es" and "12 Oval Dishes."[3] The latter may have included dishes similar to the following example in graduated sizes.[4]

A pair of similar plates of 1765/66 by Thomas Heming of London are also in the collection (1954-562, 1–2), as well as a set of sixteen plates and two matching meat dishes in fused silverplate (Nos. 259–60).

1954-321, 1–8

1. Davis, R. B., p. 382. Fitzhugh had ordered from his London agent in 1688, among other silver articles, "1 doz. Silver plates. Four Silver Dishes 2 pretty large for a good joint of meat, & two of a smaller sort, if my money falls short let it be wanting in the Dishes, if there be any remaining let the Overplus be what it will, laid out in silver plates" (ibid., p. 244). In the following year, he repeated the order and specified "Two Silver Dishes weighing 50 oz. a piece or thereabouts, two Ditto weighing 70 oz. a piece or thereabouts" (ibid., p. 259). He further ordered in 1698 "Two large Silver Dishes containing about 80 or 90 ounces each dish" and "A Dozen Silver plates" (ibid., p. 362).
2. Botetourt Inventory.
3. Packing list, May 27, 1771, MS, Botetourt Papers, Virginia State Library, Richmond (photostatic copy, Department of Research, Colonial Williamsburg Foundation).
4. Michael Clayton has stated that it was customary for a dinner service to include approximately twelve oval dishes ranging in length from twelve to twenty inches (Clayton, p. 104).

143 MEAT DISH OR PLATTER
Magdalen Feline
London. 1754/55

Fully marked on underside of rim.

Arms of the Scottish families of Durham impaling Gordon engraved on face of rim.

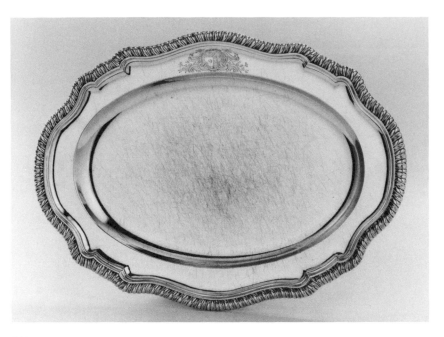

143

H: 1⅛″ (2.9 cm); L: 16¼″ (41.3 cm); W: 12⅜″
(31.1 cm). Wt: 58 oz. 12 dwt. (Nᵒ₁ 9 /60 ¹¹ 2¹¹ ″
engraved on underside).

PROVENANCE: Museum of Fine Arts, Boston

PUBLISHED: Wenham, p. 207; Edward Wenham, "Women
Recorded as Silversmiths," *Antique Collector* 17 (March–
April 1946):63, fig. 6 (the other of the pair is illustrated)

A matching dish was retained by the Museum of Fine
Arts, Boston.

1954-322

144 SUGAR OR SPICE BOX
London. 1610/11

H: 3½″ (8.9 cm); L: 6¹⁄₁₆″ (15.4 cm); W: 4⅞″
(11.3 cm). Wt: 13 oz. 6 dwt.

*Fully marked both on interior of base in front compartment
and on underside of cover near hinge.*

PROVENANCE: How (of Edinburgh), London (1941);
Knight, Frank & Rutley, London (1962); How (of Edin-

burgh), London (1963); Garrard & Co. Ltd., London

PUBLISHED: Advertisement, How (of Edinburgh), London,
Connoisseur 107 (January 1941): back cover, ill.; "International Saleroom," *Connoisseur* 151 (September
1962):47, ill.; Mrs. G. E. P. How, "Old Silver—on a
Shoe-String," *Antique Collector* 33 (December 1962):
263, 265, fig. 1; "The Connoisseur Catalogue to the

Twenty-third Antique Dealers' Fair and Exhibition," *Connoisseur* 153 (June 1963):127, ill.; "Accessions of American and Canadian Museums, July–September, 1963," *Art Quarterly* 26 (Winter 1963):495, 499, ill.

Boxes of this type are among the most handsome articles of late Elizabethan and Jacobean silver. They are of consistent form with a hasp-fitted cover in the shape of a scallop shell, its rear extension usually chased with smaller shells and a wave motif, stamped formal moldings of Renaissance type at the cover and base, and four cast shell or snail feet. They are customarily referred to in contemporary documents as sugar boxes, though occasionally as spice boxes. Some references mention an accompanying spoon, such as "a sugar boxe, and one sugar boxe spoone" in the Unton inventory of 1620.[1] The transverse partitioning of the interior of these boxes is believed intended to accommodate the spoon. Commander G. E. P. How has suggested that the small hoof spoons of the period may have served this purpose.[2] His supposition seems to be supported by a spoon of that type and a sugar box of 1627/28, both engraved with the same owners' initials, which were sold at auction in 1969.[3] Jackson and Hughes each illustrate a sugar box practically identical to the Williamsburg example and dating from the same year and by the same maker.[4]

David Fox of Lancaster County, Virginia, drew up a deed of gift in 1662 leaving all of his silver to his daughter upon his death. It included "one sugar box in the form of a scollup shel," undoubtedly an earlier box of this type.[5]

1963-74

1. Hughes, p. 32.
2. G. E. P. How, "Rarities," *Notes on Antique Silver*, no. 3 (Summer 1943):13; How, 1:302.
3. Christie's (October 29, 1969), lot 165, frontispiece.
4. Jackson, 2:831, fig. 1075; Hughes, fig. 47.
5. Lancaster County, Deeds, no. 2 (1654–1702), p. 241 (microfilm copy, Virginia State Library, Richmond).

144

145 SCROLL SALT
London. 1635/36

Fully marked in well for salt; leopard's head crowned, lion passant, and date letter on body above base; lion passant on each of the scrolls.

H: 3½″ (5.9 cm); Diam (rim and base): 4³⁄₁₆″ (10.6 cm). Wt: 9 oz. 13 dwt. 19½ gr.

PROVENANCE: Christie, Manson & Woods, London (1931; purchased by Painter); Parke-Bernet Galleries, New York (1965)

PUBLISHED: Christie's (July 29, 1931), lot 104; Parke-Bernet (February 6, 1965), lot 238, ill.; Oman (a), pl. 48, pl. 46A

The large standing salt had been, both in social and in artistic terms, one of the most important forms in Gothic and Renaissance domestic silver. By the reign of Charles I, the standing salt had diminished in size and importance with the increasing use of individual trencher salts. The scroll salt, distinguished by voluted brackets or scrolls at the edge of the rim, usually three in number before about 1660 and four thereafter, was the last major type of standing salt. It was introduced into England from the Continent about 1630.[1] The function of the scrolls, as indicated by seventeenth-century Dutch still-life paintings, was to support a dish or bowl of fruit, presumably installed after the main course and before the dessert course. As N. M. Penzer has observed, "It was, in fact, the idea of an epergne in embryo. The beauty of the bowl holding the fruit would be lost when placed on an already crowded table, but the standing salt only required some form of support above the salt pan to transform it into a centre piece holding the bowl high up in the view and reach of all."[2] Samuel Pepys confirmed this use in describing, on April 27, 1662, the famous Seymour Salt now at Goldsmiths' Hall, stating that the four large eagles at the rim, substituted for the customary scrolls, were "to bear up a dish." The contention of some that these scrolls were intended for a draped napkin lacks supporting literary or pictorial evidence.[3]

Early scroll salts of this straight-sided cylindrical form are considerably rarer than those with indrawn pulley-shaped bodies. Penzer records only two examples, one of 1633/34, owned since 1638 by the Bridgwater Corporation,[4] and the other of 1635/36, formerly in the collection of Walter Cunliff, which may indeed be the present example. The Bridgwater Salt, the earliest recorded English scroll salt, stands almost twice the height of this unusually small example. It is amusing that the scrolls on this salt, as on other examples, are each marked with a lion passant to denote their requisite fineness, for there are in the records of the Goldsmiths' Company several early instances of complaints and violations in this regard.[5] An early London scroll salt of pulley form, given in 1644 to Harvard College, has indistinct marks, but it probably dates from between 1632 and 1638.[6]

1965-76

146 SCROLL SALT
London. 1686/87

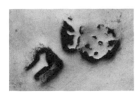

Leopard's head crowned and date letter in well for salt; date letter repeated on underside of base; maker's mark and lion passant absent.

Owner's initials pounced on face of rim; collector's name engraved on underside of base.

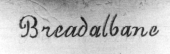

H: 5⁵⁄₁₆″ (13.5 cm); W (base): 5½″ (14 cm). Wt: 13 oz. 17 dwt.

PROVENANCE: Gavin Campbell (1851–1922), 1st marquess and 7th earl of Breadalbane; Christie, Manson & Woods, London (1961), How (of Edinburgh), London

PUBLISHED: Christie's (July 5, 1961), lot 161, frontispiece

Most standing salts of the reign of Charles II are of this tall spool form with four scrolls at their rims and their rims and bases of polygonal plan. The form recalls the elaborate covered Gothic salts of the late fifteenth and early sixteenth centuries. This late example, dating from the reign of James II, is one of the last English standing salts. It is incompletely marked, lacking both the maker's mark and the lion passant mark. The date letter is repeated on the underside of the base in apparent error for the usual lion passant mark. The "1 Table Salt" listed in the 1703 inventory of the estate of William Fitzhugh of Stafford County, Virginia, may very well have been of this form.[1] The

1. The earliest references to English scroll salts appear in the records of the Goldsmiths' Company. They are included in N. M. Penzer, "Scroll Salts," *Apollo Annual* (1949):48–49. They include complaints of 1630 against Dickinson, a goldsmith, for selling a scroll salt untouched (unmarked) and of 1631 against Valerius Sutton and of 1640 against John Hancock for putting scrolls on salts already marked. In the last instance, the scrolls were below standard and were applied to two "Pulley" salts. Thomas Borne bequeathed in 1632 £6 13s. 4d. to the Barber-Surgeons' Company, and it was ordered by the company that "there shalbe a faire Salt white, with scroules of the new fashion bought and his name ingraven theron" (ibid., p. 49).

2. Ibid., p. 53.

3. Penzer (ibid., p. 51) attributes this contention to Wilfred Cripps, who stated that the "projecting arms were for supporting a napkin with which it now became usual to cover the salt celler" in the 1st edition of his *Old English Plate* (London: John Murray, 1878), p. 260.

4. Penzer, "Scroll Salts," p. 49, fig. II; Goldsmiths' Company, *Catalogue of Corporation Plate of England and Wales* (London, 1952), pp. 17–18, no. 31, ill.; Delieb, p. 64, ill.; Clayton, p. 229, fig. 437.

5. See fn. 1.

6. Penzer, "Scroll Salts," p. 49; Harvard University, *Harvard Tercentenary Exhibition. Catalogue of Furniture, Silver, Pewter, Glass, Ceramics, Paintings, Prints, Together with Allied Arts and Crafts of the Period 1636–1836* (Cambridge, 1936), p. 20, no. 74, pl. 14.

146

three surviving American standing salts, all of Boston origin, are of related design.[2]

1965-132

147 PAIR OF SALTS
Edward Wood
London. 1742/43

147

H: 1⅜″ (3.5 cm); L: 3⅛″ (7.9 cm); W: 2⁹⁄₁₆″ (6.5 cm). Total wt: 6 oz. 18 dwt.

1. Davis, R. B., p. 382. Fitzhugh had instructed his London agent in 1689 in an order for silver, "what remains if any, let it be laid out in a large Salt" (ibid., p. 258). Also listed in the inventory were "6 Silver Trencher Salts" and "3 Silver Salts," the former probably the "Half a doz. of Trenches Salts" ordered by Fitzhugh in 1687 (ibid., pp. 228, 382).

2. Examples by Jeremiah Dummer and Edward Winslow are in the Museum of Fine Arts, Boston (Kathryn Buhler, *American Silver, 1655–1825, in the Museum of Fine Arts, Boston* [Boston: Museum of Fine Arts, 1972], 1:23–24, 81–82, nos. 20, 67, ill.), and the third by John Allen and John Edwards is in the Metropolitan Museum of Art (Graham S. Hood, *American Silver; A History of Style, 1650–1900* [New York: Praeger Publishers, 1971], p. 66, fig. 54; "Outstanding Recent Accessions," *Metropolitan Museum of Art Bulletin* 31 [Summer 1973]: unp., ill.). All three are enriched with bands of gadrooning, a feature not found on the Williamsburg or other English examples of this type.

Fully marked on underside of each well.

Owner's initial engraved on face of each body.

PROVENANCE: Garrard & Co. Ltd., London (purchased from Mrs. M. Besant, Forest Row, Sussex, 1953)

The most common pattern of salt between 1710 and 1740 is of this low oblong shape with canted corners and profiled sides. Whereas larger forms of related polygonal design, such as casters and various hollow-ware articles for tea and coffee, were rarely made after 1730, salts of this type continued to be made concurrently with more fashionable tripod salts into the 1740s. A pair of plain tripod salts of 1739/40 also by Edward Wood, a prolific specialist maker of salts, are in the collection (1954-567, 1–2). David Hennell, who completed his apprenticeship under Wood in 1735 and commenced business as a salt maker the following year, although he probably made tripod salts from the start of his career, continued to fashion salts of this earlier pattern as late as 1749.[1]

1954-533, 1–2

---

1. Percy Hennell, "The Hennells—a Continuity of Craftsmanship," *Connoisseur* 158 (February 1973):79. A tripod salt of 1737/38 by David Hennell is illustrated (ibid., fig. 2).

148 PAIR OF SALTS
Gilt-lined
London. 1752/53

H: 1⅝″ (4.1 cm); Diam (rim): 2⅜″ (6 cm).
Total wt: 4 oz. 19 dwt. 9 gr.

PROVENANCE: Gift of Katharine Brooke Fauntleroy Bundy in memory of Sally Conrad Fauntleroy Johnson

PUBLISHED: Davis, J. D., p. 136, ill.

148

Fully marked on the underside of each.

These salts have a tradition of Virginia ownership since the eighteenth century. They are believed to have belonged to Major Burr Powell (1768–1839) and his wife, Katharine Brooke (1770–1851), of Middleburg, Virginia. The tradition is uncertain as to whether they descended to the Powells from his parents, Levin Powell (1737–1801) and Sarah Harrison (1746–1790), or from her father, Colonel Humphrey Brooke (1739–1802). They apparently passed to the Powell's daughter, Elizabeth Whiting Powell (1809–1872), and her husband, Robert Young Conrad (1805–1875); to their daughter, Sally Harrison Conrad (1843–1908), and her husband, Dr. Archibald Magill Fauntleroy (1837–1886); to their daughter, Katharine Brooke Fauntleroy (b. 1882), and her husband, Henry Clay Miller; and to their daughter, the donor.

Other London tripod salts in the collection include four of 1734/35 by John Pero (1967-169, 1–4), a pair of 1739/40 by Edward Wood (1954-567, 1–2), a pair of 1749/50 by William Williams (1953-802, 1–2), and four of 1769/70, probably by Jacob Marsh (1967-613, 1–4).

G1968-307, 1–2

149 FOUR SALTS
Probably Samuel Meriton
London. Probably 1771/72

149

Fully marked on underside of each body (marks worn).

H: 1¾" (3.5 cm); Diam (rim): 2½" (6.3 cm).
Total wt: 7 oz. 11 dwt.

PROVENANCE: George H. Burwell III, Millwood, Virginia

These salts of standard tripod type descended in the Burwell family of Virginia and are believed to have been originally owned by Nathaniel Burwell (1750–1814) of Carter's Grove, James City County.

London tripod salts of 1739/40 and of 1754/55 with histories of Virginia ownership in the Nelson family of Yorktown and the Belches family of Surry County are known.[1]

1964-499, 1–4

---

1. Davis, E. M., p. 112.

150 FOUR SALTS
David and Robert Hennell
London. 1767/68

150

Fully marked on underside of each body.

Owner's crest engraved on face of each body.

H: 2" (5.1 cm); L: 3¼" (8.3 cm); W: 2⁹⁄₁₆" (6.5 cm). Total wt (excluding liners): 8 oz. 17 dwt. ½ gr.

PROVENANCE: S. J. Shrubsole Corp., New York

David Hennell and his son Robert, on the completion of the latter's apprenticeship, formed a partnership in 1763 and entered the mark that appears on these salts. The firm continued to specialize in the production of salts. From the late 1760s, they made large numbers of pierced oval salts in the neoclassical taste, of which these are early examples. The dark blue glass liners are probably original.

1967-642, 1–4

151 SIX SALTS
Gilt-lined
John Wakelin and William Taylor
London. 1787/88

151

Fully marked on underside of each base.

*Owner's crest en-
graved on face of
each body.*

H: 3⅛″ (7.9 cm); L: 5″ (12.7 cm); W: 2½″ (6.4
cm); L (base): 2⁹⁄₁₆″ (6.5 cm); W (base): 1¹¹⁄₁₆″
(4.3 cm). Total wt: 22 oz. 2 dwt.

PROVENANCE: Anonymous gift

Boat-shaped salts, which imitate in miniature the
form of neoclassical sauce and soup tureens, were
popular from about 1785 until about 1810.

G1971-2061, 1–6

152 CASTER
London. 1685/86

152

*Fully marked on face of body below rim; maker's mark and
lion passant on face of cover.*

*Owners' initials en-
graved on underside
of base.*

H: 7⁷⁄₁₆″ (18.9 cm); Diam (base): 3½″ (8.9 cm).
Wt: 10 oz. 0 dwt. 22½ gr.

PROVENANCE: Firestone and Parson, Boston

Cylindrical casters of "lighthouse" type, apparently introduced during the Commonwealth period,[1] remained the standard form of caster until the beginning of the eighteenth century. The covers of most are pierced with floral and foliate designs, sometimes enhanced, as in this instance, with engraving. The covers are usually firmly secured by "bayonet" fittings, a pair of shaped lugs soldered to the applied rim molding or moldings of the cover and fitting over that of the body. A short break in the latter molding aids in the attachment and removal of the cover. A circular well in the top of the cover above a shoulder of cyma reversa profile, an applied molding placed low on the body, and a bold sequence of moldings immediately above the foot, which repeats the contour of the shoulder of the cover, are features found together on casters dating mainly from the 1680s.

From the reign of Charles II onward, casters were commonly made in sets of three, a large one for sugar of the approximate size of this example and a smaller pair for pepper and mustard or two types of pepper. William Fitzhugh of Stafford County, Virginia, ordered through his London agent in 1689 "a Sett of Castors that is to say for Mustard, Pepper & Sugar about 24 or 26 ounces."[2] When the cover piercings have been voided by an inner sleeve or the cover has been chased or engraved to simulate piercings or left plain and unpierced, it is thought that the caster was intended for mustard.[3]

A similar set of three casters of 1684/85 by an unidentified London maker "WB" are illustrated in Commander G. E. P. How, "Values," *Notes on Antique Silver*, no. 1 (Summer 1941):11.

1963-123

---

1. An unmarked example of this type with engraved arms, motto, and the date of 1658 is illustrated in Clayton, p. 51, fig. 98.
2. Davis, R. B., p. 258.
3. N. M. Penzer, "Mustard and the First Silver Mustard Pots," *Antique Collector* 38 (October 1957):186–92.

153 SET OF THREE CASTERS
Charles Adam
London. 1719/20

H (no. 1): 7⁵⁄₁₆″ (18.6 cm); W (base): 2⁷⁄₁₆″ (6.2

153

Fully marked on underside of each base; maker's mark and lion's head erased on bezel of each cover.

cm); H (nos. 2 and 3): 5¹³⁄₁₆″ (14.8 cm); W (base): 2″ (5 cm). Total wt: 20 oz. 6 dwt.

PROVENANCE: Garrard & Co. Ltd., London (purchased from Bracher & Sydenham, Reading, 1958)

PUBLISHED: Advertisement, Bracher & Sydenham, Reading, *Apollo* 118 (October 1958):ix, ill.

Most casters during the first three decades of the eighteenth century are of baluster form, either plain or eight sided, as in this handsome and representative set. A similar set of 1724/25 by Thomas Bamford of London, who served his apprenticeship under Adam and, in turn, was Samuel Wood's master, is also in the collection (1955-261, 1–3). Other similar London casters in the collection include a large and a small caster from a set of 1718/19 by Charles Adam (1936-445, 1–2) and small examples of 1715/16 by Charles Adam (1954-527) and of 1722/23 by Samuel Welder (1954-528).

1958-615, 1–3

154 CASTER
Paul Crespin
London. 1736/37

Fully marked on underside of base; lion passant on bezel of cover.

H: 8¹⁄₃₂″ (20.4 cm); Diam (base): 3⅛″ (7.9 cm). Wt: 17 oz. 16 dwt.

PROVENANCE: Garrard & Co. Ltd., London (purchased from E. T. Biggs & Sons, Maidenhead, Middlesex, 1954)

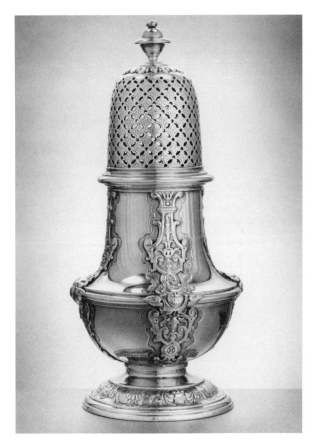

154

Owner's crest engraved on face of body.

The Huguenot makers generally employed a heavy gauge of silver and favored the use of applied ornament, both cast and cut from sheet. The vertical straps on this piece were cast in three parts with a winged cherub's mask connecting and concealing the join between the upper and lower sections. The straps are visually enhanced by a conforming border of matting. Their formal design and disposition complement the controlled contours and refined proportions of this piece. Paul de Lamerie used straps of similar design at this time.[1]

This caster may have been originally the largest of a set of three. A set of identical design by Crespin of the same year includes a small caster for mustard with an unpierced cover engraved to match the others.[2]

Another caster by Crespin of identical design, also of the same year, is recorded.[3]

1954-526

___

1. See those illustrated in Phillips, plates LXXXVIII–LXXXIX, XCV, CII–CIII.
2. Advertisement, S. J. Phillips, London, *Connoisseur Souvenir of the Antique Dealers' Fair and Other Exhibitions* (June 1952), p. xxi, ill.
3. Wenham, pp. 203, 205–6, fig. 2.

155 CASTER
Richard Gurney and Thomas Cook
London. 1737/38

155

Maker's mark and lion passant on interior of cover; leopard's head crowned, lion passant, and date letter on underside of base.

H: 4³⁄₁₆" (10.6 cm); Diam (base): 1¹³⁄₁₆" (4.6 cm). Wt: 2 oz. 16 dwt.

PROVENANCE: Garrard & Co. Ltd., London (purchased from Miss E. Sankey, Kensington, 1951)

Owners' initials engraved on face of body.

Most of these modest casters of "bun-top" type date from the second quarter of the eighteenth century and undoubtedly served as pepper pots. A set of three such casters, however, a large one and a smaller pair of 1731/32 by Starling Wilford is known.[1] A pair of 1732/33 by James Kerr of Edinburgh, one of which was left unpierced for mustard, is in the National Museum of Antiquities of Scotland.[2]

1954-568

___

1. Clayton, p. 197.
2. N. M. Penzer, "Mustard and the First Silver Mustard Pots," *Antique Collector* 28 (October 1957):191, fig. 7.

156 SET OF THREE CASTERS
Peter Archambo, Sr.
London. 1739/40

Fully marked on underside of each base; maker's mark and lion passant on bezel of cover.

H (no. 1): 9¹¹⁄₁₆" (24.6 cm); Diam (base): 3" (7.6 cm). H (no. 2): 7²³⁄₃₂" (19.6 cm); H (no. 3): 7⅛" (20 cm); Diam (bases, nos. 2 and 3): 2½" (11.4 cm). Total wt: 55 oz. 19 dwt. 14 gr.

PROVENANCE: Garrard & Co. Ltd., London

Peter Archambo, Sr., the noted Huguenot maker, fashioned this magnificent set of large and unusual casters in the early rococo taste. Like much high-

156

styled Parisian work of that period, they exhibit a
stately elegance in which their elaborate decorative
enrichment is firmly controlled by a strong formal
emphasis. Restrained chased and matted panels separate the openwork cover sections of flowing grape-
vines. Moldings of bold, repetitive design are evenly
distributed: at the rim of the cover, at the contraflexure of the body, and at the foot. The drawn mold-

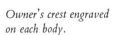

*Owner's crest engraved
on each body.*

ing at the rim of the body is forcefully repeated
below the mid-band. The fluted and slotted lattice
banding chased on the neck both separates and unites
the cast elements of the cover and lower part of the
body.

The combining of various techniques with the intent of creating dramatic effects of relief and recession
and an interplay of contrasting textures gives these
casters an unusually rich sculptural quality. The
extensive use of cast elements permitted Archambo to
avoid the conventional piercing of the covers and the
conventional rimming and joining of plain wrought
covers and body sections with simple moldings. The
covers, exclusive of their cast finials and wrought
bezels, are cast in four parts, each incorporating an
openwork section with the seams extending vertically
through the centers of the intervening panels. The
alternating oval and rosette moldings at the rims,
overlapped by extensions of the panels between the
openwork sections, are part of these castings, with

the edges of the latter chased with undercuts to simulate overlays. The alternating oval and rosette mid-bands, the applied shells and floral swags of the bodies, and the feet are also cast. Additional leaves and stems are applied as overlays on the initial castings of the covers, as well as additional leaves and flowers on the applied swags of the bodies. The cast openwork rim of Archambo's salver of 1744/45 is built up with overlays in the same manner (see No. 135).

These casters represent an early use of the double-bellied or inverted pear-shaped body, which was adopted during the rococo period for a number of hollowware forms other than casters, especially those associated with tea and coffee.

These casters are related in both form and decoration to a set of 1740/41 by Paul de Lamerie of London in the Untermyer collection.[1]

1963-38, 1–3

1. Hackenbroch, rev. edn. only, p. 93, no. 181, ill.; ———, "New Acquisitions of English Silver in the Irwin Untermyer Collection," *Antiques* 94 (September 1968):368–69, fig. 8.

157

157 PAIR OF CASTERS
Samuel Wood
London. 1758/59

Fully marked on underside of each base; maker's mark and lion passant on bezel of each cover.

Crest of the Carroll family of Maryland engraved on neck of each body.

H: 5⅜" (13.7 cm); Diam (base): 1¾" (4.5 cm). Total wt: 7 oz. 17 dwt. 16 gr.

PROVENANCE: Farris C. Pitt, Baltimore (sold to Mrs. Waldo Newcomer, Baltimore, 1907); John D. Walton, Inc., New York

A 1907 bill of sale for these casters notes that they were "once the property of the father of Charles Carroll of Carrollton with his crest engraved."[1] Grouped with these casters in the bill is a "Sugar Sifter or Muffineer" of the same date, perhaps the large caster completing an original set of three.

Samuel Wood was the principal specialist caster and cruet stand maker in London from the early 1730s until the mid 1760s, and many examples from this period bear his mark. He commenced his apprenticeship in 1721 under Thomas Bamford, a caster maker, and he entered his first mark in 1733.

1971-25, 1–2

1. Department of Collections, Colonial Williamsburg Foundation. Charles Carroll (1737–1832) of Carrollton, Anne Arundel County, was the son of Charles Carroll (1702–1782) of Annapolis.

158 CRUET STAND
Isaac Liger
London. 1726/27

158

Fully marked on underside of frame and on face of body of each caster below rim; maker's mark and lion passant on face of each cruet cover; lion passant on bezel of each caster cover.

Unidentified arms engraved on central post and on body of each caster and on covers of cruets.

H: 8¼″ (21 cm); H (cruets): 7¼″ (18.4 cm); H (casters): 4¹³⁄₁₆″ (12.2 cm). Wt (exclusive of glass cruets): 32 oz. 5 dwt. 5½ gr. ("33=13" engraved on underside of frame).

PROVENANCE: Garrard & Co. Ltd., London

Cruet stands, consisting usually of a flat shaped plate elevated on feet with a central handle and an open frame fitted with two glass cruets with silver covers and a set of three casters, appear during the first decade of the eighteenth century. The two wire rings usually mounted on the front of the frame are to accommodate the cruet covers when in use. This ex-

ample is unusual in having only two casters. The plates supporting the casters are attractively pierced with a flowering urn design.

1967-168, 1–5

159 CRUET STAND
Samuel Wood
London. 1750/51 to 1753/54

H: 8¹³⁄₁₆″ (22.4 cm); H (cruets): 7⁵⁄₁₆″ (18.6 cm) and 7⁷⁄₁₆″ (18.9 cm); H (large caster): 7¼″ (18.4 cm); H (small casters): 6¹⁄₁₆″ (15.4 cm). Wt (exclusive of glass cruets): 50 oz.

Fully marked on underside of frame and on underside of each caster; maker's mark and lion passant on handle, both cruet covers, and bezel of both small casters; maker's mark twice on bezel of large caster cover.

159

Owner's crest engraved on cartouche of frame and on neck of each caster.

PROVENANCE: Garrard & Co. Ltd., London (purchased from S. G. Schwersee, Finchingfield, Essex, 1954)

Cruet stands fitted with two cruets and three casters are commonly referred to as of "Warwick type." Michael Clayton has suggested as the possible origin of this term the cruet stand of 1715/16 with five casters from the earl of Warwick's collection, which was at one time thought to be the earliest extant example.[1]

The large caster and one of the smaller pair bear the date letter for 1750/51, the frame bears the date letter for 1751/52, and the remaining caster that for 1753/54. The crest engraved on the stand and casters indicates their use as an ensemble.

George Washington acquired in 1757 a cruet stand of this conventional rococo form. Fashioned by Jabez Daniel of London, it survives without its original casters, though it is fitted with an earlier caster of 1736/37 by Samuel Wood, engraved with Washington's crest.[2] An incomplete cruet stand of 1752/53 by Samuel Wood, engraved with the arms of the Munford family of Virginia, was exhibited in 1940 at the Virginia Museum of Fine Arts, Richmond.[3] A cruet stand of 1746/47 by Samuel Wood is also in the Colonial Williamsburg collection (1954-328).

1954-575, 1-6

1. Clayton, p. 84.
2. Buhler, pp. 12–14, fig. 1. This is listed as "A Neat cruit stand & Casters wt 28 oz a[t] 7/4 10-5-4" in an invoice of goods shipped, dated August 20, 1757.
3. Virginia Museum (a), p. 21, no. 99; Davis, E. M., p. 118.

160 CRUET FRAME (incomplete)
London. 1771/72

160

Fully marked on underside of plate.

H 1½″ (3.8 cm); L (inclusive of front feet): 7 3/16″ (18.3 cm). Wt: 12 oz. 2 dwt. 3 gr.

PROVENANCE: Joseph A. Miller, Hallieford, Virginia

PUBLISHED: Ivor Noël Hume, *Here Lies Virginia: An Archaeologist's View of Colonial Life and History* (New York: Alfred A. Knopf, 1963), pp. 229–31, fig. 88

*Cypher of Josiah
Granberry (1728–1772)
and his wife, Christian
Gregory, of Suffolk,
Virginia, engraved on
cartouche.*

Fully marked on underside of base.

For information relating to the history of this and
related pieces see No. 138.

1965-155

161 MUSTARD POT, WITH BLUE GLASS LINER
Probably John Neville
London. 1770/71

161

H: 3⅛″ (7.9 cm); Diam (cover): 2⅜″ (6 cm);
Diam (base): 2⅛″ (5.4 cm). Wt (excluding liner):
3 oz. 16 dwt.

PROVENANCE: Garrard & Co. Ltd., London (purchased
from Nayler Bros., London, 1954)

Lidded mustard pots with a thumbpiece and handle,
usually notched at the rim of the cover to accommo-

date a spoon, are rare in England before 1750. The
earliest surviving example is a pair—of barrel form—
of 1724/25, possibly by Jacob Margas.[1] One with
applied strap decoration by Edward Wakelin is in
the Farrer collection in the Ashmolean Museum,
Oxford. Lacking a date letter, it was probably made
shortly after Wakelin entered his first mark in 1747.[2]
Even though seventeenth-century Dutch mustard
pots are known,[3] the English persisted in using casters with blind covers, either unpierced or having the
piercings voided by an inner sleeve, for mustard.
Both that type of caster and the more specialized
container, such as this example, are referred to as
"mustard pots" in contemporary documents. The
inclusion of a spoon in references is not a guarantee
that a mustard pot of the latter type is intended,
even though small spoons were sometimes used
with mustard pots of caster form.[4] After about 1765,
mustard pots of this modest tankard form, their
bodies often attractively pierced and fitted with contrasting dark blue glass liners, are quite common.
A pierced mustard pot of about 1790 by William
Plummer of London, engraved with neoclassical
decoration and the arms of the Carter family, is
part of the Carter family silver at Shirley, Charles
City County, Virginia. A plain example of 1775/76
by Burrage Davenport of London is also in the
Colonial Williamsburg collection (1954-578).

1954-565

1. N. M. Penzer, "Mustard and the First Silver Mustard Pots,"
Antique Collector 28 (December 1957):229–31, fig. 11; Hughes, fig.
143; Clayton, pp. 187, 189, fig. 379; Judith Banister, "Pots for a
Pungent Spice: Two Centuries of Silver Mustard Pots," *Antique
Dealer and Collectors Guide* 38 (August 1973):62–64, fig. 1. Charles
Oman also cites a mustard pot of the same year and of similar
barrel form by Paul de Lamerie of London (Oman [b], p. 113).
2. Jones (a), p. 28, pl. xv, no. 1.
3. Examples of 1681 and 1687 are illustrated in J. W. Fredericks,
*Dutch Silver, Embossed Ecclesiastical and Secular Plate from the Renais-
sance until the End of the Eighteenth Century* (The Hague: Martinus
Nijhoff, 1961), vol. 4: nos. 188 and 202.
4. A mustard pot of caster form with spoon of about 1670, both
bearing the same maker's mark, is illustrated in an advertisement,
How (of Edinburgh), London, *Antique Collector* 9 (January 1939):
back cover.

162 PAIR OF SAUCEBOATS
William Darker
London. 1729/30

Fully marked on underside of each base.

Owner's crest engraved on face of a handle of each.

H: 4½″ (11.4 cm); L: 8⅞″ (22.5 cm); W: 8½″ (21.6 cm). Wt (no. 1): 21 oz. 1 dwt. ("23–4" engraved on underside of base); (no. 2): 22 oz. 3 dwt. 20 gr. ("23–1" engraved on underside of base).

PROVENANCE: Museum of Fine Arts, Boston

Sauceboats were not in general use in England before the reign of George I. The earliest principal type is of this handsome baroque form of Huguenot introduction, usually dating before 1730. The oval body, with a curved pouring lip at either end and a boldly shaped rim of scrolled outline, physically and visually strengthened by an applied molding at the edge, rises upward and flares outward in the center of both sides to receive a scrolled handle. The bodies and feet of some sauceboats of this type are polygonally treated, usually, in that case, having an applied midband echoing the contour of the rim. This pair, like most other examples of the general type, are of large size and good weight.

1954-327, 1–2

163 PAIR OF SAUCEBOATS
Francis Pages
London. 1735/36

Fully marked on underside of each base.

163

H: 3⅞₆″ (8.7 cm); L: 6¼″ (15.9 cm); W: 3½″ (8.9 cm). Total wt: 14 oz.

PROVENANCE: Garrard & Co. Ltd., London (purchased from C. J. Vander Ltd., London, 1952)

By the late 1720s sauceboats of reduced size, with a single pouring lip and a single handle at opposite ends of the body, make their appearance. This pair is representative of a standard type, dating mainly from the 1730s. The deep oval body and the stepped oval foot are retained, but the enlarged pouring lip is now raised from the same sheet of silver as the body and not separately let in as before.

1954-525, 1–2

164 FOUR SAUCEBOATS
William Grundy
London. 1760/61

Fully marked on the underside of each body.

H: 5″ (12.7 cm); L: 8¼″ (21 cm); W: 3⅞″ (9.8 cm). Total wt: 57 oz. 15 dwt. 10 gr.

PROVENANCE: Garrard & Co. Ltd., London

Sauceboats supported on short legs first appear in the mid-1720s, increase in number during the 1730s, and are quite plentiful between 1740 and 1780. Early ones are usually supported on four legs, three being customary after 1740. After that date they vary greatly as to weight and quality. This substantial set with cast and applied gadrooned rims and well-articulated handles and feet are good examples of a conventional

Unidentified arms engraved on face of each body.

164

165

mid-century type. A similar pair of 1762/63 by Sebastian and James Crespel of London are also in the collection (1954-541, 1–2). Other London sauceboats in the collection of this general type with an unmounted rim include one of 1748/49 with an indistinct maker's mark (1953-805) and a pair of 1760/61 by William Shaw and William Priest (1954-532, 1–2). A modest cream boat of the same form, of 1777/78 probably by Thomas Smith or Thomas Satchwell, is included in this catalog with the articles for tea, chocolate, and coffee (No. 100).

1967-165, 1–4

Owner's crest and coronet engraved on face of body.

165 SAUCEPAN
Fuller White
London. 1766/67

Fully marked on underside of base.

H (rim): 4″ (10.2 cm); Diam (body): 5½″ (14 cm). Wt (including handle): 20 oz. 3 dwt. 12 gr. ("21=5" engraved on underside of base).

PROVENANCE: Museum of Fine Arts, Boston

This piece is representative of the most common form of eighteenth-century saucepan: a squat baluster-

shaped body with a triangular pouring lip placed at right angles to a turned wooden handle. Also included in the collection are similar London examples of 1728/29 by James Goodwin (1954-549), of 1737/38 by William Justis (1954-320), and of 1767/68 by an unidentified maker "WS" (1954-318). A similar saucepan of 1750/51 by Thomas Parr of London is part of the Carter family silver at Shirley, Charles City County, Virginia.[1]

1954-319

---

1. Virginia Museum (a), p. 20, no. 94; Davis, E. M., p. 118.

166 CHAFING DISH
Robert Cooper
London. 1708/9

H: 4⅛″ (10.5 cm); Diam (rim): 6³⁄₁₆″ (15.7 cm). Wt (excluding handle): 19 oz. 12 dwt. 9 gr.

166

Fully marked on face of body to right of handle; lion's head erased on handle socket.

Unidentified arms engraved on face of body opposite handle.

PROVENANCE: Ronald A. Lee, London

Chafing dishes in a variety of materials were more generally used in the seventeenth and eighteenth centuries than surviving examples indicate. English silver chafing dishes are comparatively rare. This example is of conventional form. Its circular body is pierced below the rim and at the base to facilitate the burning of the charcoal fuel. The charcoal was placed on a pierced circular plate (now missing), which rested on an applied molding above the lower band of piercing on the interior. The projecting edge of the base plate curves upward to retain the ashes. Voluted brackets at the rim supported a plate, dish, or pan. The insulating wooden pads of the feet are replacements. The turned fruitwood handle is original, and its inner end is bound in brass with a bolt attachment to a plate within the socket. The socket is attached to the body with foliate cut-card work.

William Fitzhugh of Stafford County, Virginia, wrote in the spring of 1697 to Nicholas Hayward, his London agent, for, among other silver articles, "2 silver chafing dishes."[1] The 1719 inventory of the estate of Edmund Berkeley of Middlesex County, Virginia, also listed "2 silver chafing dishes."[2] "Four Chaffing Dishes" appear in the 1769 list of silver mortgaged by William Byrd III of Westover, Charles City County, Virginia.[3] In 1780 Betty Randolph of

Williamsburg willed "the Silver Chafing Dishes" to Edmund Randolph, her nephew.[4]

1967-418

1. Davis, R. B., p. 344.
2. "Library of Edmund Berkeley, Esq.," *William and Mary Quarterly*, 1st ser. 2 (April 1894):252.
3. Westover Plate.
4. York County, Wills and Inventories, no. 23 (1783–1811), p. 4 (microfilm copy, Department of Research, Colonial Williamsburg Foundation).

167 CHAFING DISH
Paul de Lamerie
London. 1724/25

Fully marked on face of body and on underside of lamp; maker's mark and Britannia on bezel of lamp cover; removable trivet unmarked.

Crest and motto of Baillie engraved on face of body and lamp cover.

H (with trivet): 3⁵⁄₁₆" (8.4 cm); H (rim): 3" (7.6 cm); Diam: 7¹³⁄₁₆" (18.3 cm). Wt: 44 oz. 5 dwt. 12 gr.

PROVENANCE: Sotheby & Co., London (1961)

PUBLISHED: Sotheby's (October 19, 1961), lot 155, pl. XI; "Accessions of American and Canadian Museums, July–September, 1962," *Art Quarterly* 25 (Winter 1962):411; Barry A. Greenlaw, "The English Furniture," *Antiques* 95 (January 1969):150, ill.

Chafing dishes of this form would appear to derive from footed dish rings or stands, of which an example of 1697/98 by Samuel Hood of London was sold at

167

Christie's in 1971.[1] Dish rings and chafing dishes of this type persisted until the mid-eighteenth century, at which time they were supplanted by the unfooted dish ring and dish cross.

Two similar chafing dishes by de Lamerie are recorded. One of 1727/28 has pierced sides and similar scrolled legs elevated on shell feet.[2] The other of 1740/41 has broadly pierced sides, short legs, lion masks, and ball-and claw feet.[3] Both of them are fitted, like this example, with removable trivets having a central ring held by scrolled brackets that repeat the design of those supporting the lamp. Another similar example of 1744/45 by Paul Crespin of London is in the Museum of Fine Arts, Boston. It has a gadrooned rim, pierced sides, bracket feet, and swing handles. It is not fitted with a trivet.

Paul Crespin also utilized a dish ring of this form in 1740/41 as the stand for an epergne having a central dish and four arms with saucers.[4] An unmarked dish ring in the Victoria and Albert Museum, London, with similar mounts for possible arms, although capped, may have originally been fitted with arms.[5]

1961-234

_____
1. Christie's (March 31, 1971), lot 103, ill.

2. Phillips, p. 84, pl. LIII.
3. Houston Museum of Fine Arts, *Silver by Paul de Lamerie in America* (Houston, 1956), no. 42, ill.
4. Parke-Bernet (October 20, 1966), lot 83, ill.
5. Clayton, pp. 112, 114, fig. 213.

168 CHAFING DISH
Probably Emick Romer
London. 1763/64

Fully marked on underside of body; lion passant on each hinged flap; removable plate unmarked.

H: 4⅜″ (11.1 cm); Diam (rim): 7″ (17.8 cm).
Wt (including handle): 27 oz. 9 dwt. 6½ gr.

PROVENANCE: Firestone and Parson, Boston

PUBLISHED: Clayton, p. 52

This chafing dish, as Clayton has observed, is a late English example. By its time, the dish cross with

168

lamp (No. 170) had largely usurped the function of the chafing dish. The hinged flaps on the rim, reminiscent of the pan supports on iron trivets, are an unusual feature. They can be flipped inward or outward, depending on the size and form of the object

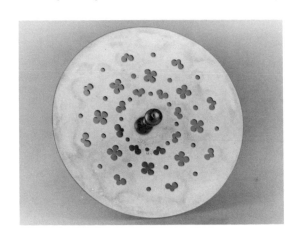

to be supported. This example retains the pierced plate on which the charcoal fuel was burnt; it fits above the lower piercing of the body.

1963-174

169 DISH CROSS
Edward Aldridge and John Stamper
London. 1759/60

H: 5¼″ (13.3 cm). Wt: 46 oz. 4 dwt. ("46=5" engraved on underside of cylinder for arms).

PROVENANCE: Garrard & Co. Ltd., London

PUBLISHED: Davis, J. D., p. 136, ill.; "Accessions of American and Canadian Museums, January–March, 1969," *Art Quarterly* 32 (Autumn 1969):330, 339, ill.

Fully marked on underside of lamp reservoir; maker's mark and lion passant on underside of lamp cover, on underside of cylinder for arms, and on underside of each arm.

Crest of Bromflet or Bronslet, Lancashire, engraved on face of lamp cover and lamp reservoir.

The dish cross, usually fitted with a central lamp, combines the advantages of the dish ring or stand and the chafing dish. Its adjustable arms lend it added flexibility. Dish crosses of this early form appear in English silver in the 1730s. London examples of 1738/39 by Paul Crespin and of 1739/40 by James Shruder are recorded.[1] They differ from the later interpretation of the form, as seen in the following example, in the number and nature of the supports

169

and arms, the means of adjustment, and the use of multiple wicks.

1968-71

___

1. Clayton, pp. 112, 114, fig. 242. The example by Shruder is also illustrated in an advertisement of Thomas Lumley Ltd., London, *Connoisseur* 130 (November 1952):xxvi. It was considered at that time to be a unique example. It was advertised in the following year by Wellby, London, *Connoisseur* 131 (April 1953):xxviii. A related dish cross of 1754/55 by Thomas Heming of London was owned in 1957 by Tiffany and Company, New York ("Shop Talk," *Antiques* 71 [June 1957]:520, ill.).

170 DISH CROSS
Probably John Neville
London. 1772/73

Fully marked on underside of lamp; lion passant on lower section of each leg; lamp cover unmarked.

H: 4¹⁄₁₆″ (10.3 cm); L: 12¼″ (30.8 cm). Wt: 17 oz. 3 dwt. 6 gr.

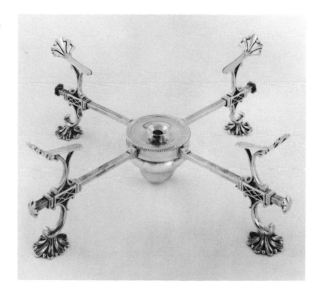

170

PROVENANCE: Garrard & Co. Ltd., London

This is the more common interpretation of the form, which was particularly popular in both sterling and fused silverplate between 1765 and 1800.[1] A similar example of 1775/76, probably by Burrage Davenport of London, is also in the collection (1967-426), as is a rare American example of about 1790 by Richard Humphreys of Philadelphia (1954–140).[2] Another example of 1782/83 by William Plummer of London with beaded circular feet and unpierced dish supports is engraved with the crest of the Carter family of Virginia, and is part of the Carter family silver at Shirley, Charles City County, Virginia.[3]

1967-730

———

1. Dish crosses of this type date from before 1750. An example of 1740, unascribed as to maker, is listed in Christie's (February 27, 1957), lot 94. An example of 1749/50 by Frederick Kandler of London is illustrated in Arthur G. Grimwade, *The Queen's Silver: A Survey of Her Majesty's Personal Collection* (London: Connoisseur, 1953), pp. 18, 74, pl. 18.

2. Marshall B. Davidson, *The American Heritage History of Colonial Antiques* (New York: American Heritage Publishing Company, 1967), p. 252, fig. 380.

3. Barbara Snow, "Living with Antiques: Shirley, Charles City County, Virginia," *Antiques* 133 (May 1963):545, ill.

171 DISH RING
London. 1771/72

171

Fully marked on upper face of body.

H: 4¾″ (12.1 cm); Diam (rim): 8½″ (12.6 cm); Diam (base): 9¾″ (24.8 cm). Wt: 20 oz. 11 dwt. 13½ gr.

PROVENANCE: James Robinson Inc., New York; William Randolph Hearst (sold at Parke-Bernet Galleries, New York, 1963)

PUBLISHED: Parke-Bernet (April 5–6, 1963), lot 250

By 1750 in England, the more versatile dish cross had largely replaced the dish ring. A considerable number of dish rings, however, were produced in Ireland and of fused silverplate in Sheffield during the second half of the eighteenth century. An unusual example of 1773/74 by Matthew Boulton and John Fothergill of Birmingham in the Birmingham Assay Office is fitted with a central lamp and a turned wooden handle.[1] A wire dish ring of fused silverplate of about 1790 is in the Sheffield City Museum.[2]

This example is unusual in having London marks. The leaf bandings at the rim and base are cast and applied. The medial banding with paterae is chased.

1963-75

———

1. Eric Delieb, *The Great Silver Manufactory: Matthew Boulton and the Birmingham Silversmiths, 1760–1790* (London: Studio Vista, 1971), color pl. facing p. 89.

2. G. Bernard Hughes, "Keeping Georgian Food Hot," *Country Life* 144 (December 26, 1968):1703, fig. 5.

172 SPOON
Parcel-gilt
London. 1604/5

Fully marked with leopard's head crowned on face of bowl below juncture with handle and maker's mark, lion passant, and date letter on underside of handle.

Pounced owner's initials on upper face of finial.

L: 6⅞″ (14.5 cm); W (bowl): 1³¹⁄₄₂″ (5 cm). Wt: 2 oz. 0 dwt. 12 gr.

PROVENANCE: Noble W. Hiatt (purchased from Marshall Field & Co., Chicago, 1951); John D. Harris, Haddonfield, New Jersey

Seal-top spoons enjoyed a long period of popularity with surviving examples dating from as early as the

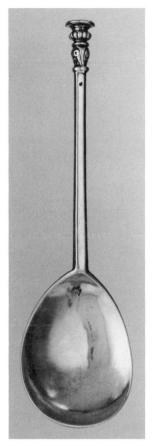

172

usually gilded, as in this instance, even if the remainder of the spoon is left plain. This spoon bears customary London marking with the leopard's head crowned on the face of the bowl below the juncture with the handle and the other marks clustered at the base on the underside of the handle.

1971-139

1. A spoon in the Benson collection has been ascribed by Commander and Mrs. G. E. P. How to the mid-fifteenth century (How, 1:212, 214–15, ill.).

2. Martha Gandy Fales, *American Silver in the Henry Francis du Pont Winterthur Museum* (Winterthur, 1958), no. 70, ill.

3. John L. Cotter, *Archaeological Excavations at Jamestown Colonial National Historical Park and Jamestown National Historic Site* (Washington: United States Government Printing Office, 1958), pl. 87.

4. How, 1:143.

173 SPOON
Silver-gilt
John Quycke
Barnstaple. About 1620

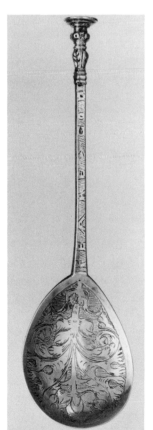

173

mid-fifteenth century.[1] Made in large numbers in the seventeenth century, they, along with those of slip-top form, were the principal types of spoons used by the earliest colonists. Although no seal-top spoons of American manufacture are known, an English provincial example of about 1700 owned by Governor Brewster of Plymouth Colony is in the Henry Francis du Pont Winterthur Museum.[2] Latten metal or tinned-brass examples have been excavated at Jamestown.[3]

This representative London example has the form of seal introduced at the close of the sixteenth century and found on most seventeenth-century examples. Like the various types of cast finials on most London spoons from the early sixteenth century onward, the seal is joined to the handle by a V-shaped joint, the seam barely discernible on the front and back facets of the handle. In contrast, a lapped joint is used, as in the following example, on most spoons with finials made in provincial areas.[4] The finials of spoons are

Maker's mark on face of bowl below juncture with handle and secondary mark stamped three times on underside of handle.

Pounced owners' initials and date on underside of bowl.

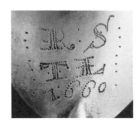

L: 7⅟₁₆″ (17.9 cm); W (bowl): 2″ (5.1 cm). Wt: 1 oz. 10 dwt. 13 gr.

PROVENANCE: How (of Edinburgh), London

PUBLISHED: "Notable Works of Art Now on the Market," *Burlington Magazine* 111 (June 1969):pl. XXXVIII; "The Connoisseur Catalogue to the Antique Dealers' Fair and Exhibition, Grosvenor House, London, June 11–26," *Connoisseur* 171 (June 1969):119, ill.

This is one of a small group of highly important gilt seal-top spoons with engraved religious mottoes on their handles and bold foliate engraving in their bowls.[1] Forming one of the most distinctive groups of English spoons and provincial decoration, they are the work of John Quycke of Barnstaple, a member of a large family of silversmiths. According to the Barnstaple parish register, he was married in 1603 and died in 1632.[2] They bear his maker's mark of a leafed strawberry within a shaped shield on the face of their bowls, a rebus for "quycke," a local Devonshire word for berry. The secondary mark "RM" in either of two forms is stamped three times on the underside of their handles. This is a debased form of Barum, the Latin name for Barnstaple.

Considering their engraved mottoes and the consistent elaborate enrichment of their bowls, these spoons were probably intended for ceremonial purposes, such as christening and wedding presents. That hypothesis is supported by the pounced initials, usually accompanied by a date, on the bowls of most of them. Some, as in this case, bear initials and a date later than manufacture. From the seventeenth century

onward, as Commander How has observed, it would appear customary to give an old spoon on such occasions and to pounce or engrave the spoon at that time.[3] The double set of pounced initials and date on this example probably indicate that it was given as a wedding present in 1660.

The engraved bowl decoration on this spoon is very similar to that on a female terminal spoon from the Cookson collection.[4] The handle of the latter is engraved with the motto "HONNOR GOD." The face of its bowl is marked with the leafed-strawberry maker's mark of the Colonial Williamsburg spoon. A virtually identical spoon, but with handle and bowl unengraved,[5] and a further spoon with the same terminal figure but an elaborate knopped stem and engraved bowl,[6] both bear an "IQ" maker's mark. The use of these maker's marks on spoons obviously by the same maker led Commander How to attribute them and the group of seal-top spoons to John Quycke,[7] whom he considered "the greatest English spoon-maker of all time."[8]

This spoon, except for the detailing of its seal, is of standard seventeenth-century form. The knop below the end of the seal, as in the other spoons of the group, is embellished with strapwork rather than the usual gadroons, as in the previous example.

1971-246

1. Four examples are illustrated in How, 1:240–43, plates 14 and 15. The left and right spoons in plate 14 are also illustrated in How, "On Early Spoons," *Notes on Antique Silver*, No. 2 (Summer 1942): 19. The center spoon in plate 14 is also illustrated in Commander How's catalog of the Ellis collection of spoons (Sotheby's [November 13–14, 1935], lot 210). A further example, formerly in the Gask collection and presently in the Victoria and Albert Museum, London, is illustrated in Norman Gask, *Old Silver Spoons of England: A Practical Guide for Collectors* (London: Herbert Jenkins Ltd., 1926), pl. XII, fig. 5. The various mottoes engraved on the handles of spoons in this group include: "FEARE GOD," "PRAISE GOD," "PRAISE GOD ALWAIES," "HONOR [or 'HONNOR'] GOD," and "HONOR GOD ONLI."

2. How, 2:379; [Mrs. G. E. P. How] "Notable Works of Art Now on the Market," *Burlington Magazine* 111 (June 1969): unp., caption to pl. XXXVIII.

3. How, 1:5.

4. Ibid., 2:202–3, pl. 1.

5. Ibid., 2:204–5, pl. 2.

6. Ibid., 2:206–7, pl. 3. This magnificent spoon is in the museum at Barnstaple.

7. Ibid., 2:202, 378–79.

8. Ibid., 2:379.

174 SPOON
London. 1634/35 or 1636/37

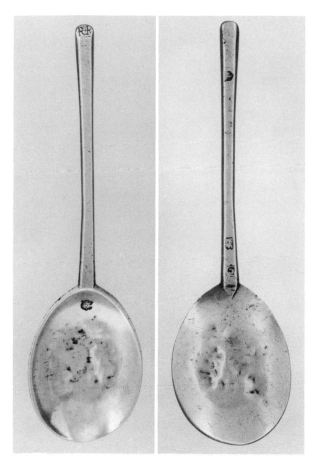

171

Fully marked with leopard's head crowned on face of bowl below juncture with handle and maker's mark, lion passant, and date letter on underside of handle.

Owner's initials engraved on end of handle.

L: 6¾″ (17.1 cm); W (bowl): 1¹⁵⁄₁₆″ (4.9 cm). Wt: 1 oz. 12 dwt. 3 gr.

PROVENANCE: Gift of Dr. William A. R. Goodwin, Williamsburg, Virginia

Slip-end or slip-top spoons, distinguished by the oblique termination of their handles, resembling a gardner's slip, were made throughout a long period. The earliest recorded London one is that of 1487/88,[1] with late examples extending into the reign of Charles II. They share with other sixteenth- and seventeenth-century spoons a pear-shaped bowl and a narrow stalklike handle of hexagonal section, the front and back facets being of greater width, and having a short V-shaped drop on the underside at the juncture with the bowl. The shape of the bowls of late slip-end spoons reflects the changing form of contemporary Puritan and trefid spoons. This example is conventionally marked with the date letter placed high on the handle, which, as Commander How has noted, indicates that spoons of this type were never intended to have a finial.[2]

The spoon was found in an old house foundation near Jamestown, Virginia. The precise site is not known, and the colonial records for James City County have been destroyed. The engraved initials "R·K" on the end of the handle may be those of Richard Kemp or Richard Kingsmill, both of whom were prominent citizens of Jamestown and its vicinity in the first half of the seventeenth century. A silver slip-end spoon of Continental origin has been found in a seventeenth-century context at Jamestown.[3]

G1930-666

1. How, 1:84–85, ill. The spoon is in the collection of Mrs. G. E. P. How, London.
2. Ibid., p. 277. Some slip-end spoons of very small or large size do not have the date letter so placed.
3. John L. Cotter, *Archeological Excavations at Jamestown Colonial National Historical Park and Jamestown National Historic Site, Virginia* (Washington: United States Government Printing Office, 1958), p. 189, pl. 87; ——— and J. Paul Hudson, *New Discoveries at Jamestown, Site of the First Successful English Settlement in America* (Washington: United States Government Printing Office, 1957), pp. 33–34, ill.

175 SIX SPOONS
London. 1660/61

L: 7½″–7⁹⁄₁₆″ (19 cm–19.2 cm); W (bowl): 1¹⁵⁄₁₆″–2¹⁄₃₂″ (4.9 cm–5.2 cm). Total wt: 12 oz. 8 dwt.

PROVENANCE: Christie, Manson & Woods, London (1923); William Randolph Hearst (sold by Parish-Watson & Co., New York, 1938)

175

Fully marked with leopard's head crowned on face of each bowl below juncture with handle and maker's mark, lion passant, and date letter on underside of each handle.

Unidentified arms and crest of an unmarried lady engraved on the underside of each bowl.

PUBLISHED: Christie's (April 24, 1923), lot 79; How, 1: 296–97, pl. 2; Clayton, p. 279

These six superb spoons constitute the largest known set of English stump-end or stump-top spoons. No surviving examples of this comparatively rare type are recorded with a date before the reign of James I.[1] They are the only early English spoon type with handles of octagonal, rather than hexagonal, section. Superficially, they resemble slip-end spoons, but their handles of differing section are generally longer than those of the latter, and they terminate in a faceted point rather than an oblique face. The bowls of this set are of oval form, closely resembling in outline and profile those of other spoon types of the mid-seventeenth century. These spoons are marked in the customary fashion with the date letter still placed relatively high on the handle, as on spoons without finials, but at an intermediate height, indicating their mid-seventeenth-century date. Contemporary engraved armorials with conventional plumed mantling dominate the undersides of their bowls.

1938-41, 1-6

————

1. How, 1:293.

176 SPOON
Stephen Venables
London. 1664/65

Fully marked on underside of handle.

L: 5 7/16″ (13.8 cm); W (bowl): 1 1/4″ (3.2 cm). Wt: 13 dwt. 12 gr.

PROVENANCE: How (of Edinburgh), London

The trefid (trifid, lobed-end, trefoil-top, *pied de biche*) spoon, its broad handle ending in a tripartite division and its oval bowl having level edges and long rattail on the underside, initiates the modern phase of spoon design. Introduced in about 1660 from France in a fully developed state, spoons of this type were referred to in 1663 as "French spoons" in the accounts of Child and Rogers, the London goldsmiths and bankers.[1]

This is an extremely early English trefid, dating two years after the earliest recorded example.[2] The marks, as on most London trefids, are all on the

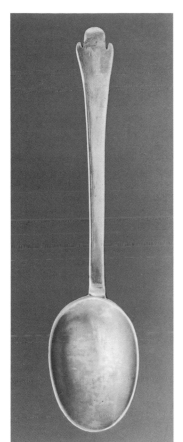

176

177 SPOON
Stephen Venables
London. 1671/72

177

underside of the handle with the date letter on early examples, such as this, elevated above the other marks.[3] Stephen Venables, its maker, was a prolific mid-seventeenth-century spoonmaker. It, like a number of his spoons, displays carelessness in execution with the shoulders of the bowl not symmetrical and the handle and rattail not centered with the bowl.[4]

This spoon is of intermediate porringer or dessert size. It was during the late seventeenth century that spoons were first made in a variety of sizes and that the distinction between tea, dessert, and table spoons was established.

1971-237

<hr />

1. Jackson, 2:522.

2. How, 1:326–27, pl. 1.

3. The leopard's head crowned is often struck in the bowls of London trefids of unusual size, such as condiment and basting spoons, as was the customary marking procedure on earlier London spoons (ibid., p. 328).

4. Commander How has commented on this aspect of Venables' work (ibid., pp. 250, 312).

Fully marked with leopard's head crowned on face of bowl below juncture with handle and maker's mark, lion passant, and date letter on underside of handle.

Owner's initials engraved on underside of handle at end; engraving removed from underside of bowl.

L: 7 1/32" (18.3 cm); W (bowl): 1 7/8" (4.8 cm). Wt: 2 oz. 3 dwt. 2 gr.

PROVENANCE: Garrard & Co. Ltd., London

The Puritan spoon, first appearing during the reign of Charles I, enjoyed its main popularity during the Commonwealth period. It is the first English spoon type with a handle of rectangular section and a relatively broad handle face. Its bowl is usually of pronounced oval outline, though, when viewed in profile, the rim still exhibits the concave contours associated with bowls of modified fig or pear form of earlier types. It retains the short V-shaped extension of the handle onto the back of the bowl, a feature of early English spoons, which on trefid ones was replaced by a long, ridged rattail. On London examples, the leopard's head crowned continues to be struck on the face of the bowl and the date letter to be elevated above the other marks on the underside of the handle. In this instance, the marks on the handle are fairly evenly spaced with the date letter at an intermediate height, perhaps attributable to this spoon's late date.

This massive example, like a number of Puritan spoons, is in virtually pristine condition. That is probably due, in part, to the brief period of their popularity and their formal obsolescence after the introduction of the trefid about 1660. This late London example was out of fashion when it was made. Stephen Venables, however, who fashioned the preceding spoon of early trefid form, continued to make Puritan and seal-top spoons well into the reign of Charles II.[1]

1971-395

---

1. A massive Puritan spoon of 1664/65 by Venables with an unusually broad handle for a London example is illustrated in How, 1:312–13, pl. 1. Commander How also illustrates seal-top spoons of 1677/78 and 1681/82 by Venables (ibid., pp. 250–53, plates 19 and 20). Venables, as Commander How observes, was the most prolific maker of seal-top spoons during the reign of Charles II (ibid., p. 250).

178 SPOON
Provincial. About 1680

Maker's mark and repeated secondary mark on underside of handle.

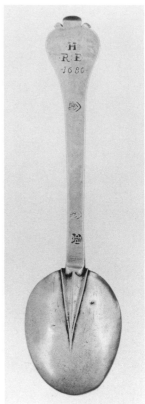

178

Owners' initials and date engraved on underside of handle.

L: 7$\frac{15}{32}$" (19 cm); W (bowl): 1$\frac{27}{32}$" (4.7 cm). Wt: 1 oz. 9 dwt. 18 gr.

PROVENANCE: A. V. Sutherland-Graeme, London

The identity of the maker and the origin of this provincial spoon have not been determined. The maker's and secondary marks, as are those on many provincial trefid spoons, are unrecorded.[1]

1955-160

---

1. This spoon, when acquired, was thought to be possibly by Peter Pemberton of Chester. Neither the maker's nor the secondary mark is recorded in Maurice H. Ridgway, *Chester Goldsmiths from Early Times to 1726* (Altringham: John Sherratt & Son Ltd., 1968).

179 SPOON
London. 1681/82

179

Fully marked on underside of handle.

Pounced owner's initials on underside of handle.

L: 8¹¹⁄₁₆″ (22.1 cm); W (bowl): 1²⁷⁄₃₂″ (4.7 cm). Wt: 1 oz. 9 dwt. 23 gr.

PROVENANCE: How (of Edinburgh), London

Trefid spoons bear a variety of decoration, either stamped in low relief, as in this example, punched with repeated small circles or devices, as encountered most often in provincial examples, especially of West Country origin, and engraved. This extremely fine spoon is of characteristic "lace-back" type, with scrolled foliate and beaded decoration in low relief on the end of the handle face and the underside of the bowl. The inclusion of a mask within the handle decoration is an unusual feature, although representative of a small group of mainly London spoons. Such decoration is achieved by hammering the spoon into handle and bowl swages cut with the designs.

This spoon still retains certain aspects of early trefid spoons. The sides of its handle remain almost parallel until they splay outward to form the end, and the date letter on the underside of the handle is still elevated above the other marks clustered below.

1971-236

180 TEASPOON
Silver-gilt
London. About 1690

Maker's mark only on underside of handle.

L: 4⅛″ (10.5 cm); W (bowl): ¹⁵⁄₁₆″ (2.4 cm). Wt: 5 dwt. 19 gr.

PROVENANCE: S. J. Shrubsole Corp., New York

Teaspoons first appear during the reign of Charles II. Seventeenth- and eighteenth-century ones are considerably smaller than their modern counterparts. Fully marked examples are uncommon, and, until 1782, it is customary for teaspoons to bear only the maker's mark and usually the lion's head erased or the lion passant, depending on whether the spoon is of Britannia or sterling standard.

This spoon is of a conventional late seventeenth-century type of probably Huguenot introduction

180

181

with overall foliate engraving on either side of the handle and a large acanthus leaf enclosing the rattail on the underside of the bowl. Such engraved spoons were usually gilded.

Small spoons of this sort were probably used interchangeably for coffee and chocolate, as well as tea. Nicholas Blundell of Lancashire acquired in London in 1703, just before his marriage, six "gilt Coffy Spoones" for 18s.[1] These may very well have been similar engraved teaspoons.

1971-150

1. Clayton, p. 277.

181 TABLESPOON
John Chartier
London. 1698/99

L: 7¹⁵⁄₁₆″ (20.2 cm); W (bowl): 1²¹⁄₃₂″ (4.2 cm).
Wt: 2 oz. 9 dwt. 5 gr.

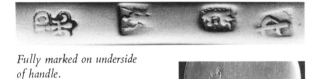

Fully marked on underside of handle.

Owner's crest engraved on underside of handle at end.

PROVENANCE: How (of Edinburgh), London

This magnificent spoon of fine proportions and weight is enriched with superlative engraving of an individual character. The fineness of the engraving can be readily appreciated when compared with the preceding and following spoons. This dense engraving of foliated scrolls and flowers is in the elegant French manner, associated in England with the work of Simon Gribelin. It exhibits unusual freedom and an embryonic rococo element in the ruffling of some of the scrolls. Not surprisingly, the spoon bears the mark of John Chartier, a notable Huguenot maker.

Shield-end (wavy-end, dog-nose) spoons occupy an intermediate position between trefid and Hanoverian spoons. In comparison with the trefid, this spoon, like developed examples of its type, has a more languid rhythm to the unbroken contour of its outline, due to the elimination of the clefts and ears of the trefid handle end, the gentler curve of the handle sides, the rounding of the handle edges and shank, and the flaring of the shank to receive the softened shoulders of the longer, narrower bowl. The extremely long plain rattail on the underside of the bowl is consistent with the bowl's attenuation.

1971-248

Fully marked on underside of handle (lion's head erased and Britannia indistinct).

L: 7⁷⁄₁₆″ (18.9 cm); W (bowl): 1¹¹⁄₁₆″ (4.3 cm). Wt: 1 oz. 9 dwt.

PROVENANCE: How (of Edinburgh), London

The engraving on this spoon exhibits an uncommon flow and crispness for engraving of this conventional late seventeenth-century type (see No. 180). The gradual taper of the sides to the end of the handle, the long, narrow oval bowl, and the even spacing of the marks on the lower half of the underside of the handle are characteristics of late trefids.

1971-247

182 TABLESPOON
Silver-gilt
John Ladyman
London. 1699/1700

183 BASTING OR SERVING SPOON
Anthony Nelme
London. 1700/1701

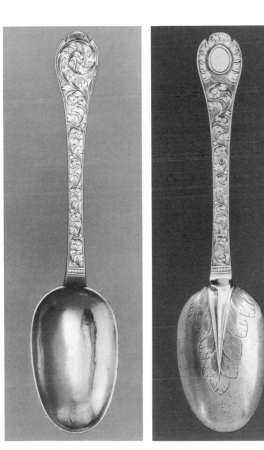

182

183

Fully marked on underside of handle.

Owner's crest engraved on underside of handle at end.

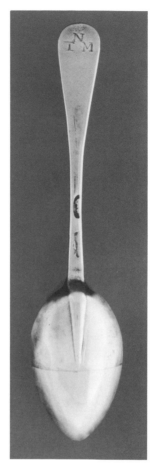

184

L: 13¹⁵⁄₁₆″ (35.4 cm); W (bowl): 2⁷⁄₁₆″ (6.2 cm). Wt: 7 oz. 1 dwt. 16 gr. ("7=4" engraved on underside of handle).

PROVENANCE: How (of Edinburgh), London

Large spoons of the late seventeenth and eighteenth centuries, which usually closely follow the design of contemporary spoons for table use, were probably intended for basting and serving purposes. Some late seventeenth- and early eighteenth-century examples are fitted with tubular handles. This example of shield-end type, like the tablespoon by Chartier (No. 181), is of good proportions and well made.

1971-238

184 TEASPOON
London. About 1715

Indistinct maker's mark and lion's head erased on underside of handle.

Owners' initials engraved on underside of handle.

L: 4″ (10.2 cm); W (bowl): 1³⁄₁₆″ (2.1 cm). Wt: 5 dwt. 12 gr.

PROVENANCE: Gift of Mrs. William B. Sanders, Alexandria, Virginia

Thomas Nelson (1677–1745) of Yorktown, Virginia, and his wife, Margaret Reade, whom he married in 1710, originally owned this spoon. It descended through the Digges and Pendleton families of Virginia and West Virginia to the donor. The lower part of the bowl has been replaced and the outline of the bowl altered.

G1972-185

185 PAIR OF TABLESPOONS
London. 1720/21

Fully marked on underside of handle.

Owners' initials engraved on underside of handle; lower set added.

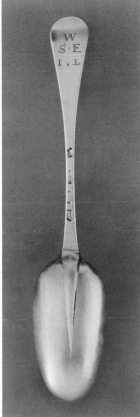

185

L: 8⅜″ (21.3 cm); W (bowl): 1⅝″ (4.1 cm).
Total wt: 3 oz. 15 dwt.

PROVENANCE: Museum of Fine Arts, Boston

Spoons of "Hanoverian" type first appeared during the reign of Queen Anne. Firmly established when George I came to the throne in 1714, this remained the principal pattern for flatwares until about 1770. They are characterized by a handle of loop-shaped outline turned up at the end with a raised crest and central rib on the face, rounded shank of D-shaped section, and a long, narrow, oval bowl. The plain rattail on the underside was retained until about 1730. The turning-up of the handle end, the raised crest and central rib on the handle face, and the attenuation of the bowl tend to be more pronounced on early examples, such as these.

1954-334, 1–2

186 BASTING OR SERVING SPOON
Edinburgh. 1734/35

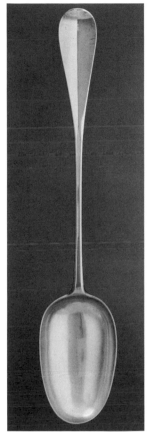

186

Fully marked on underside of handle.

Owner's initials engraved on underside of handle at end.

L: 14¾″ (37.5 cm); W (bowl): 2¹⁵⁄₁₆″ (7.5 cm).
Wt: 6 oz. 9 dwt. 5 gr.

PROVENANCE: Anonymous gift

Michael Clayton has observed that large spoons of this sort were very popular in Scotland and that early eighteenth-century examples are known from practically every Scottish provincial center. He notes that they appear to have been called "hash spoons" in Scotland and Ireland.[1] They were sometimes referred to as "ragout spoons" in England and America. William Byrd III of Westover, Charles City County, Virginia, owned in 1769 "four Ragooe Spoons" with a value of £4.[2] These would appear to be the "two raguel spoons" and "two ragoul spoons" listed in the 1813 will of his widow, Mary Willing Byrd.[3]

This pleasing spoon with a generous bowl bears customary Edinburgh marks. Instead of a hallmark to indicate that a piece is of required fineness, Edinburgh work before 1681 is stamped with the deacon's mark, which was replaced in that year by the mark of the assay master, in this instance, Archibald Ure.

Similar London basting or serving spoons of 1731/32, of 1746/47 by Samuel Roby, and of 1757/58 by William Turner with respective histories of ownership in the Ambler, Jones, and Randolph families of Virginia were exhibited in 1940 at the Virginia Museum of Fine Arts, Richmond.[4] A similar spoon of 1755/56 by Elias Cachart of London is also in the Colonial Williamsburg collection (1954-543).

G1971-2083

1. Clayton, p. 272.
2. Westover Plate.
3. "The Will of Mrs. Mary Willing Byrd, of Westover, 1813, with a List of the Westover Portraits," *Virginia Magazine of History and Biography* 6 (April 1899):350–51.
4. Virginia Museum (a), pp. 19–21, nos. 79, 90, 107; Davis, E. M., pp. 110–11, 115.

187 DESSERT SPOON
Elias Cachart
London. 1747/48

Fully marked on underside of handle.

L: 6⅛″ (15.6 cm); W (bowl): 1¹⁵⁄₃₂″ (3.3 cm). Wt: 1 oz. 0 dwt. 21 gr.

187

Crest of the Lewis family of Virginia engraved on underside of handle at end.

PROVENANCE: Gift of Mrs. George D. Baylor, Richmond, Virginia

This spoon is believed to have been originally owned by Warner Lewis I (b. 1720) of Warner Hall, Gloucester County, Virginia. In 1745 he married Eleanor Bowles Gooch, the widow of William Gooch, Jr., the only son of Sir William Gooch, who served as governor of Virginia from 1741 to 1749. It probably descended to their son, Warner Lewis II, who married Mary Chiswell; to their daughter, Eleanor Lewis, who married John Fox; to their daughter, Elizabeth Fox, who married Dr. George Daniel Baylor; to their son Dr. Warner Lewis Baylor; and to his son, George Daniel Baylor, husband of the donor.

G1961-303

188 SIX TEASPOONS AND SUGAR TONGS, WITH CASE

John Wirgman
London. About 1750

188

Maker's mark and lion passant on underside of each spoon handle.

L (spoons): 4⅜″ (11.1 cm); W (bowl): 1⁵⁄₁₆″ (2.4 cm); L (case): 6⅝″ (16.8 cm); W: 2⅜″ (6 cm). Total wt (spoons): 3 oz. 13 dwt.

PROVENANCE: Garrard & Co. Ltd., London (purchased from C. J. Vander Ltd., London, 1954)

These spoons are decorated in the rococo taste, their handles chased with scrolls, shells, and flowers and their bowls stamped with beaded and foliated scrolls.

Contemporary shagreen-covered case with brass hardware and lined with green silk and velvet.

From middle to late eighteenth century the bowls of spoons, especially teaspoons, were stamped with a variety of decorative and pictorial devices and subjects.[1] This, like the raised decoration on lace-back trefids, was achieved by hammering the bowl into a swage cut with the design.[2] Known as fancy-back or picture-back spoons, most examples are of "Hanoverian" type, their popularity diminishing with the use of various decorative border treatments, principally feather-edged and bright-cut, on the handles of "Old English" spoons during the last quarter of the century. The chased decoration on the handles of these, although typical, is less frequently encountered than the decoration of the bowls.

Part of a handwritten label (EG./Spoons/gar Tongs,/ged to Mrs Ray/my Mother) remains on the interior of the cover of the case. The sugar tongs are illustrated and discussed with the tea and coffee accessories (No. 112).

Lord Botetourt, who served as governor of Virginia from 1768 to 1770, owned a similar set: "1 Shagreen case contain^g 8 Chas'd silver tea spoons and 1 p^r of tongs" is listed in "His Lordship's Bed Chamber" in the Governor's Palace in Williamsburg in the 1770 inventory of his estate. Another "30 Tea spoons" are listed with the "Plate, in the Pantry."[3]

Illustrated are bowls of other picture-back teaspoons in the collection. They date from the third quarter of the eighteenth century, and their handles are of plain "Hanoverian" type. The last example with a squirrel sitting on an oak branch is from one of three matching teaspoons given by Mrs. G. Fred Smith, Rolfe, Iowa (G1969-122; G1971-34, 1–2).

1954-563, 1–8

189 TABLESPOON
Thomas Northcote
London. 1785/86

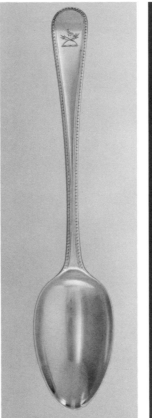 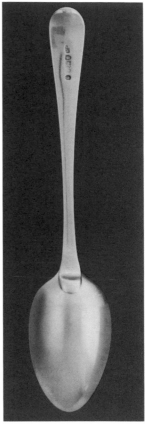

189

Fully marked on underside of handle.

Owner's crest engraved on face of handle.

L: 8¹⁵⁄₃₂″ (21.5 cm); W (bowl): 1²³⁄₃₂″ (4.4 cm). Wt: 2 oz. 2 dwt. 2 gr.

PROVENANCE: Garrard & Co. Ltd., London

"Old English" spoons with downturned handles and oval to egg-shaped bowls first appeared about 1760

---

1. G. E. P. How lists twenty-seven different devices or subjects appearing on picture-back spoons (How, "The Cult of the Teaspoon," *Notes on Antique Silver*, no. 4 [1944–45]:39).

2. A steel spoon swage engraved with an eagle, which belonged to John Vogler (1783–1881) of Salem, North Carolina, is owned by Old Salem, Inc. (Louise C. Belden, "Liberty and the American Eagle on Spoons by Jacob Kucher," *Winterthur Portfolio*, 3 [1967]: 108, fig. 15).

3. Botetourt Inventory.

or shortly thereafter.[1] By the early 1770s they had largely displaced those of "Hanoverian" type. Their handles are often enhanced with various decorative borders, such as stamped beading, as in this example, or chased feather-edging and bright-cut engraving, as in the following two examples. Feather-edging was the first of these decorative treatments to be employed. An early feather-edged spoon of 1766/67 is in the Victoria and Albert Museum, London.[2] Charles Harris, the Charleston silversmith, in an early American reference to such spoons, advertised in the *South Carolina Gazette* for August 1, 1768, that he "Makes and sells all sorts of new fashioned . . . tablespoons, feathered on the handle."[3] Angular shoulders flanking the base of the handle, when encountered on "Old English" spoons, appear only on feather-edged examples, though they are a regular feature of later spoons of fiddle and king's patterns. This spoon and the following two examples are marked toward the ends of their handles, as was customary after 1780.

1971-399

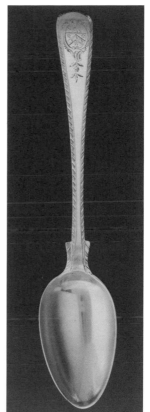
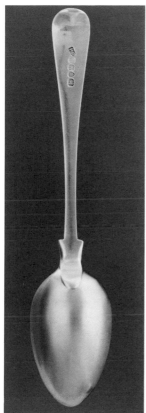

190

L: 8¹⁷⁄₃₂″ (21.7 cm); W (bowl): 1¾″ (4.4 cm). Total wt: 4 oz. 15 dwt. 13 gr.

PROVENANCE: Garrard & Co. Ltd., London

1971-398, 1–2

---

1. An extremely early reference, probably to spoons of this type, is the entry of March 28, 1760 "To 12 Turned back teaspoons" in the Wickes-Wakelin-Garrard ledgers (Clayton, p. 279).

2. Victoria and Albert Museum, *A Picture Book of English Silver Spoons* (London, 1927), pl. 19.

3. Alfred Coxe Prime, ed., *The Arts & Crafts in Philadelphia, Maryland, and South Carolina, 1721–1785* (Topsfield, Massachusetts: Wayside Press, 1929), p. 67.

190 PAIR OF TABLESPOONS
Charles Hougham
London. 1791/92

Fully marked on underside of each handle.

Unidentified arms engraved on face of each handle.

191 TABLESPOON
London. 1799/1800

Fully marked on underside of handle.

Owners' initials engraved on face of handle.

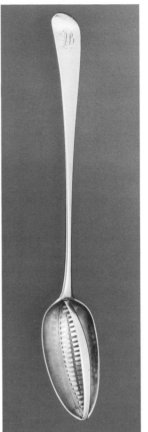

191

192

L: 8⁵⁄₁₆″ (18.6 cm); W (bowl): 1¹³⁄₁₆″ (4.6 cm). Wt: 1 oz. 13 dwt. 18 gr.

PROVENANCE: Garrard & Co. Ltd., London

1971-397

L: 11¾″ (28.8 cm); W (bowl): 2″ (5 cm). Wt: 3 oz. 19 dwt. 15 gr.

PROVENANCE: Anonymous gift

These spoons are generally considered to have been used for serving gravy with the pierced partition separating and retaining the coarser elements. They achieved a certain popularity in the late eighteenth century, but appear to have been limited in use to Great Britain and Ireland.[1] Contemporary with the argyle, this specialized form reflects the same attention given to the serving of gravy.

G1971-2080

192 DIVIDED SERVING SPOON
London. 1799/1800

Fully marked on underside of handle (maker's mark indistinct).

Owner's cypher engraved on face of handle.

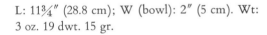

1. Erik Lassen, *Ske, Kniv og Gaffel: Knives, Forks & Spoons* (Copenhagen: Høst, 1960), no. 76; Kurt Ticher, "Irish Silver," *Proceedings of the Society of Silver Collectors*, no. 7 (Spring 1965):6–7.

193 SUCKET FORK
London. 1674/75

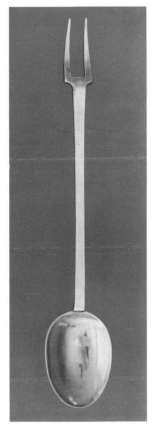

193

Fully marked on underside of handle.

L: 6¹³⁄₁₆″ (17.3 cm); W (bowl): 1⁷⁄₃₂″ (3.1 cm).
Wt: 15 dwt. 12 gr.

PROVENANCE: S. J. Shrubsole Ltd., London

Sucket forks, intended for the eating of preserved fruit, were used from at least the first half of the sixteenth century.[1] Most surviving examples date from the second half of the seventeenth century, after which time they fell into disuse.

This example is of representative form having an oval bowl with a ridged rattail, a handle of rec-

tangular section (as on contemporary trefid spoons), and two tines (occasionally three were used) with angular shoulders and square shaping between the tines (as on contemporary trefid forks). Fully marked examples, such as this, are uncommon.

1971-3302

---

1. Clayton notes the following from the 1549 inventory of Edward VI: "Item one Suckett Spone wt a forke Joyned together of silver gilte. weing iij oz. Item one Spone wt a suckett forke uppon one stele [stem] gilt. pos. iij oz." (Clayton, p. 279).

194 TABLE FORK
John Brooke
London. 1698/99

194

Fully marked on underside of handle.

Unidentified arms engraved on underside of handle.

L: 7¹³⁄₃₂″ (18.8 cm). Wt: 2 oz. 2 dwt. 6 gr.

PROVENANCE: William Bruford & Son, Ltd., Exeter (1944); How (of Edinburgh), London

PUBLISHED: Advertisement, William Bruford & Son, Ltd., Exeter, *Antique Collector* 15 (July–August 1944):139, ill.; G. Bernard and Therle Hughes, *Three Centuries of English Domestic Silver* (London: Lutterworth Press, 1952), pl. 13; G. Bernard Hughes, "Evolution of the Silver Table Fork," *Country Life* 126 (September 24. 1959):365, fig. 6

Knives and spoons have long been standard eating implements. Even though forks for specialized purposes were used at an early date, they were not generally adopted for individual table use in England until the second half of the seventeenth century. The majority of early silver forks were made in one piece, their handles based on those of contemporary spoons. The earliest known English silver table fork is that of 1632/33 in the Victoria and Albert Museum, London.[1] Engraved with the crests of the earl of Rutland, it has a handle of notched-end Puritan type and two tines. The only other recorded English fork of this pattern is one with London hallmarks of 1683/84, engraved with the crest of Charles, earl of Dorset, formerly in the collection of Charles G. Rupert of Wilmington, Delaware.[2] French examples have survived in greater number.

The number of tines on a fork does not follow a chronological sequence. Silver forks of trefid type with two, three, and four tines appear in the reign of Charles II. The earliest recorded four-tined examples are of trefid form and date from 1674/75.[3] Five years earlier, Madame Prujean had purchased "12 Four Tyned Forks weighing xxxiii ounces ii dwt at V^s 11^d ounce."[4] After 1760 the use of four tines did become fairly standard on silver forks, though two or three tines remained customary on hafted forks with steel tines.

The shank and tines of this fork are extremely

heavy. The outer tines, as on most seventeenth-century examples with three or four tines, incline inward. The shoulders of the lower or tined section and the short intervals between the tines are characteristically less angular than on trefid forks before about 1690.

1971-239

1. C. T. Bailey, *Knives and Forks* (London: Medici Society, 1927), p. 7, fig. 72; G. Bernard Hughes, "Evolution of the Silver Table Fork," *Country Life* 126 (September 24, 1959):364, fig. 1.

2. "Notes," *Connoisseur* 79 (November 1927):162–64, ill.

3. At least two examples of this date by an unidentified London maker "IK" are recorded. One is illustrated in W. W. Watts, "A Collection of Silver Spoons and Forks," *Apollo* 23 (May 1936):266, fig. III; G. E. P. How, "Flat Silver," *Notes on Antique Silver*, no. 3 (Summer 1943):24, fig. 1; G. Bernard Hughes, "Evolution of the Silver Table Fork," p. 364, fig. 3. The other is part of the Grenville canteen and is illustrated in Jackson, 1:244, fig. 254 and Clayton, p. 323, fig. 683. Jackson apparently did not realize that the fork and spoon in this canteen bear the date letter for 1674/75.

4. Hughes, "Evolution of the Silver Table Fork," p. 364.

195 SET OF TEN TABLE FORKS
Paul Hanet
London. 1723/24

195

Fully marked on the underside of each handle.

Owner's crest and initials, possibly for a member of the Gordon family, engraved on underside of each.

L: 7¹³⁄₁₆″ (19.8 cm). Total wt: 20 oz. 11 dwt.

PROVENANCE: Museum of Fine Arts, Boston
1954-339, 1–10

196 KNIFE AND FORK, WITH SHEATH
London, About 1690

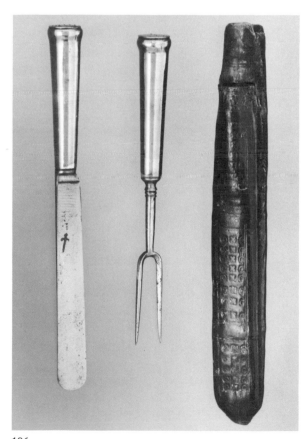

196
Contemporary leather sheath tooled with vertical rows of Xs and Os within outlined panels on front and back.

L (knife): 5²³⁄₃₂″ (14.5 cm); L (fork): 4¹⁵⁄₁₆″ (12.5 cm); L (case): 6⅜″ (16.2 cm).

PROVENANCE: How (of Edinburgh), London

Knives and forks with matching silver handles and steel blades and tines first appear in the reign of Charles II. These seal-end examples are of the earliest type, characterized by a tapering tubular handle of circular section with a bulge before a flush end. Their handles, unlike later cast and stamped ones, are wrought out of a strip of silver with a single seam running lengthwise and a flat disc soldered to and forming the end. They were fashioned by an unidentified London small-plate worker, whose mark appears on other flatware handles and small accessory items, such as nutmeg graters. Like most forks of this type and date, this example has two rather long slender tines. The knife blade with nearly parallel edges is original. During the late seventeenth century, curved blades of early scimitar form were being introduced. The blade bears the dagger mark of the London Cutlers' Company, which was struck on

Maker's mark on each handle; cutler's mark and secondary marks on knife blade.

Owner's initials engraved on end of each handle.

London knife blades after 1607 and soon was misappropriated by some Sheffield and Birmingham cutlers. Sheathed knives and forks probably served as personal traveling accessories. Pairs of knives in sheaths, however, were common wedding presents during the late sixteenth and seventeenth centuries.[1]

William Fitzhugh of Stafford County, Virginia, ordered from London in 1688 a set of silver flatware, including "One dozen silver hafted knives. 1 doz: silver forks One dozen silver spoons large & strong."[2] There were difficulties in processing the order, and he reminded his London agent the following year that he still desired "a Case containing a dozen hafted knives, & a dozen silver hafted forks."[3] These he apparently obtained, for "1 Dozn. Silver hafted Knives 1 Dozen Silver Forks . . . 1 Doz: Silver Spoons" are listed in the 1703 inventory of his estate.[4] The knives and forks probably had handles of this seal-end type.

1972-323

---

1. Charles R. Beard, "Wedding Knives," *Connoisseur* 85 (February 1930):91–97.
2. Davis, R. B., p. 244.
3. Ibid., p. 258.
4. Ibid., p. 382.

197 SET OF TEN KNIVES AND TEN FORKS
Blades by How
About 1760

197

Maker's mark and lion passant on each handle; cutler's mark and dagger mark of the London Cutlers' Company on each blade.

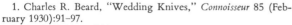

Owner's crest engraved on each handle.

L (knives): 10½" (26.7 cm); L (forks): 7¾" (19.7 cm).

PROVENANCE: Museum of Fine Arts, Boston

These are of representative mid-eighteenth-century type with handles of conventional pistol-grip form. Handles of this design from earlier in the century were quite substantial, being cast lengthwise in halves and then soldered together. During the second half of the century, handles, as on this set and the following example, were stamped from thin sheet silver and filled with composition for weight and reinforcement. Sheffield with its die-stamping industry produced vast quantities of such handles.

Even though two tines rarely appear on silver forks after the opening years of the eighteenth century, they remained common throughout the century on steel forks fitted with handles of various materials. The steel blades of these knives are of developed scimitar form, having an angular break to the upper edge. They were fashioned by the firm of How, which under Ephraim How and his son, John, was one of the most important and prolific cutlery firms from its inception in the late seventeenth century.[1] Fragments of knife blades with this firm's mark have been excavated in 1750–70 contexts at the Anthony Hay site in Williamsburg and at Carter's Grove, James City County, Virginia.[2]

The 1760 inventory of the estate of Henry Wetherburn, the prosperous Williamsburg tavern-keeper, lists "10 Silver Hand Knives and 11 Forks with a Case 1.14.0" among the large quantity of silver.[3] From their low evaluation, it would seem they were probably knives and forks of this type, with steel blades and tines. The inventory of the furnishings of the Governor's Palace in Williamsburg taken after the death of Lord Botetourt, who served as governor of the colony from 1768 to 1770, included the following knives and forks among "Plate, in the Pantry:"

> 54 large Knives & 55 forks with 3 prongs
> 2 black Shagreen Cases containg each
> 1 Doz large Knives & 1 doz. forks & 1 doz large table Spoons.
> 1 Case containing 1 doz Knives & 1 doz Forks with China Handles.
> 1 small Shagrine Case contg 1 doz Desert Gilt Silver handled Knives; 1 doz Silver Forks & one doz Spoons
> 1 do contg 1 doz Silver handled desert Knives & Forks & 1 doz Spoons.
> 1 do contg eleven Silver handled desert Knives—[4]

1954-338, 1–10; 342, 1–10

1. John F. Hayward, *English Cutlery, Sixteenth to Eighteenth Century* (London: Victoria and Albert Museum, 1956), p. 11.
2. Colonial Williamsburg Foundation, Department of Archaeology, E.R. 247G. 28D and C.G.E.R. 460B.
3. York County, Wills and Inventories, no. 21 (1760–71), pp. 36–43 (microfilm copy, Department of Research, Colonial Williamsburg Foundation).
4. Botetourt Inventory.

198 KNIFE
Blade by How
About 1760

L: 10⅞″ (27.6 cm).

PROVENANCE: Garrard & Co. Ltd., London (purchased from C. J. Vander Ltd., London, 1954)

Pistol handles on knives and forks of the second half of the eighteenth century are usually more elaborate than their counterparts from earlier in the century. Their sides are often boldly ribbed and their voluted ends wrapped with scrolled leaves. The handle of this knife, like those of the previous set, is stamped in halves and soldered together.

George Washington received from London in 1757 "2 Setts best Silver handle Knives & Forks best London Blades 11-0-0." Of dinner and dessert size,

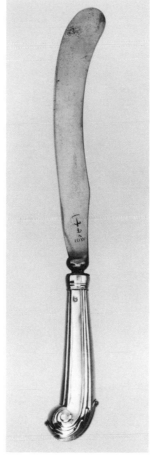

Maker's mark and lion passant on handle; cutler's mark and dagger mark of the London Cutlers' Company on blade.

198

with each set numbering twenty-four pieces each, they are fitted with handles identical to that of this example, and they bear the same unidentified maker's mark.[1]

1954-641

1. Buhler, pp. 13–15, fig. 2. These are part of Washington's earliest known purchase of silver. A cruet stand of 1757 by Jabez Daniel of London was also included in the order (ibid., pp. 12–14, fig. 1).

199 PAIR OF SAUCE LADLES
London. 1753/54

L: 7⅗₁₆″ (18.6 cm); Diam (bowl): 2⁵⁄₁₆″ (5.9 cm). Total wt: 7 oz. 12 dwt.

PROVENANCE: Garrard & Co. Ltd., London (purchased from C. J. Vander Ltd., London, 1954)

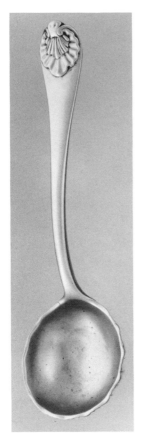

199

Fully marked on underside of each handle.

Owner's crest engraved
on underside of each
handle.

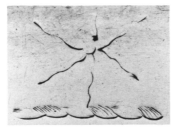

These ladles are unusual in construction, in that their handles and bowls are cast elements. Usually ladles of this type are, for the most part, wrought, with the shaping of the bowl being visible on either side, as in the following example. A pair of salt spoons (No. 203) from the 1770s have cast bowls of similar design with a scalloped rim and alternating swirled ribs and flutes on their undersides. During the middle

decades of the eighteenth century, one encounters an increased use of casting in the more individual and plastic rococo elements of ladle handles, as can be seen in the following two examples.

1954-581, 1–2

200 SOUP LADLE
William Cripps
London. 1760/61

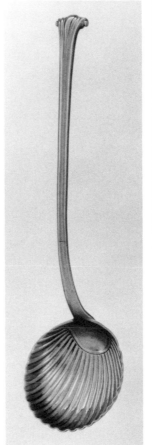

200

Fully marked on underside of handle.

L: 15⅟₁₆″ (38.3 cm); Diam (bowl): 4″ (10.2 cm).
Wt: 9 oz. 12 dwt.

PROVENANCE: Garrard & Co. Ltd., London (purchased from C. J. Vander Ltd., London, 1954)

Owner's crest engraved on underside of handle.

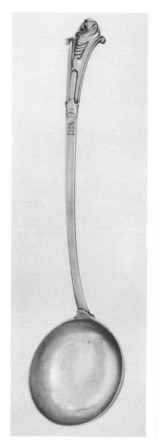

201

Fully marked on underside of handle.

Owner's crest engraved on face of handle.

This ladle is of Onslow type, characterized by a downturned handle terminating in a ribbed volute. Deriving its name from Arthur Onslow, who served as speaker of the House of Commons from 1728 to 1761, examples date mainly from the 1740s to the 1770s. Spoons and ladles are the most common articles in the Onslow pattern in both English and American silver. The ladles usually have fluted bowls.

Even though the Onslow pattern did not seriously challenge flatwares of "Hanoverian" type, which remained the standard pattern through the 1760s, it is important not only as an expression of rococo taste but also as the first English flatware pattern with a downturned handle, a feature that characterizes most of the immediately subsequent patterns.

The handle of the ladle is constructed in an interesting fashion. The upper two-thirds is hollow, having been cast in halves with the seam extending up the sides, through the volutes, and across the top. A vent hole, necessary for soldering the halves together, is immediately below the top on the underside. The lower third of the handle is solid and wrought. The construction appears contemporary, not a later modification.

1954-569

201 SOUP LADLE
John Swift
London. 1762/63

L: 14¼" (36.2 cm); Diam (bowl): 3¹¹⁄₁₆" (9.4 cm).
Wt: 7 oz. 4 dwt.

PROVENANCE: Garrard & Co. Ltd., London (purchased from C. J. Vander Ltd., London, 1951)

The distinctive handle of this ladle is basically of

Onslow form, embellished with shell and imbricated decoration. The decorated end of the handle from above the engraved crest and the projecting tip at the lower end are cast. The intervening plain section appears to be wrought.

1954-580

202 SAUCE LADLE
John Leslie
Aberdeen. About 1790

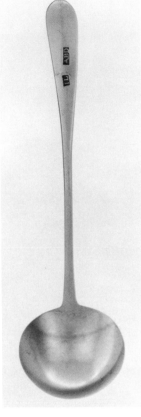

202

Maker's mark and town mark on underside of handle.

Owners' cypher engraved on face of handle.

L: 6⁵⁄₁₆″ (16 cm); Diam (bowl): 1⁵⁄₈″ (4.1 cm). Wt: 14 dwt. 9½ gr.

PROVENANCE: Henry P. Strause, Richmond, Virginia (sold by Thalhimer Brothers, Richmond, 1945)

From the early seventeenth century onward, most Aberdeen silver bears in addition to the maker's mark the town mark "AB" or "ABD" or three

castles. Sometimes, both town marks appear on a piece. This type of marking is characteristic of most Scottish provincial centers, where there were not formal guilds or assay offices but merely associations of hammermen.

1945-9

203 PAIR OF SALT SPOONS
Hester Bateman
London. About 1780

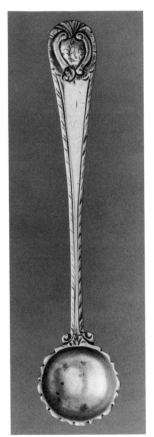

203

Maker's mark and lion passant on the underside of each handle.

Owner's crest engraved within cartouche on face of each handle.

L: 4³⁄₁₆″ (10.6 cm). Total wt: 16 dwt. 13 gr.

PROVENANCE: S. J. Shrubsole Corp., New York

The cartouche and the feather-edged borders of the wrought handles of this pair are chased. The shell bowls and the shoulders at the base of handles are cast. A similar pair of salt spoons by Hester Bateman is illustrated in David S. Shure, *Hester Bateman, Queen of English Silversmiths* (London: W. H. Allen, 1959), pl. XXXIX.

1971-148, 1–2

204 FISH SLICE OR TROWEL
William Plummer
London. 1762/63

L: 13⅜″ (34 cm); L (blade): 6⁹⁄₁₆″ (16.7 cm); W (blade): 4¾″ (12.1 cm). Wt (including handle): 5 oz. 16 dwt.

PROVENANCE: Garrard & Co. Ltd., London (purchased from S. G. Schwersee, Finchingfield, Essex, 1954)

Even though a fish slice or trowel of 1741/42 by Paul de Lamerie of London is in the Farrer collection in the Ashmolean Museum, Oxford,[1] the implement did not become fashionable until the 1760s. Most

Fully marked on underside of blade.

Owners' crests engraved on underside of blade.

examples from early in the reign of George III, such as this one, have a triangular blade pierced and engraved with foliated scrolls in the rococo taste, sometimes incorporating fish. They have a handle either of silver fashioned like those of contemporary spoons, sometimes with a cast openwork end, or of turned wood or ivory. The handles at this date are usually elevated above the blade by a curved shank

204

with a shell attachment to the rear of the blade.

They were referred to in the eighteenth century as "fish slices" and "fish trowels." A "Fish Slice" appears in the 1769 listing of the silver mortgaged by William Byrd III of Westover, Charles City County, Virginia.[2] Presumably, this is the same piece termed a "fish trowel" in the 1813 will of his widow, Mary Willing Byrd.[3] A London fish slice of 1767/68, engraved with the arms of the Tayloe family of Virginia, was exhibited in 1940 at the Virginia Museum of Fine Arts, Richmond.[4]

Trowels, probably distinguished from those for fish by their unpierced blades, were used for serving pudding. George Wickes of London supplied the earl of Kildare with "a Pudding Trowle" in 1745.[5] A pair of silver-gilt London trowels of 1751 with unpierced blades and turned wooden handles, quite similar in form to this example, is at Goldsmiths' Hall, London.[6] Engraved with the arms of the Goldsmiths' Company and the donor's inscription, they are probably the latter two mentioned in July 1751 in committee minutes of the company as "Four curious silver trowels presented by Mr. Warden Pugh, two for fish and two for pudding, engraved with the Company's Arms."[7]

1954-552

1. Jones (a), pp. 119, 121, fig. 256.
2. Westover Plate.
3. "The Will of Mrs. Mary Willing Byrd, of Westover, 1813, with a List of the Westover Portraits," *Virginia Magazine of History and Biography* 6 (April 1899):350.
4. Virginia Museum (a), p. 23, no. 127; Davis, E. M., p. 113.
5. Grimwade, p. 11.
6. Worshipful Company of Goldsmiths, *The Sterling Craft* (London, 1966), pp. 22–23, no. 55, ill.
7. John B. Carrington and George R. Hughes, *The Plate of The Worshipful Company of Goldsmiths* (Oxford: Oxford University Press, 1926), p. 115.

205 FISH SLICE
Hester Bateman
London. 1783/84

Fully marked on blade near handle; unidentified maker's mark and lion passant on handle.

Owner's cypher engraved on face of blade.

L: 12⅛" (30.8 cm). Wt: 5 oz. 3 dwt. 8 gr.

PROVENANCE: S. J. Shrubsole Corp., New York

Narrower blades, often fish-shaped, replaced those of triangular form about 1780. Knife handles, mainly beaded or reeded and usually joined to the end of the blade by a short bolster, replaced those of spoon type or of turned wood or ivory. As in this instance, handles were often made by specialist makers independently of the blades.

This handsomely pierced and engraved blade of unusual design is marked by Hester Bateman, the famous eighteenth-century woman silversmith. From 1761 to 1790, her firm produced a large and varied body of domestic wares. Generally quite standard in character, it lacks the interest of the work of some other woman silversmiths, notably Elizabeth Godfrey (see No. 105).

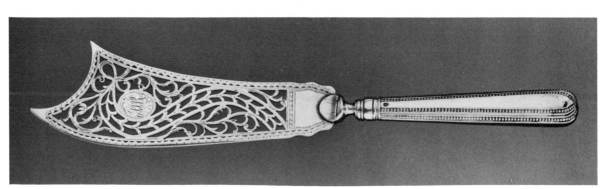

205

A similar fish slice of 1786/87 by Hester Bateman is illustrated in David S. Shure, *Hester Bateman, Queen of English Silversmiths* (London: W. H. Allen, 1959), pl. XXXVI.

1971-149

206 SKEWER
Samuel Herbert
London. 1758/59

Fully marked on face of blade.

L: 12¾″ (32.4 cm). Wt: 4 oz. 2 dwt.

PROVENANCE: Garrard & Co. Ltd., London (purchased from C. J. Vander Ltd., London, 1954)

1954-545

207 SKEWER
J. Hampston and J. Prince
York. About 1785

Maker's mark, leopard's head crowned, and lion passant on face of blade.

Owner's crest engraved on face of blade.

L. 9⅛″ (23.2 cm). Wt: 2 oz. 2 dwt. 5 gr.

PROVENANCE: Henry Philip Strause, Richmond, Virginia (sold by Thalhimer Brothers, Richmond, 1945)

1945-8

208 MARROW SPOON
London. About 1718

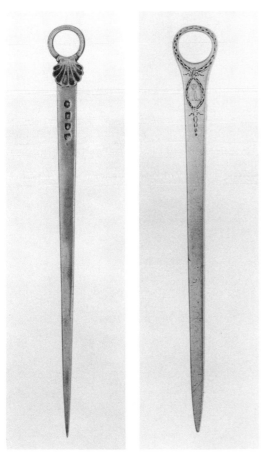

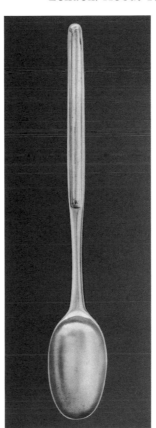

206   207   208

Fully marked on underside of handle (date letter indistinct).

Owner's initials and date engraved on underside of handle.

L: 6⅟₁₆″ (15.4 cm); W (bowl): ²⁹⁄₃₂″ (2.3 cm). Wt: 14 dwt. 22 gr.

PROVENANCE: Garrard & Co. Ltd., London

Marrow spoons with conventional spoon bowls and narrow channeled handles for the removal of marrow from bones first appear about 1690. Early examples, often included in traveling sets, are sometimes engraved and gilded. Late seventeenth-century examples are rarely fully marked. During the first two decades of the eighteenth century, they increase in number and are usually fully marked.

1971-396

209 MARROW SPOON
John Wirgman
London. 1740/50

Fully marked on underside of waist.

L: 8⅟₁₆″ (21.4 cm). Wt: 1 oz. 12 dwt.

PROVENANCE: Garrard & Co. Ltd., London (purchased from C. J. Vander Ltd., London, 1951)

Marrow spoons with both ends channeled and of uneven widths were produced in large numbers from the early years of the eighteenth century. They soon displaced the earlier form with a spoon bowl at one end, as in the previous example. Both varieties appear to have been called "marrow spoons" in the eighteenth century, the term "marrow scoop" not commonly used until the following century.[1]

A similar London example of 1707/08 is part of the Carter family silver at Shirley, Charles City

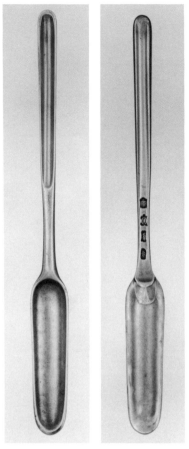

209

County, Virginia. A London example of 1799/1800 is also in the Colonial Williamsburg collection (G1965-88; Gift of Charles Terwilliger, Bronxville, New York).

1954-582

1. Hughes, pp. 199–200.

210 ASPARAGUS TONGS
London. About 1790

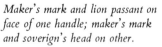   

Maker's mark and lion passant on face of one handle; maker's mark and soverign's head on other.

Owner's crest and coronet engraved on face of arm at end.

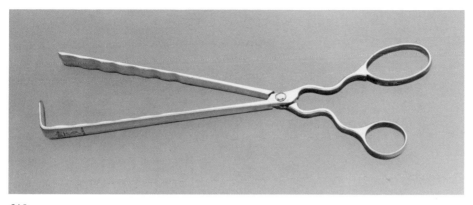

210

L: 9¹⁵⁄₁₆″ (25.2 cm). Wt: 5 oz.

PROVENANCE: Garrard & Co. Ltd., London (purchased from C. J. Vander Ltd., London, 1954)

1954-558

211 BOX

Pierre Harache, Sr.
London. About 1700

Maker's mark only on underside of base.

H: 2¹³⁄₁₆″ (7.2 cm); L: 5¹³⁄₁₆″ (14.8 cm); W: 4⅜″
(11.1 cm). Wt: 21 oz. 19 dwt. 6 gr. ("22ᵒⁿ4 p"
engraved on underside of base).

PROVENANCE: Sotheby & Co., London (1974)

PUBLISHED: Sotheby's (February 28, 1974), lot 122, ill.

Pierre Harache, Sr., from Rouen was the first of the
Huguenot silversmiths to gain admittance to the
Goldsmiths' Company, obtaining his freedom in
1682 by order of the lord mayor and court of alder-
men of London. The high calibre of his varied out-

put places him among the most important of the
first generation of these immigrant craftsmen.[1] This
exquisite box exhibits the exacting proportions and
precise control of contour that characterizes the best
of their work. It is fashioned from metal of extremely
heavy gauge, the gadrooned bands of the cover and
base being cast. The applied molding on the top of
the cover not only visually terminates the profiled
ascent of the cover's shoulder but also—through
forming a framed recess—lends added importance to
the fine armorial engraving. The fifteen-knuckle

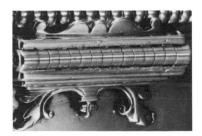

hinge and the scrolled leaves and central gadrooned
drop, which echo the cartouche and cast moldings,

194

Arms of Capell impaling Bennet engraved within a lozenge with a baron's coronet above and lion supporters on either side for Dorothy, Lady Capell (d. 1721) of Tewksbury, Gloucestershire.

indicate the piece's high level of technical and visual finish. The box's original weight is engraved on the base with unusual abbreviations as "22ᵒⁿ4 p," reminiscent of the inscribed weights of "13 on. 12 peni." and "14 on. 9 pe." on two of Harache's set of four candlesticks of 1683/84 at Althorp, Northamptonshire, the earliest recorded examples of his work,[2] and of "14-ON 9 PE" on his cup of 1686/87 at Bruton Parish Church, Williamsburg (see below).

The box, though it bears only Harache's mark, can be closely dated between 1697, when he entered this mark, and about 1700, when he is believed to have retired. The reason for its incomplete marking, short of deceit, appears to be either a continuation of the practice of not necessarily having silver made to private order hallmarked, technically legal between 1575 and 1697, or its possible separation from a toilet service, in which some of the larger pieces may have been fully marked.

Dorothy, Lady Capell, the original owner, was the widow of Henry Capell, who was created Baron Capell of Tewksbury in 1692 and served as lord deputy of Ireland from 1695 until his death in the following year. She was the daughter of Richard Bennet of Kew Green, Surry, and died in 1721. Her husband had acquired from Harache in 1692/93 a

large sideboard dish with the engraved scrolls of its cartouche in like manner upholding his baron's coronet and incorporating an architectural plinth on either side for a lion couchant.[3] The engraving on this dish (formerly in the collection of Rex Beaumont), like the related but more complex overall engraving on the dish (Lutton Hoo, Bedfordshire)[4] and comb box of 1695/96 by Harache, formerly part of the toilet service at Burghley House,[5] has been attributed to the Huguenot designer and engraver, Simon Gribelin. The engraving on another sideboard dish of 1700/1701 by Harache (formerly in the collection of the Earl Bathurst), with elements of the cartouche and plinth similar to those of the Burghley box, has also been ascribed to Gribelin.[6] The same format of cartouche with coronet, plinth, and supporters appears on a further sideboard dish and ewer by Harache with the arms of the duke of Devonshire (Wilding Bequest, British Museum)[7] and on a gold dish and ewer of 1701/02 by Pierre Platel of London, also bearing the arms of the duke of Devonshire and still retained at Chatsworth, Derbyshire.[8]

The gilt two-handled covered cup of 1686/87 by Harache, which was given to the College of William and Mary in Williamsburg in 1775 by Lady Gooch, whose husband served as governor of Virginia from 1727 to 1749 and whose son attended the college, is illustrated in the introduction. It is on permanent loan to Bruton Parish Church in Williamsburg.

1974-69

1. Judith Banister, "The First Huguenot Silversmith," *Country Life* 137 (June 10, 1965):1463–65.

2. Arthur G. Grimwade, "Silver at Althorp—II: The Candlesticks and Candelabra," *Connoisseur* 152 (March 1963):159.

3. Christie's (December 2, 1964), lot 21, ill.; Banister, "The First Huguenot Silversmith," p. 1465, fig. 5.

4. Hayward, p. 71, pl. 88.

5. Christie's (June 22, 1960), lot 135, pl. XII and frontispiece; Banister, "The First Huguenot Silversmith," p. 1463, fig. 2; Clayton, p. 35, fig. 54.

6. Christie's (April 28, 1965), lot 128, pl. 29 and frontispiece; Clayton, p. 120, fig. 253.

7. Clayton, p. 133, fig. 279; Hugh Tait, "Huguenot Silver Made in London (c. 1690–1723): The Peter Wilding Bequest to the British Museum. Part 1," *Connoisseur* 180 (August 1972):268–69, figs. 2–3.

8. E. Alfred Jones, *Old English Gold Plate* (London: Bemrose & Sons Limited, 1907), p. 10, plates XII and XIII; Jackson, 2:583–84, figs. 803 and 804; Hayward, p. 44, frontispiece; Clayton, p. 132, color pl. 29.

212 PAIR OF CHAMBER POTS
David Willaume, Jr.
London. 1743/44

H: 5″ (12.7 cm); L: 10⅜″ (26.4 cm); Diam (rim): 7⁹⁄₁₆″ (19.2 cm). Wt (no. 1): 33 oz. 19 dwt. 11 gr.

("34 = 6" engraved on underside); (no. 2): 33 oz. 19 dwt. 19½ gr. ("34 = 7" engraved on underside).

Fully marked on underside of each.

Cypher and coronet of George Booth (1675–1758), 2nd earl of Warrington, engraved on each body opposite handle.

PROVENANCE: Descended from George Booth (1675–1758), 2nd earl of Warrington, the original owner, to Catherine, Lady Grey and Sir John Foley Grey of Enville Hall, Stourbridge (sold at Christie, Manson & Woods, London, 1921; purchased by Crichton Bros., London); Christie, Manson & Woods, London, 1937 (purchased by Hyman, London); gift of Mr. and Mrs. Harry A.

212

Prock, Fort Washington, Pennsylvania

PUBLISHED: Christie's (April 20, 1921), lot 147; Christie's (June 22, 1937), lot 20.

Silver chamber pots are known to have been used in England from the reign of Elizabeth I. In fact, an early English reference appears in her Household Books for 1576–80 as "A round basin and Ewer wth a piss-pot of silv^r weigh^g 57 Oz. paid for the weight 5^s p^r Oz and 6^d an Oz. for the fashion."[1] Their use, at least in court circles, was sufficient for John Marston, the satiric poet, to write in 1598 in his *Scourge of Villanie:*

> When Hermus makes a worthy question,
> Whether of Wright, as Paraphonalion,
> A silver pispot fits his Lady dame?
> Or i'st too good? a pewter best became.[2]

The earliest extant English example is that of 1670/71 by Marmaduke Best of York, which was presented to the city of York for the use of the lord mayors and is still part of the corporate plate.[3] It differs little in form from this pair and other surviving ones. Even though they had become a standard article of domestic plate by the early eighteenth century and were often included in the issue of plate to ambassadors and other high government officials, most have been consigned to the melting pot.[4] No fewer than eleven silver chamber pots, however, were contained in the Grey sale of 1921, including this well-made and matched pair and one of 1714/15 by Isaac Liger of London, engraved with the arms of George Booth.[5] Lord Botetourt owned a silver chamber pot, listed with the "Plate, in the Pantry" of the Governor's Palace in Williamsburg in the 1770 inventory of his estate.[6]

G1965-169, 170

---

1. N. M. Penzer, "The Silver Chamber-pot; A Sidelight on English Social History. Part I," *Antique Collector* 29 (October 1958):176. Clayton (p. 59) dates this reference 1575.

2. Penzer, "The Silver Chamber-pot; Part I," p. 176.

3. Ibid., pp. 176–78, ill.; Oman (a), p. 51, pl. 58B.

4. Penzer, "The Silver Chamber-pot; Part II," *Antique Collector* 29 (December 1958):226–27.

5. Ibid., pp. 225, 227, fig. 1; Jonathan Stone, *English Silver of the Eighteenth Century* (London: Cory, Adams & MacKay Ltd., 1965), p. 57, pl. 12; Clayton, pp. 59–60, fig. 116.

6 Botetourt Inventory.

213 PINCUSHION
Unmarked
London. About 1675

Owner's cypher and coronet engraved on underside of frame.

213

H (excluding cushion): 2⁵⁄₁₆″ (5.9 cm); L: 8¼″ (21 cm); W: 6¹¹⁄₁₆″ (17 cm). Wt (excluding cushion): 13 oz. 18 dwt. 8 gr.

PROVENANCE: Thomas Lumley Ltd., London

Large pincushions of this type, either individual, as in this instance, or mounted in the covers of boxes, often were originally part of large toilet services. This example is of conventional form, being of rectangular plan with inclined, shaped sides and supported on short scrolled feet at the corners. Like much of the enriched plate of the late Commonwealth period and the reign of Charles II, it is high-chased with naturalistic decoration. Swirling acanthus leaves with flowers and playful cherubs was a popular baroque device. The probable design sources for this decoration are the engraved designs of Polifilo Zancarli of about 1625. Influential in France and Holland, they were issued in England in 1672 as *A Booke of Foldages designed by the famous Italian Polifilo Zancarli, Sould by John Overton at the White horse without Newgate*.[1] Related decoration appears in the cast borders with seated cherubs of the set of eight sconces (No. 2). The velvet cushion and backing, secured on the underside with four threaded studs and nuts, are replacements.

1972-461

1. Oman (a), p. 17, pl. 94. A similar ornamental border, engraved by Edward Pearce and also sold by John Overton, is illustrated in Hackenbroch, rev. edn. only, p. xxiii, fig. 9.

214 SPOUT CUP
John East
London. 1717/18

Fully marked on face of body below rim; maker's mark twice on bezel of cover.

Owner's initials engraved both on underside of cover flange and base of body.

H: 5½″ (14 cm); W: 6¾″ (16.2 cm); Diam (base): 2⅝″ (6.7 cm). Wt: 11 oz. 14 dwt. 18 gr.

214

PROVENANCE: Preston G. Saywell, Sydney, Australia (sold at Parke-Bernet Galleries, New York, 1969)

PUBLISHED: Parke-Bernet (February 25, 1969), lot 126, ill. p. 31

The purpose of slender spouts, not only on cups but also on tankards and mugs, is conjectural. They are believed to have assisted in the feeding of invalids, and may also have served to draw off in drinking or serving the liquid of beverages with thick floating matter, such as various possets. A spouted tankard of 1642/43 by Timothy Skottowe of Norwich in the Victoria and Albert Museum, London, may be the earliest surviving English vessel of the kind.[1]

1969-38

1. Oman (c), pl. 52; Clayton, pp. 284, 286, fig. 566.

215 PAP BOAT
Probably Richard Bigge
London. 1725/26

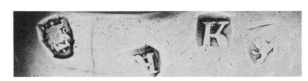

Fully marked on face of body opposite lip.

215

Owner's initials engraved on underside of body.

H: 1⅟₁₆″ (2.7 cm); L: 4¼″ (10.8 cm); W: 2½″ (6.4 cm): Wt: 2 oz.

PROVENANCE: Garrard & Co. Ltd., London (purchased from Walter H. Willson Ltd., London, 1954)

Pap boats of this conventional, plain form appeared in the first quarter of the eighteenth century. They were used in the feeding of and the administering of medicine to small children and undoubtedly to invalids on occasion. Like other small silver items, they appear in listings of imported articles in the advertisements in the *Virginia Gazette* of Williamsburg milliners, such as Catherine Rathell ("Silver Pap Boats" [October 10, 1771; October 22, 1772]) and Sarah Packe

Pitt ("silver pap boats" [October 15, 1772]). Examples of 1727/28, 1751/52, and 1775/76, all by unidentified London makers, are also in the collection (1954-340, 1954-531, 1945-13).

1954-530

216 PORRINGER
London. 1683/84

Fully marked on face of rim to right of handle; leopard's head crowned and lion passant on underside of handle.

Owners' inscriptions engraved on face of handle and on underside of body.

L: 7½″ (19.1 cm); Diam (rim): 5⅟₁₆″ (12.9 cm); Diam (body): 5¹¹⁄₁₆″ (14.5 cm). Wt: 6 oz. 4 dwt. 13 gr.

PROVENANCE: Spink & Son Ltd., London

PUBLISHED: Advertisement, Spink & Son Ltd., *Apollo* 77 (June 1963): vi, ill.

1963-127

216

217 NUTMEG GRATER
Probably Thomas Kedder
London. About 1690

Maker's mark only on underside of body and grater.
Owner's initial engraved on underside of body.

L: 2¾″ (7 cm); Diam (cover): ¹⁵⁄₁₆″ (2.4 cm); Diam (base): ⅞″ (2.2 cm); L (grater): 2⁵⁄₁₆″ (5.9 cm). Wt: 18 dwt. 5 gr.

PROVENANCE: Michael Noble (sold at Christie, Manson & Woods, London, 1967; purchased by Garrard & Co. Ltd., London)

PUBLISHED: Christie's (December 13, 1967), lot 14

This and the following nutmeg grater, like most late seventeenth- and early eighteenth-century examples, have cylindrical cases with pull-off covers containing tubular graters. Both are conventionally engraved with medial bands of stylized leaf decoration and their covers with tulips. The maker of this example, tentatively identified as Thomas Kedder by Mrs.

G. E. P. How, was a prolific maker of small wares, such as nutmeg graters, small boxes, penners, and strainers.[1]

1968-73

1. Mrs. G. E. P. How, "Old Silver—on a Shoe-string," *Antique Collector* 33 (December 1962):265.

218 NUTMEG GRATER
Alexander Hudson
London. 1708/09

Fully marked on face of body below cover; maker's mark and lion's head erased on underside of cover and on face of grater.

L: 2⅝″ (6.7 cm); Diam (cover): ¹⁵⁄₁₆″ (2.4 cm); Diam (base): ⅞″ (2.2 cm); L (grater): 2¼″ (5.7 cm). Wt: 15 dwt. 6 gr.

PROVENANCE: Garrard & Co. Ltd., London

1968-72

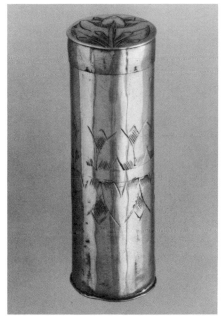

218

219 NUTMEG GRATER
Probably London. About 1750

219

Maker's mark only on interior of both covers.

H: 1⅛″ (2.9 cm); L: 1¾″ (4.4 cm); W: 1⅜″ (3.5 cm). Wt: 1 oz. 6 dwt. 3 gr.

PROVENANCE: The Quarters, Fredericksburg, Virginia

Among the most persistent patterns of nutmeg

graters during the late seventeenth century and throughout the eighteenth century are those of heart and related tear-drop forms.

1939-179

220 NUTMEG GRATER AND
CORKSCREW
Probably London. About 1770

Maker's mark only on underside of cover and case for corkscrew.

L: 3¼″ (8.3 cm). Wt: 18 dwt.

PROVENANCE: Henry Hardcastle, York, England

The unidentified maker of this piece produced a considerable number of graters of acorn form, both with and without a steel corkscrew; all of them bear only his maker's mark. Their resemblance to a ceremonial mace has been considered a possible visual pun on the spice—also called mace—that is rendered from the dried outer covering of the nutmeg.[1] A barrel-shaped grater by this maker at the Virginia Historical Society, Richmond, is believed to have been originally owned by John Robinson (1704-1766) of

220

Mount Pleasant, King and Queen County, Virginia, who served as speaker of the House of Burgesses and treasurer of the colony from 1738 until his death in 1766.

1947-182

───────

1. Hughes, p. 61, fig. 86; Elizabeth B. Miles, *The English Silver Pocket Nutmeg Grater; A Collection of Fifty Examples from 1693 to 1816* (Cleveland: C. W. Printing Service, 1966), pp. 31–35, ill.; Delieb, p. 118, ill.

PROVENANCE: Thomas Lumley Ltd., London

Silver nutcrackers, probably owing to the softness of the metal, are extremely rare.[1] This pair has silver handles only; the blades and hinge are of steel. The blades are burred on either side and are set off-center on the hinge, so that by reversing them the space between can be changed to accommodate a large or a small nut.

1972-460

───────

1. Among the other recorded silver nutcrackers are two, formerly on loan to the Victoria and Albert Museum, London, in W. W. Watts, "A Collection of Silver Spoons and Forks," *Apollo* 13 (May 1936):264–66, figs. I and IIf. Two London examples of 1784/85 by an unidentified maker "WC," both very similar to one of the preceding two, are illustrated in G. E. P. How, "Honest Opinion," *Notes on Antique Silver*, no. 3 (Summer 1943):22.

221 NUTCRACKER
Unmarked
Probably London. About 1770

L: 5 11/16″ (14.5 cm). Wt: 3 oz. 1 dwt.

221

222 INKSTAND
Robert Innes
London. 1745/46

Fully marked on underside of tray, ink pot, and pounce pot and on face of body of bell; covers of ink and pounce pots unmarked.

H: 5″ (12.7 cm); H (rim): 1⅝″ (4.2 cm); L: 10¹⁷⁄₃₂″ (26.8 cm); W: 7⅝″ (19.4 cm); H (bell): 3¹⁵⁄₁₆″ (10 cm); Diam (base): 2¹⁄₁₆″ (5.2 cm); H (ink and pounce pots): 2¼″ (5.7 cm); Diam (covers and bases): 1¾″ (4.4 cm). Wt: 34 oz. 9 dwt. 16 gr.

PROVENANCE: Garrard & Co. Ltd., London (purchased from E. T. Biggs & Sons, Maidenhead, Berkshire, 1954)

PUBLISHED: G. Bernard Hughes, "Silver Table Bells," *Country Life* 120 (December 13, 1956):1449, fig. 2

Eighteenth-century inkstands, such as the three in the Colonial Williamsburg collection, often have a salver-like tray with a cast and applied rim on its short sides and short, cast, corner feet. The tray is usually fitted with ink and pounce pots, sometimes flanking a central bell or taperstick. Occasionally, a wafer box is included, or the wafers can be housed in the hemi-spherical wells usually beneath the various components.

The 1770 inventory of the estate of Lord Botetourt lists "1 [silver] writing stand Bell & 2 Casters" with the "Plate, in the Pantry" of the Governor's Palace in Williamsburg.[1]

1954-571

---

1. Botetourt Inventory.

223 INKSTAND
Paul de Lamerie
London. 1749/50

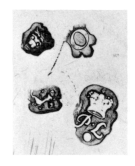

Fully marked on underside of tray, ink pot, and pounce pot.

Arms of Allen of Fornham, Suffolk, and of Bampton, Devonshire, impaling those of Holder of Wheatley, Nottinghamshire, engraved on face of tray.

223

H: 2¹¹⁄₁₆″ (6.8 cm); H (rim of tray): 1⅛″ (2.9 cm); L: 9⁷⁄₁₆″ (18.9 cm); W: 6¹¹⁄₁₆″ (17 cm); H (ink and pounce pots): 1⅞″ (4.8 cm); Diam (rim and base of ink and pounce pots): 1⅝″ (4.1 cm). Wt: 22 oz. 11 dwt. 22 gr. ("23·2" engraved on underside of tray).

PROVENANCE: Sotheby & Co., London (1960)

PUBLISHED: Sotheby's (March 24, 1960), lot 5, ill.; R. P. T. Came, "A Notable Collection of English Silver," *Apollo* 71 (March 1960):75–76, fig. 1; ———, "Sotheby's Silver Sale: A Comparison of Some of the Prices Realized," *Apollo* 71 (May 1960):141; "Accessions of American and Canadian Museums, January–March 1963," *Art Quarterly* 26 (Summer 1963):267

Two related inkstands by de Lamerie, both having shaped oval trays with cast and applied rococo rims, similar cast and applied decoration on their ink and pounce pots, and lion paw feet are recorded. One of 1734/35 has the addition of a central bell and two pen troughs.[1] The other of 1741/42 has a central taperholder.[2] De Lamerie had earlier utilized oval dishes of very similar design to the tray of this inkstand in his centerpiece of 1734/35, formerly in the Bobrinsky Collection, Moscow.[3] De Lamerie's most important and elaborate inkstand, that of 1741 made for and still owned by the Goldsmiths' Company,

London, incorporates a bell given to the company by Sir Robert Vyner in 1667.[4]

1960-181

---

1. "In the Auction Rooms," *Connoisseur* 129 (June 1952):131, ill.; advertisement, Thomas Lumley Ltd., London, *Connoisseur*, Antique Dealers' Fair and Exhibition Number (June 1958):xix, ill.
2. Phillips, p. 106, pl. CXXXVI.
3. Ibid., p. 97, plates XCV–XCVI.
4. Ibid., pp. 105–106, pl. CXXXIII; John B. Carrington and George R. Hughes, *The Plate of The Worshipful Company of Goldsmiths* (Oxford: Oxford University Press, 1926), pp. 16–17; Clayton, pp. 94–95, fig. 30.

224 INKSTAND
Edward Wakelin
London. 1753/54

Fully marked on underside of tray, ink pot, and pounce pot.

H: 2⅞″ (7.3 cm); H (rim of tray): 1⅛″ (2.9 cm); L: 7¹⁷⁄₃₂″ (19.9 cm); W: 5⅞″ (14.9 cm); H (ink and pounce pots): 2³⁄₁₆″ (5.6 cm); Diam (rims

224

and bases): 1¾" (4.4 cm). Wt: 18 oz. 10 dwt. 6 gr. ("19:12" engraved on underside of tray).

PROVENANCE: Crichton Bros., London

1936-451

225 BELL
Probably William Garrard
London. 1770/71

225

Fully marked on face of body.

H: 4¹³⁄₁₆" (12.2 cm); Diam (base): 2¹¹⁄₁₆" (6.8 cm). Wt: 5 oz. 10 dwt. 19 gr.

PROVENANCE: Viscountess Harcourt (d. 1959), Stanton Harcourt, Oxfordshire (sold by executors of her estate at Christie, Manson & Woods, London, 1961)

PUBLISHED: Christie's (November 29, 1961), lot 123, pl. xx

Small bells of this type, often placed centrally on an inkstand, were used domestically to summon servants (No. 222). Clayton cites early surviving examples of 1636/37 (Royal College of Physicians), 1637/38 (duke of Portland), about 1648 (Plaisterers' Company), and 1666/67 (Goldsmiths' Company).[1]

1961-299

1. Clayton, p. 25.

226 MAGNIFYING GLASS
Henry Haynes
London. 1771/72

L: 14½" (36.8 cm); Diam: 8¼" (21 cm). Wt (including glass): 58 oz. 14 dwt. 6 gr.

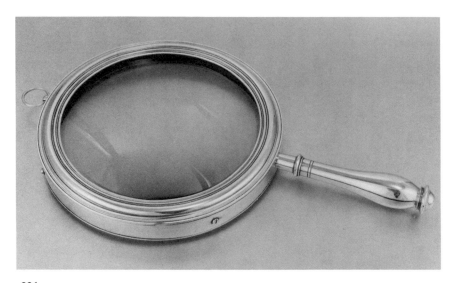

226

Fully marked on rim.

PROVENANCE: Percival D. Griffiths, Sandridgebury, St. Alban's, Hertfordshire (sold by executors of his estate at Christie, Manson & Woods, London, 1939; purchased by Webster, London); Arpad Antiques, Inc., Washington, D.C.

PUBLISHED: Christie's (May 15, 1939), lot 113

1967-692

227 POMANDER
Unmarked
England or Germany. About 1620

H: 2⅞16″ (9.4 cm). Wt: 1 oz. 15 dwt. 23 gr.

PROVENANCE: Anonymous gift

PUBLISHED: Williamsburg (a), p. 8, ill.

Pomanders, small boxes with compartments for housing aromatic substances, were worn or carried on one's person for supposed hygenic or obvious ol-

227

factory reasons.[1] The most common type of pomander is of spherical or vase form, composed of wedge-shaped sections clustered around a central post, each section individually hinged at the bottom above the foot and held in place by a screw-adjustable cap at the top, usually fitted with an eyelet or ring. The sections are filled and their scents released through slots on the interior edges, either open or fitted with sliding or hinged panels. An extremely early Rhenish spherical pomander of about 1470 is in the Bayerisches Nationalmuseum, Munich.[2] Most pomanders being unmarked, it is difficult to establish their origin even if, as are this example and others of its group, they are engraved with portraits of English monarchs.[3] By the middle of the seventeenth century, the pomander had declined in use, its function revived in the last quarter of the following century by the vinaigrette (No. 236).

G1971-2098

1. W. Turner, "Pomanders," *Connoisseur* 32 (March 1912): 151–56.

2. Erich Steingraber, *Antique Jewellery: Its History in Europe from 800 to 1900* (London: Thames and Hudson, 1957), p. 81, fig. 126.

3. Other royal pomanders are illustrated in Turner, "Pomanders," p. 151, nos. I and II; Edward Wenham, "Pomanders," *Connoisseur* 93 (August 1934):230, no. IX; Eric Delieb, *Silver Boxes* (London: Herbert Jenkins, 1968), pp. 48–49; Clayton, p. 205, fig. 410.

228

228 SNUFF BOX
London. About 1690

Maker's mark only on interior of base.

H: 11/16″ (1.8 cm); L: 1¾″ (4.5 cm); W: 1⁵⁄₁₆″ (3.3 cm). Wt: 12 dwt. 12 gr.

PROVENANCE: Anonymous gift

PUBLISHED: Williamsburg (a), p. 8, ill.

This is one of a considerable group of small oval boxes of late seventeenth-century date, their covers engraved with romantic cherubs, often in a landscape setting, and appropriate mottoes in French, as in this instance, Latin, or English. The sides of most boxes in this group are engraved with stylized leaf bandings and their undersides with overall scrolled foliate decoration. They are opened by pressing between thumb and forefinger the bosses, usually engraved with rosettes, on either end.[1]

G1971-2090

1. Boxes of this type are illustrated and discussed in Eric Delieb, *Silver Boxes* (London: Herbert Jenkins, 1968), pp. 13–14.

229 TOBACCO BOX
Edward Cornock
London. 1718/19

H: ⅞″ (2.2 cm); L: 3⅞″ (9.8 cm); W: 3″ (7.6 cm). Wt: 3 oz. 11 dwt. 23 gr.

PROVENANCE: J. Kryle Fletcher, Newport, Monmouthshire (1932); Christie, Manson & Woods, London (1934; purchased by the Goldsmiths & Silversmiths Co. Ltd., London); Firestone and Parson, Boston

229

PUBLISHED: Christie, Manson & Woods, *British Antique Dealers Association Art Treasures* (London, 1932), no. 575; Christie's (June 6, 1934), lot 72; Christie's (November 21, 1934), lot 128; "Accessions of American and Canadian Museums, April–June, 1964," *Art Quarterly* 27 (Autumn 1964):375

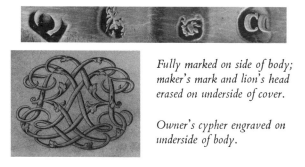

Fully marked on side of body; maker's mark and lion's head erased on underside of cover.

Owner's cypher engraved on underside of body.

elaborately engraved with coats of arms, cyphers, and inscriptions relating to ownership. This example is particularly notable for its handsome representational engraving. The seated gentleman with pipe and wineglass was taken directly from the illustrated detail reproduced here from *Essais de Gravûre Par Pierre Bourdon Maître Graveur à Paris. Ou l'on voit de beaux Contours d'ornements traités dans le goût de l'Art, propre aux Horologeurs, Orfévres, Cizeleurs, Graveurs et à toutes autres persones curieuses* (Paris, 1703), vol. 1, pl. 2.[2] The profusion of scrolls issuing

Even though tobacco has been smoked in England from the latter part of the sixteenth century, few silver tobacco boxes from before 1660 survive.[1] Most seventeenth- and early eighteenth-century examples are of relatively large size and oval plan, having either hinged or pull-off covers. Being a highly personal accessory, they are often finely and

from the pipe and enclosing the figure are an amplification of those in Bourdon and are related to the overall scrollwork shown by him in the designs of back-plates for watches. Edward Cornock, who registered his first mark with the Goldsmiths' Company in 1707, was a prolific maker of tobacco boxes.

An oval London tobacco box of 1677/78, originally belonging to Benjamin Harrison (1645–1712) of Surry County, Virginia, was exhibited in 1940 at the Virginia Museum of Fine Arts, Richmond.[3]

1964-1

1. The earliest cited example is privately owned, with the reputed date of 1643 (Delieb, p. 87). A London tobacco box of 1652/53 by an unidentified maker is illustrated in Royal Northern Hospital, no. 535, pl. IX. One by Gilbert Shepherd of London bears only Shepherd's mark but is engraved with the date July 23, 1655 (Christie's (June 26, 1974], lot 123, ill.). Another of 1655/56 by an unidentified London maker "IS" is illustrated in Jackson, 2:907–8, fig. 1187.
2. Courtesy of Marlborough Rare Books Ltd., London.
3. Virginia Museum (a), p. 18, no. 67; Davis, E. M., p. 111.

230 SNUFF OR TOBACCO BOX
Gilt-lined
Unmarked
Probably London. About 1720

230

H: ⅝″ (1.6 cm); L: 3¼″ (8.3 cm); W: 2½″ (6.4 cm). Wt: 3 oz. 10 dwt. 23 gr.

PROVENANCE: Spink & Son Ltd., London

PUBLISHED: Advertisement, Spink & Son Ltd., *The Grosvenor House Antiques Fair* (London, 1971), p. 98, fig. 3

This example is representative of a considerable

group of early eighteenth-century oval boxes of shallow depth with externally hinged covers, inset with tortoise-shell plaques inlaid with silver and usually mother-of-pearl.[1] The decorative technique is known as *piqué*. The classical scene depicted on the cover is that of Diana turning Actaeon into a stag.

1971-240

1. Boxes of related form and decoration are illustrated in H. C. Dent, "Piqué. Part IV.—Second English Period, Eighteenth Century," *Connoisseur* 58 (September 1920):30, 33, plates II and III.

231 TOBACCO BOX
Gilt-lined
Edward Cornock
London. 1723/24

231

Fully marked on side of body; lion passant on underside of cover.

H: ⅞″ (2.2 cm); L: 4 1/16″ (10.3 cm); W: 3 3/16″ (8.1 cm). Wt: 4. oz. 13 dwt. 12 gr.

PROVENANCE: Gift of Her Majesty Queen Elizabeth the Queen Mother

G1954-677

232 SNUFF BOX
Silver-gilt
London. 1750/51

232

Fully marked on interior of base.

H: 1″ (2.5 cm); L: 2¹³⁄₁₆″ (7.1 cm); W: 2⅛″ (5.4 cm). Wt. 1 oz. 18 dwt.

PROVENANCE: Garrard & Co. Ltd., London

1954-584

233 TOBACCO BOX
London. 1754/55

Leopard's head crowned, lion passant, and date letter on interior of base; maker's mark and lion passant on underside of cover.

H: 1³⁄₁₆″ (3 cm); L: 4⁵⁄₁₆″ (11 cm); W: 2⅝″ (6.7 cm). Wt: 1 oz. 10 dwt.

PROVENANCE: Garrard & Co. Ltd., London (purchased from Sotheby & Co., London, 1954)

PUBLISHED: Sotheby's (July 29, 1954), lot 170

The engraved arms, crest, and motto on the cover were apparently used without entitlement.

1954-583

233

234 SNUFF OR TOBACCO BOX
Unmarked
Probably Scotland. About 1800

234

H: 1⁵⁄₁₆″ (3.4 cm); L: 2¾″ (7 cm); W: 2¼″ (5.7 cm).

Arms of Milne impaling Duncan with motto of Milne above engraved on face of cover.

PROVENANCE: S. J. Shrubsole Ltd., London (purchased at Sotheby & Co., London, 1973)

PUBLISHED: Sotheby's (October 25, 1973), lot 19, ill.

This box is a modest expression of the long-standing tradition of mounting in silver exotic materials, both natural and man-made. Shells, especially cowries, owing to their shape and boldly figured porcelaneous surfaces, were especially popular for small boxes from the late seventeenth century onward. A white form of tiger cowrie (*Cypraea pardalis* Shaw) is the body of this example. The cover is handsomely engraved. The decorative eagle has no apparent heraldic significance.

1973-417

235 SCENT BOTTLE CASE
Samuel Pemberton
Birmingham. 1796/97

235

Maker's mark, lion passant, and sovereign's head on exterior of cover; maker's mark, anchor, and date letter on underside of base.

Owner's cypher engraved on exterior of cover.

H: 1⅝″ (4.1 cm); L: 1¹⁄₁₆″ (2.7 cm); W: ¹¹⁄₁₆″ (1.8 cm); H (bottle): 1½″ (3.8 cm). Wt (excluding bottle): 12 dwt. 5 gr.

PROVENANCE: Anonymous gift

PUBLISHED: Williamsburg (a), p. 8, ill.

G1971-2091

236 VINAIGRETTE
Gilt-lined
Samuel Pemberton
Birmingham. 1806/07

236

Fully marked both on interior of cover and base.

H: ¹¹⁄₃₂″ (.9 cm); L: 1⁷⁄₁₆″ (3.7 cm); W: 1¹⁄₁₆″ (2.7 cm). Wt: 5 dwt. 13 gr.

PROVENANCE: Anonymous gift

Vinaigrettes—small boxes of varied form containing a sponge soaked with aromatic vinegar behind an interior grille—revived the function of the earlier pomander (No. 228). They were produced in large numbers during the late eighteenth and nineteenth centuries mainly in Birmingham, the center of the English "toy" trade, and to a lesser extent in London. During the early part of this period, Samuel Pemberton was one of the most prolific makers of vinaigrettes and related small wares, such as the preceding scent bottle case. Also in the collection are a patch box of 1798/99 (G1971-2092) and a vinaigrette of 1801/02 (G1971-2096), both by Pemberton, as well as vinaigrettes of 1801/02 by "I&W" of Birmingham (G1971-2094), of 1804/05 by "TH" of London (G1971-2095), and of 1806/07 by Joseph Willmore of Birmingham, another specialist maker (G1971-2097).

G1971-2093

237 BODKIN
Unmarked
Probably London. About 1680

Pounced owner's initials on lower part of blade.

237

L: 5¹³⁄₁₆″ (13.6 cm). Wt: 7 dwt. 12 gr.

PROVENANCE: Anonymous gift

PUBLISHED: Sandra C. Shaffer, "Sewing Tools in the Collection of Colonial Williamsburg," *Antiques* 104 (August 1973):234, ill.

Bodkins were used in lacing garments and in other situations involving the threading of cord, tape, and ribbon. This example is of representative seventeenth-century size and form with conventional decorative engraving. The small ear spoon at the upper end may have served to gather earwax for treating thread before it was tightly spun.

G1971-3413, 9

238 CORAL AND BELLS
Richard May and Jane Dorrell
London. About 1775

238

Maker's mark only on underside of mouthpiece.

L: 6⅝″ (16.8 cm). Wt (including coral): 2 oz. 1 dwt.

PROVENANCE: Good & Hutchinson, Tolland, Massachusetts

Silver whistles fitted with bells and a coral for teething were a relatively common child's accessory from the seventeenth through the nineteenth centuries.[1] The 1706 will of Joseph White of Bruton Parish, York County, Virginia, mentions "One Silver Whissell Corrall & Bells.[2] James Geddy, the Williamsburg silversmith, offered for sale imported "Corals and Bells" in the *Virginia Gazette* for June 4, 1772. They also appear in the listings of imported accessory items in the advertisements of Williamsburg milliners, such as Catherine Rathell ("Silver mounted chased and plain Corals and Bells" [May 14, 1772] and "chased and plain Corals and Bells" [October 22, 1772]), Sarah Packe Pitte ("silver . . . coral and bells" [October 15, 1772]), and Mary Dickinson ("silver corals and bells" [May 12, 1774]). Mrs. John Norton, wife of the owner of the London mercantile firm, John Norton & Sons, wrote in 1775 to her son in Yorktown, the firm's resident representative in Virginia, inquiring after her granddaughter, "Pray let me know if a Corral & Bells would be acceptable as I would send one by the next opportunity."[3]

1970-122

1. Bernice Ball, "Whistles with Coral and Bells," *Antiques* 80 (December 1961):552–55.
2. York County, Orders and Wills, no. 14 (1709–16), p. 76 (microfilm copy, Department of Research, Colonial Williamsburg Foundation).
3. Frances Norton Mason, ed., *John Norton & Sons, Merchants of London and Virginia; Being the Papers from their Counting House for the Years 1750 to 1795* (Richmond: Dietz Press, 1937), p. 373.

239 PAIR OF SPURS
Benjamin Cartwright
London. 1772/73

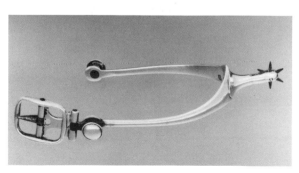

239

Fully marked inside heel of each.

L: 5″ (12.7 cm). Total wt: 3 oz. 5 dwt. 21 gr.

PROVENANCE: Berry-Hill Galleries, New York

James Geddy, the Williamsburg silversmith, advertised for sale in the *Virginia Gazette* "Spurs" (March 5, 1767); "plated spurs" (October 27, 1768); "fashionable plated spurs" (October 4, 1770); "Loop, studded, and Chain Spurs" (June 4, 1772); "Chain, Loop, and Stud plated Spurs" (July 21, 1773); and "plated Spurs" (November 11, 1773). Geddy specified that they were imported, except in the first instance, when they were included with other articles usually imported. The plated spurs were most likely close-plated on steel. All the spurs he advertised were probably of this conventional type, with slender sides, arched necks, and small rowels.

1953-557, 1–2

240 PAIR OF SPURS
Unmarked
Probably Walsall, Staffordshire
About 1830

240

Silver, with blued-steel rowels, brass rowel pins, and original leather straps and cradles with silver fittings.

L (excluding leathers): 7⅞″ (20 cm). Total wt (including leathers): 22 oz. 10 dwt. 12 gr.

PROVENANCE: Gift of Mr. and Mrs. Samuel Schwartz, Paterson, New Jersey

These massive spurs with extremely large rowels, though not of English design, appear to have been made in Walsall, Staffordshire.[1] That town has specialized for centuries in the production of harness hardware and related objects, such as spurs, both for domestic and foreign markets. There are a number of trade spurs, of a type associated with the Americas, having similar necks and terminals (the ends of the sides) in the E. M. Flint Art Gallery, Walsall. A silver spur of similar design, excavated near Silver Bluff, Georgia, about 1858, is in the Citadel Archives-Museum, Charleston.[2] A further silver spur of nineteenth-century date, like these and with similar leather straps and cradle, has a cast English inscription incorporating an apocryphal 1574 (Tower of London Armouries [VI-252]). The purpose of the ink inscription "King Geo" on the leather cradle of one of the Williamsburg pair has not been determined.

G1970-66, 1–2

_____

1. Information relating to the origin of these spurs and related examples provided by Mrs. Blanche M. A. Ellis of the Tower of London Armouries.
2. Illustrated in the *Savannah Morning News* (April 19, 1964).

241 TWELVE COCKSPURS, WITH CASE
Trade card of Samuel Toulmin
London. About 1770

Maker's mark on each, near
eyelet ("TS" on eleven and
"IM" on one); trade card of Samuel Toulmin mounted on interior of cover (ink inscription "Leon: Spenceley/May 1774.").

L (spurs; excluding leathers): 2″ (5.1 cm); H (case): 1¾″ (4.4 cm); L: 4″ (10.1 cm); D: 4″ (10.1 cm).

PROVENANCE: Gift of Mr. and Mrs. Andrew Oliver, Boston (purchased from Rupert Gentle, Milton Lilbourne, Near Pewsey, Wiltshire, 1973)

The sporting tastes of colonial Virginians placed cockfighting immediately after hunting and horse racing. Hugh Jones commented, in his *Present State*

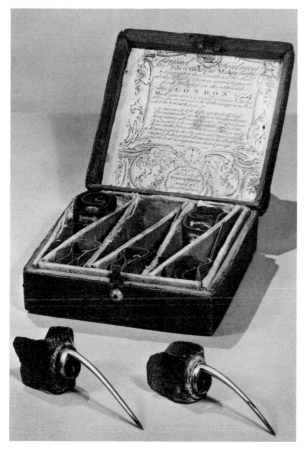

241

Mahogany case covered with black shagreen; interior divided with cardboard lined with carnation silk satin.

of *Virginia* (London, 1724): "The common planters leading easy lives don't much admire labour, or any manly exercise, except horse-racing, nor diversion, except cock-fighting, in which some greatly delight." After mid-century the *Virginia Gazette* carried accounts of cockfights between various Virginia county teams.[1] John Greenhow, the Williamsburg merchant, advertised for sale on several occasions "cock gaffs" or spurs, unspecified as to material.[2]

The case bears the trade card of Samuel Toulmin, who specialized in the production of cockspurs and also made watches and clocks. He succeeded, as the

trade card indicates, Richard Gatesfield, who in turn succeeded a Mr. Smith. The trade card is signed at the bottom "Brooke fecit Foster Lane." The incuse small-plate worker's mark "TS" on eleven of the spurs is unidentified. The "IM" mark on the twelfth may be that of John Moore of London, whose trade card illustrates two cockspurs within the cartouche and includes the note: "My Silver Spurs and Cock Spurs are marked with the two first letters of my Name, and all my Steel Spurs with my Sir Name at length."[3] Two of the spurs have attached paper labels with ink inscriptions: (1) front, "Newcastle upon Tyne/21st Jun 1795/R.D."; back, "Return/ The Duke of Hamilton/Capt O'callaghan"; (2) front, "Newcastle upon Tyne/1st May 1802/R.D. [illeg.]"; back, "This was a Subscription/main of 12 gr. Each."

G1973-64

---

1. For a discussion of cockfighting in Virginia see Jane Carson, *Colonial Virginians at Play* (Williamsburg: Colonial Williamsburg, 1965), pp. 151-64.

2. *Virginia Gazette* (April 11, 1766; June 4, 1767; September 28, 1769; April 11, 1771; December 12, 1771).

3. Sir Ambrose Heal, *The London Goldsmiths, 1200–1800* (Cambridge: University Press, 1935), pl. XLVIII.

Fused Silverplate

242 SNUFF BOX

Fused silverplate with silver-inlaid
tortoise-shell cover and tortoise-shell base
Unmarked
Sheffield or Birmingham. About 1755

242

H: 1″ (2.5 cm); Diam: 2⅛″ (5.4 cm).

PROVENANCE: Gift of Rockwell Gardiner, Stamford, Connecticut

The pieces in this section are of fused silverplate, commonly known as "Sheffield plate." The discovery about 1743 that a layer of silver could be fused to copper, and modest objects fashioned from the resulting plated sheet, is attributed to Thomas Boulsover or Bolsover, a Sheffield cutler. Basically, his process consisted of placing a sheet of silver on one side (after about 1765 on both sides) of a copper ingot; "bedding" the components under an iron weight and the blows of a sledge hammer to expel any air from between the layers; wiring them together with chalked outer sheets of copper for protection from the fire; and heating them until the silver began to melt. The silver-faced ingot was then reduced to workable sheet by passing it repeatedly through a rolling mill with the proportionate thickness of silver to copper maintained during reduction. The sheet could then be worked like silver.[1] This differed from the previous methods of silvering and from the subsequent process of electroplating, in both of which a silver coating is applied after the object has been fabricated in the carcass metal.

The industry grew rapidly, and by 1770 a broad range of domestic forms, successfully emulating in design their conterparts in sterling, were being commercially produced.[2] Labor-saving techniques and industrial organization, as well as an enlarged and self-conscious middle class, to whom both cost and appearance were important considerations, prompted this growth.

Small circular boxes with pull-off covers, such as this and the following example, are among the first articles produced in fused silverplate. The cover and base of this box are of tortoiseshell, the former inlaid with silver in a scene from Aesop's fable of the fox and the crane. Both boxes are of conventional construction. Their covers and bases are held by the overlapped edges of their swaged and seamed sides. Both covers and bases are backed with plain copper discs. Plated on only one side, their interiors are tinned.

Boxes of this early type were also made in Birmingham, which was not only the center in England of the toy trade (small personal accessories, such as boxes, buttons, and buckles) but also the other main center for the production of fused silverplate. Charleston has questioned the origin of plated boxes, especially those with enameled covers, in one of a series of papers on early Birmingham enameled wares.[3] He illustrates three circular plated boxes of probable Birmingham origin with enameled covers and bases die-stamped with rococo scrollwork, not dissimilar to that on the following example.[4] He also mentions the use of aventurine glass in the covers of such boxes, which he feels had a Birmingham source.[5] This contention is strengthened by the jux-

216

taposition in Bradbury of a gilt-copper rectangular box, more characteristic of the work of Birmingham than of Sheffield, with a die-stamped base design identical to that on a circular box with an aventurine glass and plated cover on the opposite page.[6] Charleston illustrates a plated box of similar form to this example, with a tortoiseshell cover inlaid with the same fable scene.[7] Even though certain inlaid details and the borders differ, the common inlaid elements are so similar as to indicate a common shop for the two boxes. Charleston cites references to a "Spun plater" in Birmingham in 1750, to a "buckle plater" and another "plater" in 1752, and to David Winwood, "Plater," in 1756.[8] It is not known whether Matthew Boulton, the great Birmingham industrialist and the largest single manufacturer of fused silverplate in England during the late eighteenth and early nineteenth centuries, made plated wares before the beginning of his partnership with John Fothergill in 1762.

Articles of fused silverplate were owned and sold in Virginia before the Revolution. Robert Beverley of Blanfield, Essex County, ordered in 1763 from John Bland, a London merchant, "a small sauce Pan lined with Silver such as I have seen you have from Sheffield to melt Butter in."[9] This would appear to be a reference to the early type of Sheffield saucepan with only the interior plated, such as the example marked by Joseph Hancock in the Bradbury collection.[10] Balfour & Barraud, Norfolk merchants, advertised for sale in the *Virginia Gazette* of July 25, 1766,"double plated [plated on both sides] silver tankards, cups, coffee pots, candlesticks, waiters, salts, knives and forks." Lord Botetourt owned "1 Sheffield ware tea Kitchen," listed with the "Plate, in the Pantry" of the Governor's Palace in Williamsburg in the 1770 inventory of his estate.[11] Catherine Rathell, a Williamsburg milliner, ordered in 1771 and received the following year "18 pair of Plaited Carved Shoe Buckles [possibly close-plated on steel]. I bought them in London last July for 2/ a pr.," "3 pair of Plaited Soop Ladles," and "2 pair of handsome Plaited CandleSticks from 4 to 5 pounds" and "2 pair of flat Plaited Ditto with Snuffers and Extinguishers."[12] She ordered and received in 1772 "3 pair of Plaited Snuffers & Snuff Dishes" and "4 plaited Table Crosses."[13] After the Revolution, plated wares were imported in large quantities. Washing-

ton's purchases from France and England, some of which have survived, are well documented.[14]

G1950-132

1. The processes involved in preparing the sheet and in fabricating and ornamenting various forms is best described in Bradbury (see short title list), the standard volume on fused silverplate.

2. *Sketchley's Sheffield Directory* (Bristol, 1774) proudly states: "SILVER and PLATED MANUFACTURERS. These ingenious workmen make a great variety of Articles, an account of which here, may not be improper, viz. Epergnes, tea urns, coffee and tea pots, tea kettles and lamps, tankards and measures of all sizes, jugs, goblets, tumblers, candlesticks, branches, cruet frames, water and plater plates and dishes, dish rims, crosses, casters, tea trays and waiters, bottle and writing stands, tureens, ladles, spoons, scallop shells, canisters, mustard pots, round and oval salts, bottle labels, cream pails, bread and sugar baskets, argyles, snuffer stands and dishes, wine funnels, skewers, cream jugs, lemon strainers, cheese toasters, chocolate pots, saucepans, stew ditto, snuff boxes, bridle bits, stirrups, buckles, spurs, knife and fork handles, buttons for saddles, and a great variety of other articles." (p. 18)

3. Charleston (see short title list).

4. Ibid., pp. 111–12, plates 111a and c, 112 a–d.

5. Ibid., pp. 112–13.

6. Ibid.; Bradbury, pp. 20–21.

7. Charleston, p. 114, pl. 114 a and b. Charleston compares this box with one of similar form and flat-chased decoration with an enameled cover.

8. Ibid., pp. 113–14.

9. Robert Beverley to John Bland, undated [Summer 1763], MS, Robert Beverley Letter Book (1761–75), Library of Congress (microfilm copy, Department of Research, Colonial Williamsburg Foundation).

10. Bradbury, ill. p. 32. The same or a virtually identical example in the Victoria and Albert Museum, London, is illustrated in G. Bernard Hughes, *Antique Sheffield Plate* (London: B. T. Batsford Ltd., 1970), pl. 192.

11. Botetourt Inventory.

12. Frances Norton Mason, ed., *John Norton & Sons, Merchants of London and Virginia; Being the Papers from their Counting House for the Years 1750 to 1795* (Richmond: Dietz Press, 1937), pp. 211–12.

13. Ibid., pp. 218–19.

14. Buhler, pp. 37–45, 47, 49–75.

243 SNUFF OR PATCH BOX
Fused silverplate
Unmarked
Sheffield or Birmingham. About 1760

H: 9/16" (1.4 cm); Diam: 1 19/32" (4.1 cm).

PROVENANCE: S. J. Shrubsole Corp., New York

Plated boxes with the portrait of Frederick the Great, king of Prussia, were made to commemorate Britain's alliance with Prussia during the Seven Years' War (1756–63). At least some of the boxes of this type appear to have been made in Birmingham. Charleston, in the paper cited in regard to the previous box,

243

mentions a plated box of this type, its die-stamped base design identical to that on two boxes illustrated by Bradbury which he feels are of Birmingham manufacture.[1] He also illustrates a plated snuff box of probable Birmingham origin with an inset enameled cover bearing the portrait of Frederick the Great.[2] White salt-glazed stoneware plates with molded portraits of Frederick the Great, military trophies, and inscriptions bidding success to the Prussian cause have been excavated on several Williamsburg sites.

1972-396

1. Charleston, pp. 112–13; Bradbury, pp. 20–21.
2. Charleston, p. 112, pl. 113b.

244 PAIR OF CANDLESTICKS
Fused silverplate
Probably Joseph Hancock
Sheffield. About 1765

244

Maker's mark on face of each socket.

H: 9⁹⁄₁₆″ (24.3 cm); W (base): 5⅛″ (13 cm).

PROVENANCE: Old English Galleries, Boston, Massachusetts

Passing through Sheffield in 1760, Horace Walpole noted in a letter to his friend, George Montagu, that "One man there has discovered the art of plating copper with silver. I bought a pair of candlesticks for two guineas that are quite pretty."[1] Candlesticks, both plated and sterling, were among the most important and most numerous productions of the Sheffield makers. Aided by die stamping and the use of interchangable components, Sheffield became, in fact, the center in England for the production of candlesticks after 1770, especially the more standard Adamite types (see Nos. 21, 266).

Of a conventional mid-eighteenth-century pattern, these candlesticks bear the "I·H" mark generally associated with Joseph Hancock. He, rather than Boulsover, was primarily responsible for greatly enlarging the formal scope of plated wares. Rev. Edward Goodwin, in his introduction to the Sheffield trade directory of 1797, wrote:

> Buttons of brass or copper plated with silver were made by Mr. T. Bolsover, about 50 years ago. But, about 1758 a manufactory of the composition was begun by Mr. Joseph Hancock, an ingenious mechanic, upon a more extensive scale, comprehending a great variety of articles; such as tea urns, coffee-pots, saucepans, tankards, cups, candlesticks, &c. &c. Since that time, this branch has been pursued by various companies to great advantage; which has greatly contributed to the wealth and population of the town.[2]

A candlestick of another conventional mid-century type with a shell and petal base, bearing this same mark on its socket, is illustrated by Bradbury.[3]

1939-266, 1–2

1. Bradbury, p. 2.
2. *A Directory of Sheffield, Including the Manufacturers of the Adjacent Villages* (Sheffield, 1797), p. 21. Quoted by Bradbury, pp. 27–28.
3. Bradbury, p. 33.

245 PAIR OF TAPERSTICKS
Fused silverplate
Unmarked
Probably Sheffield. About 1765

H: 6¼″ (15.9 cm); W (base): 3¼″ (8.3 cm).

PROVENANCE: Gift of Mr. and Mrs. Oliver F. Ramsey, Williamsburg, Virginia

Marked candlesticks of this contrasting early type by Joseph Hancock and Tudor & Leader, both of Sheffield, and by Boulton & Fothergill of Birmingham are recorded.[1] This pair of tapersticks lack their removable nozzles.

G1971-89, 1–2

245

1. Edward Wenham, *Old Sheffield Plate* (London: G. Bell & Sons Ltd., 1955), p. 12, fig. 6; G. Bernard Hughes, *Antique Sheffield Plate* (London: B. T. Batsford Ltd., 1970), fig. 36; Bradbury, ill. p. 33; Eric Delieb, *The Great Silver Manufactory; Matthew Boulton and the Birmingham Silversmiths, 1760–1790* (London: Studio Vista, 1971), ill. between pp. 88 and 89.

246 SET OF FOUR CANDLESTICKS
Fused silverplate
Unmarked
Sheffield. About 1765

Owner's crest engraved on face of each base.

H: 11¼″ (28.6 cm); Diam (base): 6″ (15.2 cm).

PROVENANCE: Firestone and Parson, Boston

Various patterns of figured candlesticks in the rococo taste were made in sterling during the 1740s and 1750s.[1] The stems of this handsome set, quite rare in fused silverplate, are based on a pattern made primarily, though not exclusively, by John Cafe of

246

candlesticks, unlike their substantial cast counterparts in sterling, are made almost entirely of relatively thin die-stamped parts. Wenham illustrates an identical plated candlestick, marked "IR," believed to be by John Rowbotham & Co. of Sheffield.[3] Other examples of this pattern are illustrated by Bradbury and Hughes.[4]

1972-244, 1–4

1. Figured candlesticks of the seventeenth through nineteenth centuries are discussed in John F. Hayward, "Candlesticks with Figured Stems; Some Important English and Continental Examples," *Connoisseur* 152 (January 1962):16–21. Candlesticks of a contrasting pattern by de Lamerie and Kandler are discussed in relation to a Moser drawing of about 1745 for a full-figured candlestick in Shirley Bury and Desmond Fitz-Gerald, "A Design for a Candlestick by George Michael Moser, R.A.," *Victoria and Albert Museum Yearbook* 1 (1969):27–29.
2. Two sets of six of this type by Cafe, dating between 1748 and 1756, are illustrated in Christie's (June 21, 1967), lots 75 and 76.
3. Edward Wenham, *Old Sheffield Plate* (London: G. Bell and Sons Ltd., 1955), p. 19, fig. 8.
4. Bradbury, p. 229; G. Bernard Hughes, *Antique Sheffield Plate* (London: B. T. Batsford Ltd., 1970), p. 85, pl. 36.

London, a specialist candlestick-maker.[2] Their bases, however, depart from those of most figured candlesticks in sterling of this period, which are usually shorter, more heavily scrolled, and of shaped triangular plan. This difference may be due in part to the increased interior area needed for loading, since these

247 TEAPOT
Fused silverplate
Unmarked
Probably Sheffield. About 1765

H: 5⅟₁₆″ (12.9 cm); W: 8⅛″ (20.7 cm); Diam (base): 2⁷⁄₁₆″ (8.7 cm).

247

PROVENANCE: Edgar Sittig, Shawnee-on-Delaware, Pennsylvania; S. J. Shrubsole Corp., New York

Plated teapots in the rococo taste, unlike coffeepots and hot water or coffee jugs, are extremely rare. Bradbury illustrates a bullet-shaped teapot with chased decoration at the shoulder of about 1785 by Tudor & Leador of Sheffield.[1]

The handle on this example is a replacement.

1973-48

---

1. Bradbury, p. 354.

248 HOT WATER URN
Fused silverplate
Unmarked
Probably Sheffield. About 1765

Arms of Fawside, Haddington, engraved within a cartouche on face of body and crest on face of base.

H: 18⅞″ (47.9 cm); W: 10½″ (26.7 cm); W (base): 7⅜″ (18.8 cm).

PROVENANCE: S. J. Shrubsole Ltd., London

PUBLISHED: Alwyn and Angela Cox, "Old Sheffield Plate," *Antique Dealer and Collectors Guide* (March 1972): 91, fig. 2

The hot water or tea urn is one of the most ambitious forms in fused silverplate. Early examples of this ovoid form from the late rococo period are rare in comparison with the more familiar neoclassical urn-shaped examples (Nos. 92, 262). They were used as storage vessels for hot water to replenish the much smaller teapot, in which the tea was infused. The body and base of this example are joined by a bayonet fitting that permits access to the interior chamber

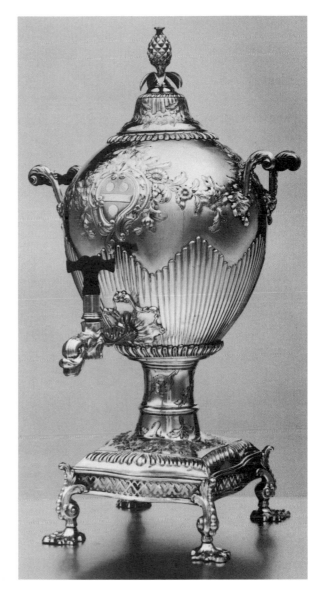

248

housing the heated cast-iron slug for keeping the water hot.

This particularly fine example is enriched with varied forms of chased and applied detail. The mounts, such as the pineapple finial, the scrolled handle arms with leaf attachments, the dolphin tap, and the scrolled legs with shell feet, all of which would have been cast on a sterling piece, are stampings filled with solder, as is customary on plated pieces because of the limitations of the medium. The green-stained ivory handles add a pleasing contrast in color and material.

This late rococo example is undoubtedly of similar form to the "1 Sheffield ware tea Kitchen," mentioned previously as listed with the "Plate, in the Pantry" of the Governor's Palace in Williamsburg in the 1770 inventory of the estate of Lord Botetourt.[1]

1972-41

_____

1. Botetourt Inventory.

249 COFFEEPOT
Fused Silverplate
Sheffield. About 1765

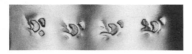

*Maker's mark four times on face of
body below rim to right of handle.*

H: 10 15/16" (27.8 cm); Diam (base): 4 9/16" (11.6 cm).

PROVENANCE: Gift of Mr. and Mrs. Oliver F. Ramsey, Williamsburg, Virginia

PUBLISHED: Helen Comstock, "Sheffield Plate: An Antiques Survey," *Antiques* 85 (February 1964):209, fig. 1

A surprising number of similar plated coffeepots in the rococo taste have survived. The maker's mark on this and the following two pieces, although unidentified, is the most common mark found on early hollowware, including many coffeepots and hot water or coffee jugs. The character, repetition, and placement of the maker's mark on this example, as on a

249

number of early plated pieces, closely imitate the maker's mark and hallmarks on sterling silver. It is conceivable that the maker used this mark of curious and indecipherable letter form, like at least two other marks recorded by Bradbury,[1] because of its superficial resemblance to the current cycle of London date letters in Gothic black-letter type—just as one of John Hoyland's marks (No. 253) and that of an unidentified maker[2] vaguely suggest a lion passant.

The misleading use of marks prompted a parliamentary committee, hearing a petition for the establishment of assay offices in Sheffield and Birmingham, to report to the House of Commons in 1773:

that Artificers are now arrived at so great a perfection in plating with Silver the Goods made of base Metal that they very much resemble solid Silver; and if the Practice which has been introduced, of putting Marks upon them somewhat resembling those used at the assay offices, shall not be restrained, many Frauds and Impositions may be committed upon the Public.[3]

The consequence was the granting of the assay offices and the prohibition of the use of any letter or letters on articles "made of metal, plated or covered with silver, or upon any metal vessel or other thing made to look like silver."[4] The ban was lifted in 1784, but the act of repeal stipulated that plated wares:

> made in Sheffield or within one hundred miles thereof [which included Birmingham], might bear the surname or partnership name of the maker, together with any mark, figure, or device at the end of the name, such figure not being an assay office device for sterling silver, or in imitation thereof [and that such marks had to be registered at and approved by the Sheffield Assay Office].[5]

Even though a number of firms registered their marks, they left most of their wares unmarked, as they had done before 1773.

G1971-82

---

1. Bradbury, p. 441. Bradbury attributes one of these marks to Matthew Fenton & Co. of Sheffield.
2. Ibid. This is the second mark listed after that attributed to Matthew Fenton & Co.
3. Ibid., p. 426.
4. Ibid.
5. Ibid.

250 PAIR OF TEA CANISTERS
Fused silverplate
Sheffield. About 1765

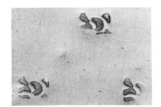

Maker's mark four times on underside of one base; the other unmarked.

Owner's crest engraved within cartouche on each body.

H: 5⅜″ (13.7 cm); L (base): 3⁵⁄₁₆″ (8.4 cm).

250

PROVENANCE: Gift of Mr. and Mrs. Oliver F. Ramsey, Williamsburg, Virginia

The earliest plated tea canisters are of this bombé form. These, like other examples of this early type, are composed almost entirely of die-stamped elements, lending a sureness to their contours and a crispness to their rather florid rococo decoration. A set of three canisters of this pattern, stamped with the same repeat of this unidentified maker's mark and housed in its original shagreen case, was formerly in the Lipton collection.[1] Another set in a satinwood case is illustrated by Frost.[2] A single example is illustrated by Bradbury.[3]

G1972-105, 1–2

---

1. Portland Art Museum, *The Lipton Collection; Antique English Silver Designed for the Serving of Tea* (Portland, 1954), no. 51, ill.; William Rockhill Nelson Gallery of Art and Atkins Museum of Fine Art, *The Lipton Collection of Antique English Silver Designed for the Serving of Tea* (Kansas City, 1955), p. 35, no. 48, ill.
2. T. W. Frost, *The Price Guide to Old Sheffield Plate* (Woodbridge, Suffolk: Antique Collectors' Club, 1971), p. 343.
3. Bradbury, p. 187.

251 TWO-HANDLED CUP
Fused silverplate
Sheffield. About 1765

Maker's mark four times on face of body below rim.

Owner's initials engraved on face of body.

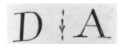

H (handles): 4⁹⁄₁₆″ (11.6 cm); H (rim): 4⁷⁄₁₆″ (11.3 cm); Diam (rim): 3¾″ (9.6 cm); Diam (base): 3⁵⁄₁₆″ (8.4 cm).

PROVENANCE: Gift of Mr. and Mrs. Oliver F. Ramsey, Williamsburg, Virginia

Bradbury illustrates an ornamented two-handled cup of similar size and of identical form and detailing, which he ascribes to Matthew Fenton & Co. of Sheffield.[1]

G1971-83

_____

1. Bradbury, p. 349.

252 THREE CASTERS
Fused silverplate
Sheffield. About 1765

Maker's mark four times on underside of base (nos. 1 and 2) and on body body below rim (no. 3).

H (no. 1): 7¹⁄₁₆″ (17.9 cm); Diam (base): 2¼″ (5.7 cm); H (nos. 2 and 3): 5¹³⁄₁₆″ (14.8 cm); Diam (bases): 1¹⁵⁄₁₆″ (4.9 cm).

PROVENANCE: Gift of Mr. and Mrs. Oliver F. Ramsey, Williamsburg, Virginia

PUBLISHED: Helen Comstock, "Sheffield Plate: An Antiques Survey," *Antiques* 85 (February 1964):210, fig. 2

The small caster on the left with an unpierced cover, although stamped and chased to correspond with pierced casters of this pattern, was probably intended for mustard (see No. 152). It was acquired separately

252

by the donors to complete the set. A plated caster of this same pattern and with the same maker's mark is in the Croft Lyons bequest, Victoria and Albert Museum, London.

G1971-85, 1–3

253 GOBLET
Fused silverplate
John Hoyland & Co.
Sheffield. About 1770

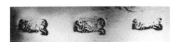

Maker's mark three times on face of bowl.
Owner's crest engraved on face of bowl below rim.

H: 5¹¹⁄₁₆″ (14.5 cm); Diam (rim) 3⁵⁄₁₆″ (8.4 cm); Diam (base): 3″ (7.6 cm).

PROVENANCE: Gift of Mr. and Mrs. Oliver F. Ramsey, Williamsburg, Virginia

253

A similar goblet by John Hoyland & Co. with the lower portion of its bowl chased with pointed bands of reeding, as on the body of the hot water urn (No. 248), is in the Sheffield City Museum.

G1971-86

254 PAIR OF CANDLESTICKS
Fused silverplate
Unmarked
Matthew Boulton and John Fothergill
Birmingham. About 1775

254

H: 12⅟₁₆″ (30.5 cm); W (base): 4⅝″ (11.8 cm).

PROVENANCE: S. J. Shrubsole Ltd., London

James Wyatt, the architect, was influential in the formation of Boulton's shop style of the 1770s, providing Boulton with designs, among others, for candlesticks of this elegant pattern, which were produced both in sterling and in fused silverplate.[1] Boulton utilized this same fluted, trumpet-shaped transition to a shaped square base with a beaded shoulder and inclined, inward-curved sides and clipped corners (the sides ornamented with a guilloche banding with

rosetted corners) in his drawings for a two-handled cup and a jug.[2] A cup of 1777/78 after the former drawing is in the Birmingham Assay Office.[3] Rowe illustrates three jugs related to the latter drawing.[4] The bases of two of these of 1774/75 and 1775/76 deviate from the drawing and from those of this pair of candlesticks in their straight sides and omission of the beading.[5] The third jug of 1776/77 retains the fluted transition, but it is supported on a circular base.

Patrick Robertson, the Edinburgh silversmith, who acted as a retail agent for Boulton in the 1770s, produced a silver hot water or tea urn in 1778/79, presently in the Royal Scottish Museum, Edinburgh, which is clearly in this Boulton manner.[6]

1971-405

---

1. A drawing for a very similar candlestick and one with a related socket and stem from an album of Wyatt designs in the collection Vicomte de Noailles, Paris, are illustrated in Frances Fergusson, "Wyatt Silver," *Burlington Magazine* 116 (December 1974):750, figs. 48 and 49. Fergusson also illustrates drawings for a candlestick of this pattern and for an abbreviated candlestick with related socket and base from the Boulton pattern books in the Birmingham Assay Office (ibid., pp. 750, 753, figs. 50, 52). Sterling candlesticks of this pattern of 1774/75 from the Museum of Fine Arts, Boston, and the Birmingham Assay Office are illustrated in Rowe (pl. 50) and Eric Delieb, *The Great Silver Manufactory: Matthew Boulton and the Birmingham Silversmiths, 1760–1790* (London: Studio Vista, 1971), color pl. between pp. 88 and 89, respectively. Wyatt's designs and these candlesticks are related in general terms to a drawing of about 1767 by Robert Adam of a candlestick in the Soane Museum, London, having a stem of this attenuated vase form and a calyx of acanthus leaves on the lower part of the socket and stem. It is illustrated in Rowe in relation to a pair of sterling candlesticks of 1767/68 by John Carter of London from Temple Newsam House, Leeds (Rowe, plates 10 and 11). Rowe also illustrates the Adam drawing of 1773 for a candelabrum with a shaped triangular base with inclined inward-curved sides and clipped corners (the sides ornamented with foliated scroll decoration) and the set of four sterling candelabra of the following year by John Carter after this design (ibid., plates 12 and 13).
2. Rowe, plates 40 and 53.
3. Ibid., pl. 52.
4. Ibid., plates 41–42, 45.
5. A set of sterling candlesticks of 1774/75 by Boulton and Fothergill at the Birmingham Assay Office have this alternative base treatment (Rowe, pl. 51A; Delieb, *Great Silver Manufactory*, color pl. between pp. 88 and 89; Fergusson, "Wyatt Silver," p. 750, fig. 51).
6. Malcolm Baker, "Patrick Robertson's Tea Urn and the Late Eighteenth Century Edinburgh Silver Trade," *Connoisseur* 188 (August 1973):289–91, fig. 1. This piece is also illustrated in Ian Finlay, *Scottish Gold and Silver Work* (London: Chatto & Windus, 1956), pl. 83.

255 SALVER
Fused silverplate
Unmarked
Probably Sheffield. About 1780

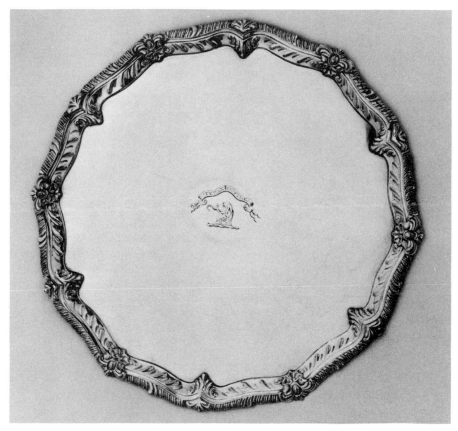

255

Crest and motto of the Smith family, barons of Carrington, Nottinghamshire, engraved on face; owners' cypher engraved on underside.

H (rim): 1½″ (3.8 cm); Diam: 12¼″ (30.8 cm).

PROVENANCE: Gift of Mr. and Mrs. Oliver F. Ramsey, Williamsburg, Virginia

Salvers are among the first of the larger forms produced by the Sheffield platers. Thomas Boulsover gave a plated shell and scroll edged salver to his daughter on the occasion of her marriage in 1760, presumably of his own manufacture.[1] The rims of most early salvers, as in this example, are composed of a double layer soldered back to back for added strength and ease of attachment to the central plate. The rim, as well as the three short cabriole legs ending in ball and claw feet, are stampings, the latter

filled with solder. The crest and motto on the face are engraved on a rubbed-in silver shield, discernible in the illustration, to permit the engraver greater depth. This was probably added later.

G1971-88

———————

1. Bradbury, ill. p. 25.

256 SUGAR BASKET
Fused silverplate
Unmarked
Probably Sheffield. About 1780

256

Possible workman's or owner's stamp on underside of handle.

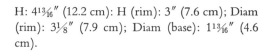

Owner's crest engraved on face of handle.

H: 4¹³⁄₁₆″ (12.2 cm): H (rim): 3″ (7.6 cm); Diam (rim): 3⅛″ (7.9 cm); Diam (base): 1¹³⁄₁₆″ (4.6 cm).

PROVENANCE: S. J. Shrubsole Corp., New York

Bradbury illustrates an identical sugar basket, which he ascribes to Richard Morton & Co. of Sheffield.[1] The clear glass liner is probably a replacement.

1971-147

———————

1. Bradbury, p. 341.

257 HOT WATER OR COFFEE JUG
Fused silverplate
Unmarked
Probably Sheffield. About 1780

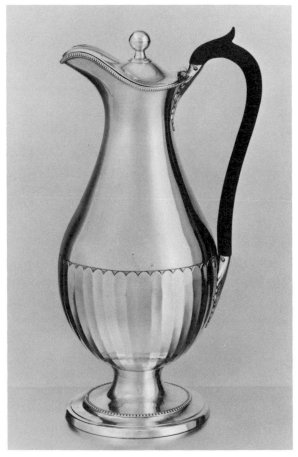

257

H (handle): 10¹³⁄₁₆″ (27.5 cm); H (finial): 10⅝″ (27 cm); Diam (base): 4⅛″ (10.5 cm).

PROVENANCE: Walter H. Willson Ltd., London

1972-345

258 SIXTEEN DINNER PLATES
Fused silverplate
Unmarked
Probably Sheffield. About 1785

*Arms and motto of
Warren engraved on face
of each rim.*

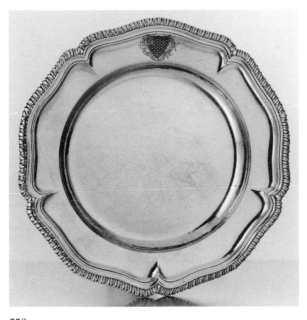

258

H (rim): ⅔″ (1.9 cm); W: 9¹¹⁄₁₆″ (24.6 cm).

PROVENANCE: Harvey & Gore, London

Unlike heavier sterling examples, with cast and applied gadrooning, these plates and the following pair of meat dishes were each stamped from a thin plated sheet, including the rims, the edges simply folded over for strength and finish.

1973-11, 1–16

259 PAIR OF MEAT DISHES OR PLATTERS
Fused silverplate
Unmarked
Probably Sheffield. About 1785

259

H (rim): 1⁹⁄₁₆″ (4 cm); L: 19¼″ (48.9 cm).

PROVENANCE: Harvey & Gore, London

Part of the same service as the previous plates and engraved with the same arms.

1973-12, 1–2

260 BREADBASKET
Fused silverplate
Unmarked
Probably Sheffield. About 1785

H: 11⅛″ (28.3 cm); L: 13⅞″ (35.2 cm); W: 10⅝″ (27 cm).

PROVENANCE: Gift of Mr. and Mrs. Oliver F. Ramsey, Williamsburg, Virginia

A plated breadbasket, with similar piercing and a tradition of ownership by George Washington, is in the Lewis collection in the Smithsonian Institution.[1]

G1971-84

1. Buhler, p. 69, fig. 36.

261 PAIR OF BOTTLE SLIDERS OR BOTTLE STANDS
Fused silverplate with mahogany bases and ivory insets
Unmarked
Probably Sheffield. About 1785

Owner's crest engraved on each.

H: 1⅞″ (4.8 cm); Diam: 4¹⁵⁄₁₆″ (12.5 cm).

261

PROVENANCE: S. J. Shrubsole Corp., New York

The decorative borders and oval surrounds for the urns and crest are stamped in imitation of bright-cut engraving, so as not to cut through to and expose the copper.

1972-107, 1–2

262 HOT WATER URN
Fused silverplate
Unmarked
Sheffield or Birmingham. About 1785

Owner's crest engraved on cover.

H: 20⅜″ (51.8 cm); L: 10¾″ (27.3 cm); W (base and feet): 6¼″ (15.8 cm).

PROVENANCE: Anonymous gift

Benjamin Henry Latrobe made an ink sketch and a watercolor of the Washington family at tea on the portico of Mt. Vernon during his visit in July 1796.[1] Although differing in detail, both views depict the same hot water urn with the tea equipage on a breakfast table. Its urn-shaped body with a wave molding at the rim is elevated on four incurved legs

with rams' heads at their attachments with the body. It is probably the "large Tea-Urn, or receptacle for the water which is to supply the tea pot, at the table" that Washington included in a list of plated goods he

262

ordered from France through Lafayette in 1783.[2] The "1 large plain beaded plated Gallon Tea Urn" he received from England the following year was probably similar to this rather plain representative example.[3]

G1971-3022

1. Both are owned by the Maryland Historical Society. The ink sketch is illustrated in *Maryland History Notes* 18 (November 1960): 9, and a detail from the watercolor in Buhler, frontispiece.
2. Buhler, p. 41.
3. Ibid., p. 45.

263 PAIR OF BASTING OR SERVING SPOONS
Fused silverplate
Unmarked
Probably Sheffield. About 1785

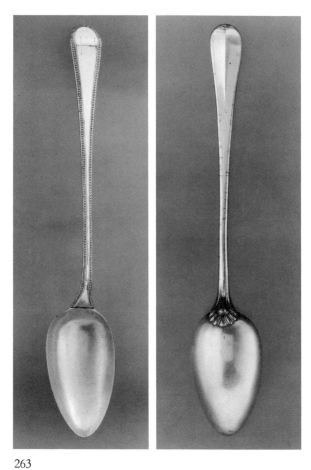

263

L: 12″ (30.5 cm); W (bowl): 2 1/16″ (5.2 cm).

PROVENANCE: S. J. Shrubsole Corp., New York

Flatware, especially spoons and forks, were among the less successful classes of fused silverplate. Their construction was by necessity clumsy in comparison with their sterling equivalents, which were made in one piece; and daily use could soon expose the underlying copper at the edges and points of wear, perhaps considered prejudicial to the taste of food.[1] This pair of spoons was fashioned in the customary manner. The handle was stamped in upper and lower halves, hard soldered together around the edges, the interior filled with soft solder through the bowl end, and then soldered to the bowl, with the lower half extending onto the underside of the bowl in a shell drop for added strength and decorative effect.

1973-103, 1–2

---

1. H. Bennet-Clark, "The Importance of Taste in Plate; Old Sheffield Plated Flatware," *Country Life* 153 (February 15, 1973): 388–89. He illustrates a similar "Old English" soup ladle with a stamped beaded handle and a shell drop on its bowl (p. 388, figs. 1 and 2). A similar ladle by Nathaniel Smith & Co. of Sheffield is illustrated in Bradbury, p. 336.

264 FISH SLICE OR TROWEL
Fused silverplate
Unmarked
Probably Sheffield. About 1785

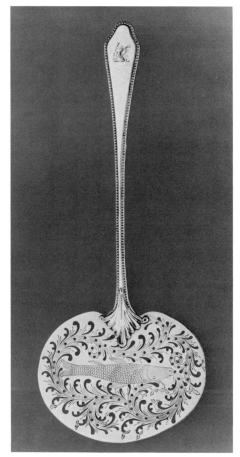

264

L: 13″ (33 cm); W (blade): 5 5/16″ (13.5 cm).

PROVENANCE: S. J. Shrubsole Corp., New York

Owner's crest engraved on face of handle.

The handle is constructed from die-stamped halves, as in the previous pair of spoons. The end of the handle is attached to the upper face of the blade with an applied shell not only reflecting similar use in sterling examples but also concealing the join.

1973-102

265 SUGAR TONGS
Gilded fused silverplate
Unmarked
Probably Sheffield. About 1790

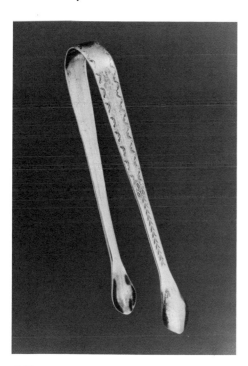

265

L: 5½″ (14 cm).

PROVENANCE: Gift of Dr. Benjamin H. Caldwell, Jr., Nashville, Tennessee

This pair of tongs, like many late eighteenth- and early nineteenth-century plated examples, was rolled from plated wire, a development of the 1780s that

eliminated the problem of exposed edges, except at the ends. Longitudinal stress lines, as is customary in articles made in this manner, are evident. The decoration is punched to simulate bright-cut engraving.[1]

G1973-178

1. The use of rolled wirework is discussed and a comparison of the punch decoration on similar tongs to an engraved sterling example is illustrated in H. Bennet-Clark, "The Importance of Taste in Plate; Old Sheffield Plate Flatware," *Country Life* 153 (February 15, 1973):388–89.

266 PAIR OF CANDLESTICKS
Fused silverplate
Nathaniel Smith & Co.
Sheffield. About 1790

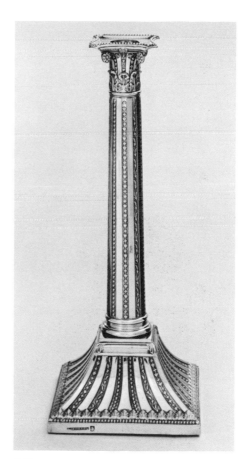

266

H: 11½″ (29.2 cm); W (base): 4¹¹⁄₁₆″ (11.9 cm).

PROVENANCE: Avis and Rockwell Gardiner, Stamford, Connecticut

Maker's mark and secondary device on face of each base.

These stamped and weighted candlesticks are of debased columnar type with the narrow alternate plain and figured panels of their sockets, stems, and bases serving decorative rather than architectural ends. Paterae have been substituted for the proper corner scrolls of their capitals. Smith's maker's mark and secondary device are in keeping with the act of 1784 which reinstituted the use of marks on plated wares and stipulated that they include the full surname of the maker or firm and devices not in imitation of hallmarks on sterling silver and that these marks be registered with the Sheffield Assay Office, which Smith did in that year (see No. 249).

1973-223, 1–2

267 GLOBE INKSTAND
Fused silverplate with blue-glass bottles
Unmarked
Probably Sheffield. About 1795

267

H: 6⅝″ (16.8 cm); W: 4¼″ (10.8 cm).

PROVENANCE: Harvey & Gore, London

Lord Melbourne purchased from John Parker and Edward Wakelin of London in 1770 a "Globe Inkstand" in sterling weighing 59 ounces 15 pennyweight. It was, as Grimwade has noted, a very early reference to this distinctive form of inkstand (most surviving examples dating between 1790 and 1810) and of surprisingly heavy weight.[1] The finials of such inkstands house a central spring-loaded post that when depressed, causes the upper half of the sphere to swing downward. Most surviving sterling examples are the work of John Robins of London, who specialized in the form. One of his of 1798/99, illustrated by Clayton, is appropriately engraved with a map of the world.[2]

The platers were especially adept in copying Robins's models. This is a particularly successful example with its handsomely pieced sphere, stamped classical masks and swags, and gracefully curved legs. Delieb illustrates a similar plated example that has a fitted leather case and additional writing accessories.[3]

1973-13

---

1. Grimwade, p. 11.
2. Clayton, pp. 156, 161, fig. 320. Also illustrated in Christie's (May 25, 1960), lot 43.
3. Delieb, pp. 140–41, ill.

268 HOT WATER URN
Fused silverplate
Unmarked
Sheffield or Birmingham. About 1800

Arms, crest, and motto of and inscription relating to the Carter family of Virginia engraved on face of cover.

H: 23⅝″ (60 cm); W: 12⅛″ (30.8 cm); W (base): 6⅞″ (17.5 cm).

PROVENANCE: Gift of Mrs. Eugene B. Simonin, Philadelphia, Pennsylvania

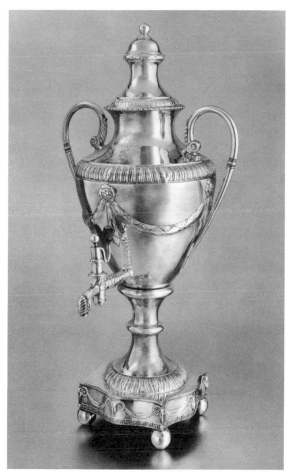

268

PROVENANCE: Gift of Mr. and Mrs. Oliver F. Ramsey, Williamsburg, Virginia

The argyle or argyll, often resembling a small teapot or coffeepot, was used to keep gravy warm until served. Various methods were employed, such as a heated slug within a central tube or hot water within a central conical reservoir or a lower chamber. In this instance, a hot water jacket is formed between the outer wall and the inner chamber. Hot water is introduced through the small triangular lip with hinged

269

This late neoclassical urn has a tradition of descent in the Carter, Stanard, Nicholas, Buffington, and Simonin families. The engraving is a later embellishment. It has been replated in this century.

G1973-371

269 ARGYLE
Fused silverplate
Matthew Boulton
Birmingham. About 1800

Maker's mark twice on underside of base.

H: 5¾6″ (13.2 cm); Diam (base): 3⅝″ (9.2 cm.)

cover opposite the spout. Possibly named for one of the eighteenth-century dukes of Argyll, their main period of popularity was during the last four decades of the century. The earliest silver argyle is a London example of 1755/56.[1] An identical plated example by Boulton is illustrated by Bradbury.[2]

G1971-87

1. This is cited in Harold Newman's comprehensive article "Argylls: Silver and Ceramic," *Apollo* 89 (February 1969):98. An example of 1756/57 by Fuller White of London is illustrated in Jonathan Stone, *English Silver of the Eighteenth Century* (London: Cory, Adams & MacKay Ltd., 1965), pl. 25.
2. Bradbury, p. 203.

270 PAIR OF CANDLESTICKS
Fused silverplate
Matthew Boulton
Birmingham. About 1805

270

Maker's mark on side of each base.

H: 11⅟₁₆″ (28.1 cm); Diam (base): 5⁷⁄₁₆″ (13.8 cm).

PROVENANCE: Gift of Mrs. Grace E. Powell, Staunton, Virginia

These candlesticks of a conventional early nineteenth-century pattern, of which Boulton made a large number both plated and sterling, have a tradition of descent in the Cuthbert, Stribling, and Powell families of Norfolk and Staunton, Virginia.

G1956-276

271 TABLE FOUNTAIN AND STAND
Fused silverplate, with glass bowl and mirrored top to stand
Unmarked
Sheffield or Birmingham. About 1815

H (fountain and stand): 33½″ (85 cm); H (fountain): 31½″ (80 cm); Diam (base of fountain): 15⅞″ (40.3 cm); Diam (stand): 19½″ (49.5 cm).

PROVENANCE: W. H. W. Tringham (sold at Sotheby & Co., London, 1959; purchased by N. Bloom & Son Ltd., London); James Robinson Inc., New York; C. J. Vander Ltd., London (purchased from Sotheby & Co., London, 1964); gift of Mr. and Mrs. Oliver F. Ramsey, Williamsburg, Virginia

PUBLISHED: Sotheby's (June 18, 1959), lot 140, pl. VII; C. G. L. Du Cann, "Lost Art of Old Sheffield Plate," *Antique Dealer and Collectors Guide* 17 (November 1962): 42, ill.; Sotheby's (May 21, 1964), lot 7, pl. 1; Frank Davis, "Jeux D'Espirit in Silver," *Country Life* 135 (June 18, 1964):1586, fig. 1; *Ivory Hammer 2: The Year at Sotheby's Two Hundred and Twentieth Season, 1963–1964* (New York: Holt, Rinehart and Winston, 1964), p. 178, ill.

This imposing table fountain is possibly a unique plated example. It derives from the long-standing use, especially on the Continent, of temples and other structures, in a variety of materials as impermanent as sugar and cardboard, as decorative centerpieces on banquet tables. They were often the focal point for an elaborate decorative scheme reflecting contemporary garden design.[1] Parson Woodforde described in his diary in 1783 the table of the bishop of Norwich dressed in this manner:

> A most beautiful Artificial Garden in the Centre of the Table remained at dinner and afterwards, it was one of the prettiest things I ever saw, about a Yard long, and about 18 Inches wide, in the middle of which was a high round Temple supported on round Pillars, the Pillars were wreathed round with artificial Flowers—on one side was a Shepherdess on the other a Shepherd, several handsome Urns decorated with artificial Flowers, etc. etc.[2]

Examples of temple centerpieces in silver are uncommon. One by William Pitts and Joseph Preedy

271

of London, which was presented to the Mercers' Company in 1794 and is engraved with that company's crest, is elevated on legs and is accompanied by a mirrored plateau and four glass-lined dishes.[3] A similar one of 1799/1800 by the same firm, with only two dishes and without a plateau, houses a central figure of Apollo.[4] Some earlier rococo epergnes echo this theme in their fanciful use of varied canopied forms on attenuated columns, sometimes wrapped with flowers, as in the 1762/63 example by Thomas Pitts of London (No. 115).

This fountain is filled through an opening with an inset strainer in the top of the dome. The interior of the dome forms the reservoir, and a small pipe extends down through one of the columns and up through the figure group within the bowl. A valve at the base of the column regulates the liquid jet issuing from the cherub's conch shell. The upper surface of the base slopes towards the center, where a perforated depression can accommodate any overflow. The underside of the base is fitted with a drainage valve. Two adjacent columns are detachable to permit removal of the bowl. The whole is supported on a mirror stand that revolves on a much smaller circular foot.

G1965-235

---

1. The use of such temple centerpieces is illustrated in drawings by Moreau of the banquet given by Madame du Barry to Louis XV

for the inauguration of the Pavilion of Louveciennes in 1771 (*Le Dix-huitième Siecle; Les Moeurs, Les Arts, Les Idées* [Paris: Chez Hachette et Cie. Libraires, 1899], ill. p. 93; Damie Stillman, *The Decorative Work of Robert Adam* [London: Alec Tiranti, 1966], pl. 173) and of the banquet given by the city of Paris to Louis XVI and Marie-Antoinette in 1782 (ibid., ill. opp. p. 136; *French Master Goldsmiths and Silversmiths from the Seventeenth to the Nineteenth Century* [New York: French & European Publications, 1966], ill. pp. 204–5).

2. Gerald Brett, *Dinner is Served; A History of Dining in England, 1400–1900* (London: Rupert Hart-Davis, 1968), p. 125.

3. Christie's (May 22, 1974), lot 146, pl. 10.

4. Christie's (April 15, 1964), lot 122, pl. 3; Clayton, p. 129, fig. 269.

Mace of the City of Williamsburg

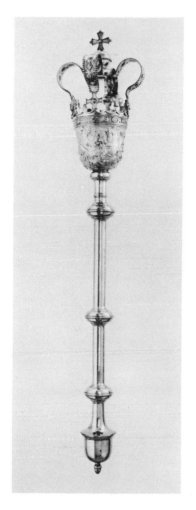

272 MACE OF THE CITY OF
WILLIAMSBURG
(partially reconstructed)
Silver-gilt
Peter Archambo, Jr., and Peter Meure
London. 1749/50

L: 41½″ (102.9 cm); Diam (rim of bowl): 5½″
(14 cm).

PROVENANCE: City of Williamsburg; Heth family (sold to
William Randolph Hearst by Miss Nannie Heth of
Washington, D.C., 1919); William Randolph Hearst
(sold by Parish-Watson & Co., New York, 1939)

PUBLISHED: Robert A. Brock, ed., *The Official Records of
Robert Dinwiddie* (Richmond, 1883; New York: AMS
Press, 1971), 1:xiv–xv; "The Mace of the Virginia House
of Burgesses," *Virginia Magazine of History and Biography*
19 (July 1911):305–6; Edward Wenham, "The Anglo-
French Silversmiths—Part 5. Peter Archambo, Father &
Son," *Antique Collector* 16 (July–August 1945):124, fig. 1

Fully marked on face of bowl of head.

English royal arms

Arms, crest, and motto of the Virginia colony

Arms, crest, and motto of the city of Williamsburg

Original elements from the colonial mace of the city of Williamsburg were acquired in 1939 from William Randolph Hearst as a standing cup. These are, in this conjectural reconstruction, the bowl of the head, the lower section of the circlet of the crown, the circular plate with royal arms within the rim of the bowl, and the short upper section of the shaft down to and including the narrow banding. These elements were in cup form in 1883, by which time Major General Henry (Harry) Heth (1825–1899), formerly of Richmond and then of Washington, D.C., had placed the cup on loan to the Virginia Historical Society, Richmond, where it remained until 1911. Robert A. Brock commented in 1883 that Colonel William Heth (1735–1808), Henry Heth's great uncle, had made the conversion of the mace into a cup.[1] The mace was reconstructed and the original elements regilded in 1941.[2]

The head of the mace is high-chased on a matted ground with the arms, motto, and crest of the Virginia colony and the arms, motto, and crest of the city of Williamsburg. Owing to the destruction of the early records of the Williamsburg Common Council, the circumstances of its acquisition and disposal are not known. This is probably the same mace that was carried on May 1, 1783, in a municipal procession celebrating the signing of the Treaty of Paris, which concluded the Revolutionary War.[3] The city of Norfolk still retains its silver mace by Fuller White of London, which Governor Dinwiddie presented to that city in 1753.[4]

1939-224

1. Robert A. Brock, ed., *The Official Records of Robert Dinwiddie* (Richmond, 1883; New York: AMS Press, 1971), 1:xv.

2. From pencil sketches of various maces in the files of the Colonial Williamsburg Foundation it would appear that the reconstruction was based primarily on the pair of maces of 1761/62 belonging to the Okehampton Corporation, Devonshire ("Notes," *Connoisseur* 19 [September 1907]:49, ill.).

3. An ink inscription in an unidentified hand on the back of a letter from Governor Benjamin Harrison in Richmond to the mayor of Williamsburg, dated April 23, 1783, and dealing with the city's observance of the event, lists under the "Order of the Procession on the Great Day, Thursday, May 1st" as "4ᵈ Sergeant bearing the mace" (*William and Mary Quarterly*, 1st ser. 14 [April 1906]: 278–79; Rutherford Goodwin, *A Brief & True Report Concerning Williamsburg in Virginia*, 3rd edn. [Williamsburg: Colonial Williamsburg: 1940], pp. 82–83).

4. "Norfolk's Historic Mace," *Arts in Virginia* 1 (Winter 1961): 20–21, ill.

Apparent original pincushion covered in dark blue velvet over a lighter blue glazed worsted fabric (tammy) mounted on a mahogany plate.

273 JEWEL BOX WITH PINCUSHION
Silver-gilt
John White
London. 1729/30

Fully marked on underside of base.

H: 4½″ (11.4 cm); L: 7⅝″ (19.3 cm); W: 5⁷⁄₁₆″ (13.8 cm). Wt (excluding pincushion): 40 oz. 14 dwt. ("40·9" engraved on underside of base).

PROVENANCE: Henry Somerset, 3rd duke of Beaufort (1707-1746), and his wife, Frances Scudamore (b. 1711), married in 1729 and divorced in 1743; his brother, Charles Noel Somerset, 4th duke of Beaufort (1709–1756), and his wife, Elizabeth Berkeley (1719–1799), married in 1740; their son, Henry Somerset, 5th duke of Beaufort (1744–1803), and his wife, Elizabeth Boscowan (d. 1828), married in 1766; their son, Henry Charles Somerset, 6th duke of Beaufort (1766–1835), and his

wife, Charlotte Sophia Leveson-Gower (d. 1854), married in 1791; their son, Henry Somerset, 7th duke of Beaufort (1792–1853), and his wives, Georgiana Frederica Fitzroy, married in 1814, and Emily Frances Smith, married in 1822; their son by his second marriage, Henry Charles FitzRoy Somerset, 8th duke of Beaufort (1824–1899), and his wife, Georgiana Charlotte Curzon (d. 1906) (sold by Christie, Manson & Woods, London, 1895; purchased by Charles Davis, London); Granville Frederick Richard Farquhar (1849–1934) and his wife, Helen Margaretta Livingstone (d. 1929), married in 1896 (sold at Christie, Manson & Woods, London, 1930; purchased by J. Rochelle Thomas, London); Charles E. Dunlap, New York (purchased from Crichton Bros., London; sold at Parke-Bernet Galleries, New York, 1963); American private collections (1963–1975); Thomas Lumley Ltd., London

PUBLISHED: Christie's (June 13, 1895), lot 68; "For the Connoisseur: English Silver," *Country Life* 67 (March 8, 1930):366; "In the Saleroom: Silver," *Connoisseur* 35 (May 1930):338; Christie's (March 19, 1930), lot 29; Parke-Bernet (April 13, 1963), lot 70, ill.

Arms of Henry Somerset, 3rd duke of Beaufort (1707–1746), of Badminton, Gloucestershire, and those of his wife, Frances Scudamore (b. 1711), only child and heir of James Scudamore of Holme Lacy, Herefordshire, borne in pretense, with ducal coronet above, Beaufort supporter to the left and Scudamore supporter to the right, and Beaufort motto below, engraved in center of plate on underside of cover. Beaufort crest engraved on face of cover.

This box was part of a large toilet service of at least twenty-five pieces.[1] Except for a pair of candlesticks of 1755/56 by John Quantock of London, all bear the mark of John White and London hallmarks for 1729/30. The service was occasioned by the marriage in 1729 of Henry Somerset, 3rd duke of Beaufort, to Frances Scudamore. He probably presented the service to his brother Charles Noel Somerset, later 4th duke of Beaufort, on the latter's marriage in 1740 to Elizabeth Berkeley. The engraved arms were altered to reflect this change in ownership—except on this piece where they appear on the interior and were left unchanged. Originally plain, the service was probably gilded at this time, explaining the discrepancy between the inscribed and present weights of this piece.

The marriage of Charles Noel Somerset to Elizabeth Berkeley was of immense importance to her brother, Norborne Berkeley, who was to serve in Williamsburg as governor of Virginia from 1768 until his death in 1770. In the year after this alliance

of influential Gloucestershire families, Berkeley became a member of Parliament. He never married and remained extremely close to his sister and the Beauforts. On the death of the 4th duke in 1756, he was an executor of the duke's estate and became, in effect, supervisor of the properties and interests and guardian of his nephew, the 5th duke, who would not reach maturity for nine years. He became Baron Botetourt in 1764 and took his seat in the House of Lords. He was Groom of the Bedchamber, 1760–64; Lord of the Bedchamber, 1767–70; and Lord Lieu-

tenant of Gloucestershire, 1762–66. His will of 1766 provided for the use of the bulk of his personal and real estate by his sister until her death, which occurred in 1799, after which it would revert to the 5th duke of

Beaufort.[2] During the latter period of her life, Elizabeth, duchess dowager of Beaufort, resided at Stoke Glifford, the Berkeley family seat.

Single rectangular boxes from toilet services, fitted with a lock and usually somewhat smaller than the customary pair of comb boxes, would appear to have been intended for jewelry. Such boxes usually house the pincushion, if not treated as an individual item. The invoice for Paul de Lamerie's famous toilet service for the Honorable George Treby, dated March 5, 1725, includes the entry: "for the lock to the Juelle Tronke."[3] Parker and Wakelin sold Sir William Draper in 1771" a toilet service which included a jewel box with blue velvet covered pin cushion lid."[4]

1975-57

---

1. The service, when sold at Christie, Manson & Woods in 1930, included, aside from this box, a ewer and dish, a pair of rectangular comb boxes, a pair of octagonal powder boxes, a pair of smaller octagonal patch boxes, a pair of octagonal two-handled covered bowls, a pair of octagonal scent vases, a pair of octagonal pomade pots, a pair of octagonal salvers, a pair of octagonal brushes, a pair of whisks, a table bell, and a "plummit" or "dressing weight," all of 1729/30 by John White of London, as well as a pair of candlesticks of 1755/56 by John Quantock of London (Christie's [March 19, 1930], lot 29, ill.). Sixteen pieces of the service were sold at Parke-Bernet Galleries in 1963 ([April 13], lot 70, ill.). One of the comb boxes was sold at Christie, Manson & Woods in 1974 ([June 26], lot 114, ill.). Selected pieces from the service are also illustrated in Edward Wenham, *Domestic Silver of Great Britain and Ireland* (London: Oxford University Press, 1931), pl. LXIX; ———, "Silver Toilet Services," *Antique Collector* 19 (May–June 1948): 105, fig. 5.
2. Bryan Little, "Norborne Berkeley: Gloucestershire Magnate," *Virginia Magazine of History and Biography* 63 (October 1955): 379–409.
3. Phillips, fig. 18. The service, in the Farrar collection in the Ashmolean Museum, Oxford, is illustrated in plates XXXI–XXXIV.
4. Clayton, p. 319.

---

274 PAIR OF BEAKERS
Gilt-lined
Gabriel Sleath
London. 1735/36

Fully marked on underside of each base.

Arms of Gooch impaling Stanton for William Gooch (1681-1751), then of Williamsburg, Virginia, and his wife, Rebecca Stanton (d. 1775), married in 1714, engraved on the face of each body.

H: 3⅞" (9.8 cm); Diam (rim): 3⅜" (8.5 cm); Diam (base): 2¹⁵⁄₁₆" (7.5 cm). Total wt: 15 oz.

PROVENANCE: Sotheby Parke Bernet South Africa, Johannesburg

PUBLISHED: Sotheby's (South Africa) (March 3, 1975), lot 38, ill.

William Gooch acquired these handsome beakers during his long and congenial term in Williamsburg as lieutenant governor of Virginia (1727–49).[1] Unfortunately, no documentary evidence has been found that would reveal the occasion for Gooch's purchase of the beakers. There is, however, a hint as to his holdings in a letter of March 3, 1744, to his brother Thomas, then bishop of Norwich. In proposing the marriage of his widowed daughter-in-law to his brother's elder son, he wrote: "My Furniture[,] and I have a great stock of all sorts, as well as a large Quantity of Plate, with my Equipage, as Coach, Chaise, Horses &c. are ready to equip an Inheritor, where as they could not be sold, without great loss."[2]

Lady Gooch specified in her will of 1775: "as a small token of my Remembrance to the place of his

274

education [her only son William (1716-1742)] I give to William and Mary College in Virginia my Gilt Sacrament Cup and put in a Red Leather case and a large Foll: Bible of Fields bound in four volumes."[3] This exquisite silver-gilt two-handled covered cup of domestic form of 1686/87 by Pierre Harache, Sr., of London, and a silver-gilt paten of 1751/52 by Richard Gurney of London, both impaled with the engraved arms of her parents, William Stanton and Margaret Gavell of Hampton, Middlesex, were transferred from the College to Bruton Parish Church in Williamsburg in 1905.[4] The cup is illustrated in the introduction.

Gabriel Sleath also fashioned the communion cup, flagon, paten, and alms dish, which are inscribed: "*The Gift of* The HON:^BLE IOHN CUSTIS ESQ:^R [1678-1749] *of Williamsburg to the Upper Church of Hungar's Parish in Northampton County 1742.*"[5]

The substantial body of each of these beakers was forged from a single billet, the rim incised and the drawn and seamed foot-ring applied.

A beaker engraved with the arms of the Randolph family of Virginia is also in the collection (No. 38).

1975-68, 1-2

1. Gooch served as deputy to George Hamilton, 1st earl of Orkney, and William Anne Keppel, 2nd earl of Albemarle, neither of whom ever came to Virginia. This was not an uncommon arrangement.

2. Collection of Sir Robert E. S. Gooch, Benacre Hall, Suffolk; microfilm copy in the Department of Research, Colonial Williamsburg Foundation. Gooch specified in his will of June 1, 1751, that "after my wife's decease I do give and devise to my nephew John Gooch Esqr. youngest son of my Brother one thousand Pounds with two dozen of silver knives forks and spoons, the four drinking silver Mugs the Case of Castors, the Bed and Chairs my Brother gave me when I furnished my House at Hampton [after his return to England from Virginia]." (Recorded April 16, 1752, Principal Probate Registry, Somerset House, London; typescript copy in the Department of Research, Colonial Williamsburg Foundation).

3. "Will of Lady Rebecca Gooch, Widow of Sir William Gooch," *William and Mary Quarterly* 23 (January 1915):174. Though the paten is not mentioned in her will, Lady Gooch did leave it to the college at this time. Samuel Athawes of London wrote on July 19, 1775, to Robert Miller in Williamsburg: "I am now to acquaint you that the Gilt Sacrament Cup & Patten together with the Bible which was left by Lady Gooch to the College of Wm. & Mary are now in my Possession & when the Times will safely permit they shall be sent to you as bursar of that Seminary." ("Letters to the College," *William and Mary Quarterly* 20 [January 1912]:210).

4. Jones (d), pp. 496–98, pl. CXL, fig. 2; Virginia Museum (b), pp. 32–33, ill.; Helen Scott Townsend Reed, "Church Silver in Colonial Virginia," *Antiques* 97 (February 1970):244–45, fig. 2.

5. Jones (d), p. 221, pl. LXXVI, fig. 2; Virginia Museum (b), pp. 78–79, ill.

INDEX OF SILVERSMITHS

(BY NAME OR MARK)

REPRESENTED IN THE COLLECTION

*(Additional references to these silversmiths,
and to others, will be found in the
General Index)*

GENERAL INDEX

(Consult entries under *Collectors and collections; Dealers; Donors;* and *Owners, former* for references to persons, firms, and museums not individually indexed.)

A

Abercromby, Robert, 3, 128
Adam, Charles, 148
Adam, Robert, 91, 226
Albemarle, 2nd earl of, 245
Aldridge, Charles, and Henry Green, 74
Aldridge, Edward, and John Stamper, 74, 162
Alexander, John, 85
Allen, John, and John Edwards, 144
Andros, Edmund, 4, 124
Archambo, Peter, Sr., 32, 62, 86, 131, 150
Archambo, Peter, Jr., 64; and Peter Meure, 138, 239
Arnett, Hugh, and Edward Pocock, 107
Ashforth & Co., George, 34
Athawes, Samuel, 245

B

Bailey, Nathaniel, 44
Baillie, Lady Grisell, 111
Balfour & Barraud, 217
Ballin, Charles, 112
Bamford, Thomas, 149, 152
Barnstaple silver, 165
Baskets: bread, 114–18, 230; dessert, 118–20; sugar, 102, 228
Basting or serving spoons, 173–76; 180; 232
Bateman, Hester, 188, 190
Bateman, Viscount William, 27
Battersea factory, 76
Bayley, Richard, 101, 123
Beakers, 49–51, 244–45
Beaufort, dukes of, 243
Beckford, William, 14
Beer jugs, 71–72
Beeton, Mrs. Isabella, 85
Behrens of Hanover, 15
Bells, 204, 206, 214
Berkeley, Edmund, 160
Berkeley, Elizabeth, 243–44
Berkeley, George, 78
Berkeley, Norborne. *See* Botetourt, Lord
Besnier, Nicholas, 26

Best, Marmaduke, 197
Beverley, Robert, 217
Bickerton, Benjamin, 77
Bigge, Richard, 198
Bignell, John, 36
Birmingham silver, 211–12. *See also* Fused silverplate.
Blair, James, 131
Blount, Thomas, 123
Blundell, Nicholas, 172
Boats: cream, 100; pap, 198–99; sauce, 156–59
Boddington, John, 14
Bodkin, 212–13
Booth, George, 2nd earl of Warrington, 196–97
Boothby, George, 69, 92
Botetourt, Lord, 19, 76, 85, 121, 138, 139, 178, 197, 203, 217, 222, 243–44
Bottle labels or tickets, 75–77
Bottle sliders or stands, 74–75, 230–31
Bougie or taper box, 38
Boulsover, Thomas, 216, 219, 227
Boulton, Matthew, 164, 217, 219, 226, 235–36
Bourdon, Pierre, 208–9
Bowls: punch, 46–49; slop or waste, 106–7; sugar, 101–2
Boxes: 194–95, 211–12; bougie or taper, 38; jewel with pincushion, 242–44; snuff and tobacco, 207–11, 216–18; spice or sugar, 140–41; sugar, 103–5; vinaigrette, 212
Britannia standard, 2, 14, 16, 24–25
Bruton Parish Church, 4–5, 124, 245. *See also* Virginia ownership.
Burwash, William, and Richard Sibley, 119

C

Cachart, Elias, 176
Cafe, John, 29, 37, 219–20
Cafe, William, 30, 31
Campbell, Colen, 121
Candelabra, 19–21

Candlesticks, 22–36, 218–20, 226, 233–34, 236
Canisters, tea, 102–6, 223
Carlisle, earl of, 124
Carter, Anne, 94
Carter, Charles, 94
Carter, John, 3, 33–34, 91, 136, 226
Carter, Robert, of Nomini Hall, 51, 75
Cartwright, Benjamin, 213
Casters, 147–54, 224–25
Chafing dishes, 159–62
Chamber pots, 196–97
Chandelier, 13–15
Chartier, John, 172–73
Chawner, Henry, 99
Chesterfield, earls of, 27, 42, 119
Chinoiserie decoration, 44, 81–82, 112, 125
Chocolate mill, 84–85
Chocolate pot, 84–86
Churchill, William, 44
"cock gaffs," 215
Cock spurs, 214–15
Coffeepots, 86–90, 222–23
Coffee or hot water jugs, 90–91, 96–97, 228
"Coffy Spoones," 172
Coker, Ebenezer, 3, 31, 32, 129, 135–37
Collectors and collections (relating to pieces not in the Colonial Williamsburg collection): Abingdon Church, 124; Abingdon Corporation, 58; Althorp House, 22, 32, 195; Anglesey Abbey, 15; Argenti, Philip, 57–58; Ashmolean Museum, 79, 84, 86, 93, 155, 189, 244; Assheton Bennett (City of Manchester Art Gallery), 86, 101; Barnstaple Museum, 166; Bathurst, Earl, 195; Beaumont, Rex, 195; Birmingham Assay Office, 91, 164, 226; Bobrinsky, 204; Bradbury, 217; Bridgewater Corporation, 143; British Museum, 79, 195; Brownlow, 14, 19, 128; Bruton Parish Church, 4–5, 124, 245; Buccleuch, duke of, 14, 17; Burghley House, 195; Carter (Ashmolean Museum), 79; Cassell, Sir Ernest, 56; Chatsworth, 14–15, 195;

Decanter labels or tickets, 75–77

de Lamerie, Paul, 2, 5, 14, 27, 32, 64, 69–70, 82, 93, 94, 111, 115–17, 149, 152, 155, 160–61, 189, 203–4, 220, 244

Denny, William, and John Bache, 22–23

Denziloe, John, 82–83

Dessert baskets or basins and stands, 118–20

Dessert spoon, 187

Devonshire, duke of, 195

Dickinson, Mary, 213

Dinwiddie, Robert, 131, 241

Dish crosses, 162–64

Dish ring, 164

Dishes: chafing, 159–62; entrée, 122–23; meat, 139–40, 229–30

Donors: Baylor, Mrs. George Daniel, 176; Bundy, Mrs. Katherine Brooke Fauntleroy, 145; Caldwell, Dr. Benjamin H., Jr., 233; Queen Elizabeth the Queen Mother, 209; Gardiner, Rockwell, 216; Goodwin, Dr. William A. R., 5, 167; Powell, Mrs. Grace E., 236; Prock, Mr. and Mrs. Harry A., 196–97; Ramsey, Mr. and Mrs. Oliver F., 219, 222, 223, 224, 225, 227, 230, 235, 236; Sanders, Mrs. William B., 174; Schwartz, Mr. and Mrs. Samuel, 214; Simonin, Mrs.

ENGLISH SILVER AT WILLIAMSBURG

was composed in Monotype Bembo by Heritage Printers, Inc., Charlotte, North Carolina, and printed by photo-offset lithography by Lebanon Valley Offset Company, Inc., Annville, Pennsylvania. The stock is Monadnock's Astrolite. The book was bound by Haddon Craftsmen, Inc., Scranton, Pennsylvania. The designer was Richard Stinely.